Understanding Linguistic Prejudice

Gladis Massini-Cagliari
Rosane Andrade Berlinck
Angelica Rodrigues

Editors

Understanding Linguistic Prejudice

Critical Approaches to Language Diversity in Brazil

Springer

editora
unesp

Editors
Gladis Massini-Cagliari (iD)
Department of Linguistics, Literature
and Classical Languages
São Paulo State University
Araraquara, São Paulo, Brazil

Rosane Andrade Berlinck (iD)
Department of Linguistics, Literature
and Classical Languages
São Paulo State University
Araraquara, São Paulo, Brazil

Angelica Rodrigues (iD)
Department of Linguistics, Literature
and Classical Languages
São Paulo State University
Araraquara, São Paulo, Brazil

ISBN 978-3-031-25808-4   ISBN 978-3-031-25806-0   (eBook)
https://doi.org/10.1007/978-3-031-25806-0

This Springer imprint is published by the registered company Springer Nature Switzerland AG
The registered company address is: Gewerbestrasse 11, 6330 Cham, Switzerland

Preface

Sadly, language is also an instrument of power; language is also an instrument of domination; language is also an instrument of oppression. I have not seen it yet, and I would like to see it someday (the utopia is part of life), language being used as a real instrument of deliverance. (Scherre, 2005: 43–44)

Language is bigger than the authoritarian impulse of the norm. (Faraco, 2008: 104)

The aim of this book is to approach language diversity in Brazil, in order to understand manifestations of linguistic prejudice, which are common in the country, concerning non-standard varieties of Brazilian Portuguese, native and other minority languages which still survive in specific geographical areas far from major cities or neighbourhoods and also in minor linguistic communities, including deaf communities. These minority languages, such as indigenous languages from various linguistic families and sign languages, especially Brazilian Sign Language (Libras), and Nonstandard Brazilian Portuguese are often taken as stigmatised forms of speaking in contrast with the major and official language of the country, Portuguese. This book brings together works and reflections on linguistic prejudice and social discrimination, departing from data and examples collected in the particular context of Brazil.

Willing to bridge the gap between academic findings and popular notions relating to linguistic diversity, which comprises both spoken and signed communication, the central tenet of the book is to promote language diversity, acceptance and mutual respect, collecting arguments to fight against division, discordance and intolerance within societies. The central ideas presented on each chapter can offer different perspective to approach the origins and motivations of linguistic prejudice and foster awareness of our own entrenched academic opinions regarding linguistic diversity and the values which some attribute to such diversity.

The first part of the book, composed of the first six chapters, will be devoted to basic sociolinguistic questions concerning linguistic prejudice and the research will be qualitative in nature.

First of all, Massini-Cagliari, Berlinck and Rodrigues, in an introductory chapter, present key notions of linguistic prejudice and language diversity, characterizing

language prejudice and discrimination as universal problems, before giving an overview of the book's contents. The main topics addressed in the Introduction are: definition of language prejudice and language discrimination; brief presentation of the
linguistic situation in Brazil: the multiple languages which are spoken/signed in
Brazil today and linguistic variation in Brazilian Portuguese; the invisibility of the
multiplicity of languages which are spoken in Brazil, in official terms and in the
media; sociolinguistic polarisation in Brazilian Portuguese.

In Chap. 2, O'Neill and Massini-Cagliari analyse the most common educational
measure to deal with language variation in a non-discriminatory way: the theory of
differences and the proposal of bidialectalism, arguing that these measures are ineffectual since they are based on naïve conclusions of sociolinguistic studies which
propose that linguistic prejudice can be combatted via a 'principle of error correction' whereby the focus is on changing beliefs of individuals. They also argue that
it is more important to analyse the political, historical, and social factors which
sustain and reinforce such beliefs and the material structures which endorse and
promote them. They therefore examine linguistic prejudice within the social theory
of Pierre Bourdieu (1973, 1977, 1986, 1991) and define it as a form of symbolic
violence, maintaining that conceiving linguistic prejudice and discrimination in this
way offers new insights on how to combat this type of prejudice and discrimination
more effectively and makes it clear that linguistic prejudice is intimately related to
other types of prejudices.

In Chap. 3, Cagliari discusses 'literacy and the problem of linguistic variation',
pointing out that it is necessary to discuss linguistic variation problems and related
social prejudice starting from the acquisition of oral language. Because literacy
classes reunite students from different varieties, different ways of speaking emerge
when the students talk to each other. Sometimes, cultural and socioeconomic differences give a complicated relationship among people that can lead to problems of
relationship among the students caused by the way they speak. Dialect variations
provoke situations of verbal discrimination leading to a situation of linguistic prejudice. If these sentiments are not adequately controlled since the beginning of schooling, the relationship between mates of the class may root bullying, discrimination,
and prejudice in subsequent years.

Chapter 4, written by Sene, Biazolli and Brandão, focuses on the analysis of
societal evidence that expresses subjective evaluations of speakers concerning linguistic uses considered 'irritating'. The data was collected using the social network-
ing platform Facebook, from the post 'Mention a Portuguese mistake that deeply
irritates you', published in the group LDRV – Taubaté New Global Era. The main
objective of the authors is to demonstrate that language is a social practice subject
to the evaluation of the speaker on the one hand and the evaluation of the listener on
the other. Therefore, along with the knowledge of how people effectively use the
language, it is necessary to include the way they perceive, evaluate and react to
diversified linguistic uses. In general, such evaluation materialises in societal evidence (Garrett et al., 2003) that may be negative or positive regarding a variety,
variant or specific linguistic item.

In a historical perspective, the purpose of Barreto and Massini-Cagliari in Chap. 5 is to promote a reflection on two phenomena that, in the contemporary Portuguese language, are the target of linguistic prejudice: rhotacism and lambdacism. In order to do so, the medieval stage of ancestral Portuguese is considered, pointing out to how the process of orthographic standardization was decisive for the construction of a discriminatory attitude in the face of variation, since, in the Middle Ages, words presenting sound change resulting from the application of both phonological processes figured systematically in the medieval Galician-Portuguese songbooks, texts written only by the most erudite and privileged of that time.

The objective of Chap. 6, authored by Costa and Nascimento, is to present a socio-semantic analysis of neologisms present in the lyrics of funk songs from Rio de Janeiro. Funk is a musical style that is linked to social issues, and, for this reason, the lyrics present some peculiarities that can be interpreted as marks of social identification. It can be noticed, in the reading of some lyrics of MCs, that, in addition to their global content, there is the use of specific words, which could be classified as slang, to identify a particular social group. Because funk is a marginalised musical style, originating in the periphery and favelas of Rio de Janeiro, the authors also intent to contribute to the dissipation of the prejudice that surrounds this type of music, showing that certain words and linguistic constructions are representative of a dialect used by a particular linguistic community, which represents part of the diversity of uses of Portuguese.

The second part of the book is composed of five chapters that analyse linguistic prejudice in Brazil in (a) major communities that speak Brazilian Portuguese varieties and (b) minor communities that speak native and sign languages.

Chapter 7, written by Almeida, Berlinck and Levey, addresses the uncritical equation of the prescriptive norms of standard Portuguese with those that underlie spontaneous spoken usage. Exemplifying with a study of the variable strategies for expressing locative relativization, quantitative analysis of spoken language data recorded in São Paulo state turns up, among other important findings, the rarity of the prescriptively ratified pied-piping strategy for forming locative relative clauses. Instead, two alternative options involving *onde* 'where' and *que + prepositional phrase-chopping* make up the bulk of the variable context in everyday spoken interactions. The results indicate that detailed analysis of spontaneous speech can considerably enrich our understanding of the variable grammatical processes that operate in actual discourse.

In their study, Pinto and Berlinck start from the well-established principle in Sociolinguistics that social evaluation of linguistic forms is determinant of the fate of these forms in the linguistic scenario of a community. The authors focus on the pronominal expression of the first person plural in the variety of Brazilian Portuguese (BP) spoken in two rural communities in the south of Minas Gerais, Brazil. The investigation conducted in a less explored context in variation studies – rural communities – revealed a particular linguistic ecosystem, in which, in addition to the variation between 'nós' and 'a gente' (*we*), general in BP, there is a phonological variation, as the inhabitants of this region also use 'nóis' and 'nói'. It also reveals that the variants are associated with local social values that do not correspond necessarily to those of urban communities, determining, then, a specific configuration of norms of usage, with prestige and stigma values specifically bond to these communities.

Rodrigues, Clempi and Felix propose in Chap. 9 a non-essentialist approach to gender and sexuality and relying on social theories advocate that the study of variation and change in Brazilian Portuguese can be enriched if the analyses are not limited to gender and sexuality stereotypes. The authors combine studies on the implementation of the periphrastic future in Brazilian Portuguese and on the use of the superlative adjectives as a possible index of *gay* identity to discuss methodological aspects related to the sex/gender and sexuality factors, emphasizing that the adoption of a social perspective of gender requires a socially sensitive choice of the research corpus, especially if one is dealing with historical data, and that the stratification of speakers based on their sexualities helps to build a database more sensible to the identities diversity avoiding taking stereotypes as reference of the gay community.

In Chap. 10, Rodrigues and Pfau discuss language prejudice on the scope of deaf community considering absent and emerging conjunctions in sign languages. The authors recover discussions about the status of languages that were considered primitive because of the absence of certain linguistic categories. The chapter essentially shows two different perspectives on the subject. Initially, based on evidence presented in numerous works on linguistic typology, the authors refute the framing of languages as being primitive. In this sense, they argue that the absence of conjunctions in sign languages, if confirmed, should not be analysed as a lack of grammatical complexity. Secondly, they present evidence of the use of conjunctions in sign languages of the world, emphasizing cases of emergence of conjunctions in Libras through processes of borrowing and grammaticalization.

The chapter enriches the language prejudice debate highlighting aspects of ableist perspectives on language analyses. Contributions from Disability Studies and Crip Theory are brought together to address that as disable people should not be described for what they lack, sign language should not be analysed as less complex because they may lack some grammatical categories often found in spoken languages. Indeed, the authors have shown that sign languages do not lack conjunctions and that restriction of their analyses only in the contrast with spoken languages would lead to an inaccurate description of their particular grammar.

In Chap. 11, Fargetti and Carvalho approach prejudice against indigenous peoples and languages in Brazil, which may be related to the lack of knowledge about them and inferred from their treatment in the media, in teaching materials and in publications on social networks. Considering the presence or absence of the subject in the media and the misconceptions widely presented also in school education, the authors point out to strategies that can be used to bring knowledge, reduce prejudice and encourage interaction with indigenous peoples and their languages, which may be relevant at the beginning of the decade of indigenous languages, proposed by UNESCO (2022–2032).

From the discussions presented in this book, we can conclude that language prejudice can also affect the way both spoken and sign language are described due to biased ideas about civilization, culture and language. Arguments in favour of the existence of more complex and developed languages opposed to primitive language with less complex grammar can be found in the linguistic literature especially in the nineteenth century. Although, thanks to several works on typological linguistics, we can assure that every language ever studied consists of a complex and highly developed system of communication.

Araraquara, São Paulo, Brazil

Gladis Massini-Cagliari
Rosane Andrade Berlinck
Angelica Rodrigues

References

Bourdieu, P. (1973). Cultural reproduction and social reproduction. In R. K. Brown (Ed.), *Knowledge, education and cultural change: Papers in the sociology of education* (pp. 71–112). Tavistock Publications.

Bourdieu, P. (1977). *Outline of a theory of practice*. Cambridge University Press.

Bourdieu, P. (1986). The forms of capital. In J. G. Richardson (Ed.), *Handbook of theory and research for the sociology of education*. Greenwood Press.

Bourdieu, P. (1991). *Language and symbolic power*. Polity/Basil Blackwell.

Faraco, C. A. (2008). *Norma culta brasileira – desatando alguns nós*. Parábola.

Garrett, P., Coupland, N., & Williams, A. (2003). Investigating Language Attitudes: Social Meanings of Dialect, Ethnicity and Performance. *International Journal of Applied Linguistics*. https://doi.org/10.1111/j.1473-4192.2005.00100d.x

Scherre, M. M. P. (2005). *Doa-se lindos filhotes de poodle*. Parábola.

Acknowledgements

The editors would like to thank the Brazilian Federal Agency for Support and Evaluation of Graduate Education [Coordenação de Aperfeiçoamento de Pessoal de Nível Superior – CAPES], in the scope of the Program CAPES-PrInt, process number 88887.310463/2018-00. The editors would like also to thank Unesp's Vice Presidency for Postgraduate Studies [Pró-Reitoria de Pós-Graduação – PROPG], External Relations Advisory [Assessoria de Relações Externas – AREX] and Unesp Publishing company [Fundação Editora Unesp] (EDITAL ProPG No. 15/2021– em parceria com AREX e FEU).

Gladis Massini-Cagliari also wishes to thank the Brazilian National Council for Scientific and Technological Development (Conselho Nacional de Desenvolvimento Científico e Tecnológico – CNPq, 302648/2019-4).

Rosane Andrade Berlinck also wishes to thank the Brazilian National Council for Scientific and Technological Development (Conselho Nacional de Desenvolvimento Científico e Tecnológico – CNPq, 306464/2019-5).

Contents

Contributors

Débora Aparecida dos Reis Justo Barreto has got a graduation degree in Language Studies from the Unesp São Paulo State University, Araraquara, Brazil, and a master's degree in Linguistics and Portuguese Language by the same institution. She is currently pursuing a PhD in Linguistics and Portuguese Language (in the same Postgraduate Program). She is a member of the Portuguese Phonology: Archaic and Brazilian research group since 2014, coordinated by Professor Gladis Massini-Cagliari.

Rosane Andrade Berlinck is professor of Linguistics at the São Paulo State University (UNESP). Her research focuses mainly on morpho-syntactic variation and change in Brazilian Portuguese, and on the correlations between textual genres, style, linguistic norm(s), identity and processes of linguistic variation and change. She coordinates Araraquara Sociolinguistics Research Group (SoLAr/UNESP).

Caroline Carnielli Biazolli has a master's and a PhD in Linguistics and Portuguese (Unesp/Araraquara/Sao Paulo/Brazil). She is a professor at the Department of Teaching Methodology, UFSCar/São Carlos/Sao Paulo/Brazil, as well as at the Graduate Program in Linguistics and the Professional Graduate Program in Education. She develops research in the areas of Language Teaching and Learning and (Variationist and Educational) Sociolinguistics and currently is the vice-leader of SoLAr – Research Center for Sociolinguistics in Araraquara.

Silvia Maria Brandão has a degree in Languages, a master's and a PhD in Linguistics and Portuguese from Unesp Sao Paulo State University. She worked as professor in the Languages undergraduate program at the State University of Paraná (UNESPAR). She develops research in Sociolinguistics and Historical Sociolinguistics, with emphasis on morphosyntactic change in Brazilian Portuguese, and is currently Secretary of Education in the city of Inconfidentes – Minas Gerais.

Luiz Carlos Cagliari got his PhD from Edinburgh University (1978). He taught at UNICAMP until his retirement in 1997. He got his professorship in 1991. He taught at UNESP from 2005 to 2015, when he retired. Now he teaches at de Postgraduate Courses. Dr. Cagliari has published books and articles in the areas of Phonetics, Phonology, Intonation, Rhythm, with special reference to Brazilian Portuguese. He also has published books and works on Literacy and Writing Systems.

Camila Bordonal Clempi holds a master's degree in Linguistics from Sao Paulo State University (Unesp) and is currently enrolled in the doctoral program of Linguistics also at Sao Paulo State University (Unesp). She develops research in Linguistics, with an emphasis on Sociolinguistics, and is a member of the Research Group in Sociolinguistics (SOLAR).

Daniel Soares da Costa has a PhD in Linguistics and Portuguese Language and teaches at Unesp Sao Paulo State University, Araraquara, São Paulo, Brazil. He develops research in Phonology and Morphology with an emphasis on the interface between these areas, Morphophonology. He also works in the area of Neology, investigating the creation of new words in lyrics of Brazilian songs in their various styles.

Milena Aparecida de Almeida is a PhD student in Linguistics and Portuguese at Unesp Sao Paulo State University, Araraquara, Brazil. She obtained her master's degree in Linguistics and Portuguese at Sao Paulo State University, Araraquara, Brazil. She conducts research in Sociolinguistics under the supervision of Prof. Dr. Rosane Andrade Berlinck and is a member of SoLAr – Araraquara Sociolinguistics Research Center since 2017.

Mateus Cruz Maciel de Carvalho is professor at the Federal Institute of Education, Science and Technology of São Paulo – Salto campus, where he teaches courses in general linguistics, phonology and morphology. He obtained his PhD in linguistics with a thesis describing aspects of the morphosyntax of Deni language, an Arawá language spoken in Brazilian Amazon. Currently, his research interests focus on the language and culture connection, especially on the embodiment hypothesis.

Marcus Garcia de Sene has a PhD and a master's degree in Linguistics and Portuguese from Unesp Sao Paulo State University. He is currently professor of the Languages undergraduate program at the Newton Paiva University, as well as a member of the Structuring Teaching Nucleus (NDE) and a member of the Ethics and Research Committee (CEP). He coordinates the research project 'Linguistic Diversity, Subjective Assessment and Linguistic Respect' (Div.AR), and is postdoctoral fellow at the Graduate Program in Languages at the Federal University of Roraima (UFRR).

Cristina Martins Fargetti is free lecturer in Indigenous Languages at the Sao Paulo State University (UNESP, 2015), Doctor and Master in Linguistics at the State University of Campinas (UNICAMP, 2001, 1992), where she also completed her graduation in Languages, Bachelor and Degree (1988). She is professor in RDIDP at UNESP, Faculty of Sciences and Letters of Araraquara, in the Letters course, working in the Postgraduate Program in Linguistics and Portuguese Language. Leader of the LINBRA Group – Research Group on Brazilian Indigenous Languages, by CNPq, she has been working on research on the Juruna language since 1989, initially on the project of her advisor Lucy Seki. In addition to being interested in this language and in its welcoming and friendly people, she is also dedicated to music.

Rafael de Almeida Arruda Felix holds a master's degree in Linguistics from Sao Paulo State University (Unesp) and is currently enrolled in the doctoral program of Linguistics also at Sao Paulo State University (Unesp). He is professor at Barão de Mauá University for the course of Letras (Languages and Literature).

Stephen Levey is associate professor of Linguistics at the University of Ottawa. His research interests reside primarily in morpho-syntactic and discourse-pragmatic variation and change in the English language. His funded research examines the acquisition of variation in English as a first and second language. Additional research interests include language contact as well as pidgin and creole languages.

Gladis Massini-Cagliari is professor at Sao Paulo State University, UNESP, at Araraquara, Brazil, since 1996. Her PhD in Linguistics was obtained from Campinas State University, UNICAMP, Campinas, Brazil (1995). She spent one year at the University of Oxford, England (2002-2003), doing a post doctorate. Her research activities focus mainly on the search for clues which can clarify the history of Portuguese prosody, especially addressing rhythm, from its origins to present days, in the remaining registers of the medieval secular and religious cantigas. She served as Vice President for Undergraduate Studies at UNESP (2017-2020).

Geisibel Cristina Andrade Nascimento has PhD in Linguistics and Portuguese Language by Sao Paulo State University, Araraquara, Sao Paulo, Brazil. She develops research about phonological aspects in the process of learning English as a foreign language by speakers of Brazilian Portuguese. She teaches English and Portuguese and works as text reviewer.

Paul O'Neill is senior lecturer in Hispanic Studies at the University of Sheffield, United Kingdom. His research focuses on variation and change in the Ibero-Romance Languages (Spanish, Catalan, Portuguese, Galician, Austrian, Aragonese) and specifically on the varieties of Portuguese and Spanish spoken around the world. He has a particular interest in issues related to linguistic prejudice and discrimination in Brazil.

Roland Pfau is associate professor in sign language linguistics at the Department of General Linguistics in the University of Amsterdam since 2014 and has received MA (1995) and PhD degree (2001) from the University of Frankfurt. He started with sign language research in 1995 and work mostly with sign language grammar and typology. He is the co-editor of the journal *Sign Language & Linguistics* and editorial board member of the Mouton de Gruyter *Sign Language Typology (SLT)* series.

Letícia Gaspar Pinto has a degree in Languages – Portuguese / English and a master's degree in Linguistics and Portuguese Language (Unesp/ Araraquara). Currently, she is a PhD student in the postgraduate program in Linguistics and Portuguese Language (Unesp/Araraquara) and is part of the SoLAr – Araraquara Sociolinguistics Research Group.

Angelica Rodrigues is associate professor at the Department of Linguistics, Literature and Classical languages in The São Paulo State University (UNESP) since 2011 and has received MA (2001) and PhD degree (2006) from The State University of Campinas – Unicamp. Since 2015 has been dedicated to sign language linguistics studies and is interested in sign language syntax, variation and change (specially grammaticalization) and sociolinguistics aspects of deaf communities.

Part I
Linguistic Prejudice and Discrimination

Chapter 1
Introduction

Gladis Massini-Cagliari ⓘ**, Rosane Andrade Berlinck** ⓘ**,
and Angélica Rodrigues** ⓘ

In academic circles, the social and economic benefits of plural societies are often taken for granted; there is not only a general acceptance and tolerance of diversity (be it based on one's gender, race/ethnicity, social background or language), but such diversity is celebrated and, particularly in the case of indigenous and deaf communities, it is seen as a marker of identity. However, such views are not always shared with the majority of the population. The general public can have strong and deeply entrenched beliefs about the 'correct' forms of language, and, more dangerously, these opinions can be translated into discriminatory behaviour towards speakers of non-standard varieties and minority languages (e.g. sign and native languages) as attested within the education system, the justice system and the housing market, as well as in training courses and the job market.

Beliefs about non-standard forms of Portuguese and/or minority languages can be so deeply embedded in certain sectors of the Brazilian society that scientifically grounded findings generated by researchers working on linguistic variation are routinely dismissed as politically motivated left-wing bias, or as inauthentic facts, creating divisions within society and fuelling distrust of academic research.

Despite being the ninth most spoken language in the world and the native language of approximately 232 million people, the linguistic variation present in Portuguese and its relevance to theories of language has not been prominent internationally, especially when compared with the closely related language Spanish. This book not only seeks to analyse the social problems with which such linguistic variation can be correlated and address the gap between the results of academic research and the common sense of the general public but also seeks to address the lack of representation of Portuguese and minority languages spoken in Brazil in

G. Massini-Cagliari (✉) · R. A. Berlinck · A. Rodrigues
Unesp – Sao Paulo State University, Araraquara, Sao Paulo, Brazil
e-mail: gladis.massini-cagliari@unesp.br; rosane.berlinck@unesp.br;
angelica.rodrigues@unesp.br

© The Author(s), under exclusive license to Springer Nature Switzerland AG 2023   3
G. Massini-Cagliari et al. (eds.), *Understanding Linguistic Prejudice*,
https://doi.org/10.1007/978-3-031-25806-0_1

international questions regarding language variation and change. This will be achieved by combining the specialised knowledge on Brazilian Portuguese, native languages and Libras with knowledge of trends and methodologies which are currently of international importance.

Brazil is the only official Portuguese-speaking country in South America, surrounded by official Spanish-speaking countries. It is the fifth largest country in the world, with a (projected) population of more than 214 million people.[1] This geographically gigantic country is characterised by a striking biodiversity, which is known and celebrated as a universal heritage, to be preserved. Because of this, it would be a huge surprise if, in this immense geographic area, there was not diversity in terms of people and of the language(s) spoken by them.

In spite of the fact that almost the total population is constituted of monolingual Portuguese speakers, and the vast majority of them will never learn a second language, there are more than 210 languages spoken in Brazil today. The *Inventário Nacional da Diversidade Linguística – INDL* [National Inventory of Linguistic Diversity],[2] funded by the *Instituto do Patrimônio Histórico e Artístico Nacional – IPHAN* [Institute of National Historical and Artistic Heritage], lists about 180 native languages, 30 immigration languages and sign languages used by deaf communities, besides Portuguese, which itself presents a huge variability in terms of sounds, morphology, syntax, etc., in Brazilian territory.

These languages are spoken/signed by marginalised social and linguistic minorities without a significant economic power, that is, by indigenous groups, deaf communities, speakers of non-standard varieties of Portuguese and immigrants. Moreover, they have rarely been recognised as legitimate or even as existing by the media (Massini-Cagliari, 2004: 4). In this respect, the populations of non-Portuguese speakers in Brazil are 'statistically non-significant' for TV channels, newspapers, social media and other Internet networks. Their choice is not only economic but also ideological. The media (including TV, radio, newspapers and the Internet) have always embraced the idea of Brazil being a linguistically homogeneous giant.

Recently, after many years of political and social movements, a few of the multiple languages used in Brazil have obtained the status of 'co-official' languages to Portuguese, in the geographical areas where they are spoken. Lagares (2018: 79) presents a table which summarises all the recognised co-official languages in Brazil. The first languages to obtain such a status were Tucano, Baniwa and Nheengatu (all Tupi-origin native languages, the last one considered the Amazonian general language – Rodrigues, 1996; Rosa, 2003; Bessa Freire, 2003), in 2002, in São Gabriel da Cachoeira, a county in the state of Amazonas. After that, other native and

---

[1] IBGE. Instituto Brasileiro de Geografia e Estatística. Projeção da População do Brasil e das Unidades da Federação. https://www.ibge.gov.br/apps/populacao/projecao/index.html Access: 30 Jun 2022.

[2] IPHAN. Instituto do Patrimônio Histórico e Artístico Nacional. Inventário Nacional da Diversidade Linguística. http://portal.iphan.gov.br/pagina/detalhes/140#:~:text=O%20Invent% C3%A1rio%20Nacional%20da%20Diversidade,a%C3%A7%C3%B5es%20de%20apoio%20 e%20fomento. Access: 30 Jun 2022.

immigrant languages were turned co-official in specific counties in Brazil.[3] Although being co-official side by side to Portuguese, in practical life, these languages do not offer all the opportunities and exchange situations which are available for the inter-action in Portuguese.

In what concerns sign languages, all around the world, the World Federation of the Deaf fights for their recognition and for the linguistic rights of the deaf communities. The Brazilian deaf community engaged in similar endeavour leading a movement that pushed the Brazilian government to edit Bill 10.436 (2002), which officially recognises Libras as an official 'means of communication and expression' used within urban deaf communities, and Bill 5.626 (2005) that works in order to specially promote Libras in educational contexts.

Those are important legal documents that guaranteed, at least officially, the recognition of Libras in Brazil. However, compared to spoken languages, sign languages remain more invisible even in academic fields. IPOL (Instituto de Investigação e Desenvolvimento em Política Linguística),[4] for example, documents that 21 languages of immigrants are officialised in more than 40 municipalities. Official information about officialisation of sign languages still remains unclear.

Although Lagares (2018: 78) maintains that none of the sign languages used in Brazil is considered official, with a little research, we find that in some cities in Brazil Libras have gained official status like in the city of Curitiba, in the state of Paraná (Bill 15.823/2021); Belo Horizonte, in the state of Minas Gerais (Bill 223/2021); and in Barueri, in the state of Sao Paulo (Bill 025/2019). In the city of Porto Nacional, the state of Tocantins, Libras are included in the curriculum of regular public schools along with Portuguese.

The social and geographical varieties of Brazilian Portuguese are also almost 'invisible' by the media and the social networks on the Internet. Massini-Cagliari (2004: 3) shows that, generally, Brazilians assume that everybody in Brazil speaks a unique variety of the Portuguese, pointing out to the fact that:

> The widespread belief that the language spoken in Brazil is highly homogeneous is due probably to a twofold reason: firstly because there are no apparent problems of mutual intelligibility in everyday communication between speakers of different varieties of Brazilian Portuguese, when compared with what happens to different varieties of other languages, like Italian, Chinese and English; secondly, and more probable, because the intelligibility is not jeopardised by phonological, morphological and syntactic variations. This fact gives the false impression that the language is totally homogeneous. (Massini-Cagliari, 2004: 4–5)

---

[3] Native languages: Guarani (Tacuru, state of Mato Grosso do Sul), Akwẽ Xerente (Tocantínia, state of Tocantins), Macuxi (Bonfim, state of Roraima) and Wapichana (Bonfim and Cantá, state of Roraima). Immigrant languages: Pomerano (a language originally spoken in Germany and Poland, in eight counties of the states of Espírito Santo, Santa Catarina and Rio Grande do Sul), Talian (considered a 'dialect' of Italian, co-officialised in eight counties of Rio Grande do Sul and Santa Catarina), Hunsrückisch (a German 'dialect', officialised in two counties in Santa Catarina and Rio Grande do Sul) and German (co-official in two cities in Santa Catarina.

[4] http://ipol.org.br/lista-de-linguas-cooficiais-em-municipios-brasileiros/

But, as the adoption of a specific linguistic variety has the function of marking the inclusion of an individual into the social group to which he belongs and of giving identity to the members of this specific group, as native speakers, we learn to distinguish variation, even when the official discourses insist that there is 'only one' language (Massini-Cagliari, 2004: 16). To Cagliari (1989), as native speakers, we may learn to speak our own variety, but at the same time, we learn to hear and to process all varieties of the language. To Faraco (2008: 43), each speaker dominates more than one norm, that is, more than one socially defined linguistic variety based on the speech practices and interaction networks of each community, and variably changes his/her way of speaking (his/her norm) in accordance to the relationship and activity net in which he/she is. In this sense, every speaker is necessarily a 'polyglot' in his own language (Fiorin, 2000: 28).

So, in the sense of Faraco (2008: 33), what the majority of Brazilian population cannot see and explain, although can experience, is our intrinsically heterogeneous linguistic reality. In the empirical plan, a language is constituted by a compound of varieties. In other words, there is no language beyond or above its constitutive varieties; it is also impossible to consider, on the one hand, a language and, on the other, its varieties, because linguistically they have the same status.

Nonetheless, because they are able to recognise that they do not speak every day the language that school tries to force upon then and they hear on the television and on Internet videos, the vast majority of the Brazilian people develop a very strong complex of linguistic incompetence: they believe they do not speak Portuguese, but an incorrect form that does not deserve the name of Portuguese (Perini, 2003: 36; Massini-Cagliari, 2004: 6), even when there is no clear definition of what would be the standard Brazilian Portuguese.

To Faraco (2008: 63), the contemporaneous society, in all its complexity, when creating conditions to amplify the social presence of certain varieties of the language, makes them pragmatically function as an element of relative social aggregation. These varieties tend to go beyond the limits of family restriction or regional communication, answering to the challenges imposed by intense urbanisation, by the complexification of social relations and means of mass communication. The varieties that can perform these functions can act as an 'educated' or 'standard norm' (*norma culta*, in Portuguese, which is opposed to a *norma curta*, 'short standard' norm, which is an interpretation of the standard as referring only to certain usages prescribed by school grammars[5]). Massini-Cagliari (2004: 5) shows that individuals tend to identify it with the variety adopted by important TV news programmes, especially Jornal Nacional, the most important TV news programme on TV Globo.

Faraco (2008: 56) also shows that, although there are no linguistic criteria capable of sustaining a qualitative differentiation of the norms, there occurs a social hierarchisation based on sociocultural or political factors. Being so, those who

---

[5]Faraco (2016: 176–177) considers the 'short standard' an 'imaginary language', that is, uniformising idealisation which floats over concrete and fluid diversity.

speak varieties which are more distant to the abstract standard tend to be stigmatised. Although the 'short standard' cannot be confused with the educated norm, it is closer to the way educated people speak than other varieties of Brazilian Portuguese, because those who codify and assume the functions of guarding and cultivating it come from the upper social strata (especially from the states of São Paulo and Rio de Janeiro).

In this context, the richness of Brazilian linguistic scenario is almost invisible for most people who live in the country and for the rest of the world, concerning both the multiple languages spoken/signed in Brazil and the multiple varieties of Portuguese. The reasons for this 'invisibility', according to Oliveira (2000: 83), can be related to several factors, such as a simple ignorance of the truth, in a country with a vast amount of an uneducated population, overlooking the truth as a result of a political policy that intentionally projects a convenient idea of a monolingual country or simply pure linguistic prejudice.

The concept of linguistic prejudice is as old as structuralism in linguistics and rests in the central idea of 'language system' (de Saussure, 2021[1916]), which implies that all the languages – and, consequently, all of their varieties – are functional and balanced systems, fully adapted to perform all the necessary communication tasks. Being so, in strict linguistic terms, there is no reason to consider that one language or one variety is superior (or inferior) to another; to do so is, henceforth, a prejudiced behaviour.

Already in 1916, the book compiled by Charles Bally and Albert Sechehaye from notes on lectures given by Ferdinand de Saussure at the University of Geneva between 1906 and 1911, *Course in General Linguistics*, refers to the necessity of denouncing and combating the 'mistakes' and 'errors' perpetrated by common people as an important social task for the linguists (de Saussure, 2021: 49). Although not new, in more than 100 years, linguistic prejudice has not been defeated, and the task of combating it, in order to achieve the most inclusive society in linguistic terms, is becoming even more crucial, as time passes by.

In spite of the fact that the core of the idea of linguistic prejudice goes back to the origin of Linguistics as a science, it became clearer in definition and more and more important from the development of sociolinguistic studies. Among the well-known and emblematic studies that mark the beginning of sociolinguistics in the United States are the investigations into African American Vernacular English (AAVE). This variety, typical among working-class African Americans in inner-city areas (Rickford, 1999), was extensively regarded as bad, incorrect, inferior English or, even worse, an index of speakers' cognitive and social-cultural deficiencies. This biased assessment represented an undeniable case of social and linguistic prejudice and discrimination. Against this generalised unscientific view, Labov (1972) describes the rich structure of the AAVE, revealing what he termed the 'logic of non-standard English'. The impact of this knowledge in society could be measured in the episode known as the Ann Arbor case, when parents of AAVE-speaking black students sued the school their children attended for negligence and failure to provide them with inclusive and equitable educational opportunities. The expert testimony of linguists in court was instrumental in representing AAVE as a rule-governed, systematic variety, *different* from standard English, but certainly not *deficient*. Significantly, the court ruled in favour of the students' parents.

In Brazil, the idea of linguistic prejudice becomes stronger with the introduction of investigations relating linguistic variation and social discrimination, especially in educational practices (Bortoni-Ricardo, 2005). These studies have shown that, more important than the geographic variation, there is a crucial sociolinguistic polarisation which separates two social varieties: on the one hand, the standard Brazilian Portuguese, typically urban and educated and, on the other hand, the popular Brazilian Portuguese, mostly uneducated, of rural origin, but also spoken today in the urban areas, because of internal migration movements (Lucchesi, 2015; Faraco, 2016).

The publication of Bagno (2002[1999]) was a turning point for the studies of linguistic prejudice in Brazil and, more importantly, for the diffusion of the concept of linguistic prejudice for the society, in general, but specially to basic education language teachers. Bagno (1999) investigates eight myths, which are common in day-by-day speaking of language and in educational practices in Brazil, showing their inadequacy and how prejudicial they are when assumed in educational contexts: (1) 'the Portuguese language spoken in Brazil presents a surprising unity', (2) 'Brazilian people do not know Portuguese'/'Only in Portugal people can speak Portuguese well', (3) 'Portuguese is a difficult language', (4) 'Uneducated people speaks in an incorrect way', (5) 'the place in which Portuguese is best spoken in Brazil is Maranhão', (6) 'the right way of speaking Portuguese is the way you write it', (7) 'it is necessary to know (school) grammar to speak and write well' and (8) 'to dominate the standard norm is a way for social promotion'.

Because of the complexity of Brazilian linguistic scenario and its relation to educational practices, in the beginning of the introduction of structuralist ideas in academic studies on language variation and literacy methodologies in Brazil, an easy shortcut could be to suggest that the children should be educated in their own variety. This kind of solution could also come from a comparison with native communities in which more than one language are used, where the maintenance of bilingual schools is indicated. But, as Massini-Cagliari (2004: 20) points out, in the case of stigmatised varieties of Portuguese, it is not possible, because we are not talking about 'minorities' in a strict sense, since speakers of non-standard Brazilian Portuguese are the vast majority of the population, and, in this case, we are not talking about different languages, but different varieties of the most spoken language in the country. However, as Hornberger (1998: 453) remembers, 'the whole notion of language minority has more to do with power than with numbers'.

Because of this, Massini-Cagliari (2001) reflects that choosing the linguistic variety of the community as the language for education purposes, particularly in the case of non-prestigious stigmatised varieties, can result in the confinement of the students to their own world, condemning them endlessly to poverty and preventing them from enlarging their horizons and from promoting themselves socially – in this sense, education is indeed a powerful instrument of social promotion. That is why it is possible to consider that the education system is obliged to live in an eternal contradiction: the variety spoken by the students should not be discriminated against, because it is an instrument of self-positioning and of individual affirmation as a member of a specific group inside the whole society, but the education system must promote the use of a standard variety, since the advantages the students will gain from it are evident. To summarise her position, Massini-Cagliari (2004: 20) argues that the ideal education system is the one that 'celebrates' rather than 'tolerates' the linguistic diversity.

O'Neill and Massini-Cagliari (2019) adopt a more critically reflective approach in suggesting that the 'objective' studies of language are not sufficiently addressing the core problem of linguistic prejudice in Brazil: the historical and socio-political contexts which can disadvantage and even vilify the poor. Drawing upon recent international theoretical discussions about linguistic prejudice and the role of linguistic academic research in social change, we suggest (a) that there needs to be much greater academic engagement with society and a willingness to understand why society attaches such negative values to certain linguistic variants and (b) that there is a need for a reconceptualisation in academic circles of the dichotomy between formal/informal and stigmatised/non-stigmatised speech. In this regard, the insights and expertise of sign language linguists will play a crucial role in offering an alternative perspective on such entrenched sociolinguistic categories within spoken communication. They hypothesise that such distinctions fail to successfully capture the wide array of social, semantic and pragmatic functions which non-standard forms of the language can have.

Research brought together in this book helps in the understanding that the problems about language diversity and language prejudice go beyond the identification of regional, social and modality varieties as linguistic 'problems'. We hope that it becomes clear that ignorance and prejudice, present in everyday life and even promoted in traditional and prescriptivist educational strategies, need to be confronted with naturalistic data and scientific evidence that confirm that monolingualism is nothing more than a colonised idea. The chapters collected in this book address language diversity present in different language communities, including the native Brazilian communities and deaf communities, offering a colourful portrait that we should celebrate as the result of part of the infinite possibilities of human communication that remains vivid even after more than 500 years of colonisation.

References

Bagno, M. (2002). *Preconceito lingüístico – o que é, como se faz* (16th ed.). Loyola. [1st ed: 1999].

Bessa Freire, J. R. (2003). Língua Geral Amazônica: a história de um esquecimento. In *Línguas Gerais*. Política Lingüística e Catequese na América do Sul no Período Colonial. Org. J. R. Bessa Freire and M. C. Rosa (pp. 195–209). EdUERJ.

Bortoni-Ricardo, S. M. (2005). *Nós cheguemu na escola, e agora?* Parábola.

Cagliari, L. C. (1989). *Alfabetização e Lingüística*. Scipione.

de Oliveira, G. M. (2000). Brasileiro fala português: monolingüismo e preconceito lingüístico. In *O direito à fala – A questão do preconceito lingüístico*. Org. Fábio Lopes da Silva and Heronides M. de Melo Moura (pp. 83–92). Insular.

de Saussure, F. (2021). *Curso de Linguística Geral.* Parábola. [1st ed. 1916].

Faraco, C. A. (2008). *Norma culta brasileira – desatando alguns nós.* Parábola.

Faraco, C. A. (2016). *História sociopolítica da língua portuguesa.* Parábola.

Fiorin, J. L. (2000). Os Aldrovandos Cantagalos e o preconceito lingüístico. In *O direito à fala – A questão do preconceito lingüístico.* Org. Fábio Lopes da Silva and Heronides M. de Melo Moura (pp. 23–37). Insular.

Hornberger, N. H. (1998). Language policy, language education, language rights: Indigenous, immigrant, and international perspectives. *Language in Society, 27*(4), 439–458.

IBGE. Instituto Brasileiro de Geografia e Estatística. Projeção da População do Brasil e das Unidades da Federação. https://www.ibge.gov.br/apps/populacao/projecao/index.html. Access: 30 Jun 2022.

IPHAN. Instituto do Patrimônio Histórico e Artístico Nacional. Inventário Nacional da Diversidade Linguística. http://portal.iphan.gov.br/pagina/detalhes/140#:~:text=O%20Invent%C3%A1rio%20Nacional%20da%20Diversidade,a%C3%A7%C3%B5es%20de%20apoio%20e%20fomento. Access: 30 Jun 2022.

Labov, W. (1972). *Language in the Inner City: Studies in the black English vernacular.* University of Pennsylvania Press.

Lagares, X. C. (2018). *Qual política linguística? Desafios Glotopolíticos contemporâneos.* Parábola.

Lucchesi, D. (2015). *Língua e Sociedade Partidas: A polarização sociolinguística do Brasil.* Contexto.

Massini-Cagliari, G. (2001). *O texto na alfabetização: coesão e coerência.* Mercado de Letras.

Massini-Cagliari, G. (2004). Language policy in Brazil: Monolingualism and linguistic prejudice. *Language Policy, 3*, 3–23. Kluwer Academic Publishers.

O'Neill, P., & Massini-Cagliari, G. (2019). Linguistic prejudice and discrimination. In Brazilian Portuguese and beyond: Suggestions and recommendations. *Journal of Language and Discrimination, 3*(1), 32–62.

Perini, M. A. (2003). *Sofrendo a Gramática.* Ática.

Rickford, J. R. (1999). *African American vernacular English.* Blackwell.

Rodrigues, A. D. (1996). As línguas gerais sul-americanas. *Papia, 4*(2), 6–18. Available at: http://www.etnolinguistica.org/artigo:rodrigues-1996

Rosa, C. (2003). A língua mais geral do Brasil nos séculos XVI e XVII. In *Línguas Gerais.* Política Lingüística e Catequese na América do Sul no Período Colonial. Org. J. R. Bessa Freire and M. C. Rosa (pp. 133–146). EdUERJ.

Chapter 2
Theorising Linguistic Prejudice in Brazil: Pierre Bourdieu – The Symbolic Power of Language and the Principle of Error Correction

Paul O'Neill and Gladis Massini-Cagliari (iD)

Introduction

Linguistic Prejudice and Discrimination in Brazil: An Overview

Linguistic prejudice and discrimination have most probably existed as long as human language has existed since basic linguistic abilities are intimately linked with the cognitive capacity to create complex categories which are not based on direct experience and exposure but on the descriptions and opinions of others (elves, goblins, griffins and unicorns, Eskimos, the Maasai). At times, categories can be based on limited exposure (e.g. the Portuguese or people of East Asian origin from Brazilians), and this limited experience in addition to opinions of others can be analogically extended to all of the categories. These abilities of categorisation and analogy, which underlie the creative capacity of language and are described as the fuel and fire of human cognition (Hofstadter & Sander, 2013), are also responsible for linguistic prejudice, since prejudice does not originate from exhaustive sense experience but from preconceived opinions that people have about *either* an entire category of individuals based on their use of language or an entire language/language variety and its appropriate domains of usage. These opinions are often never based on actual experience or knowledge of the language/language variety but rather on feelings and beliefs about them, which are socially and historically conditioned.

P. O'Neill
University of Sheffield, Sheffield, UK
e-mail: paul.oneill@sheffield.ac.uk

G. Massini-Cagliari (✉)
Unesp – Sao Paulo State University, Araraquara, Sao Paulo, Brazil
e-mail: gladis.massini-cagliari@unesp.br

© The Author(s), under exclusive license to Springer Nature Switzerland AG 2023
G. Massini-Cagliari et al. (eds.), *Understanding Linguistic Prejudice*,
https://doi.org/10.1007/978-3-031-25806-0_2

In a previous publication (O'Neill & Massini-Cagliari, 2019), we draw attention to the fact that whilst the discrimination and prejudice towards different languages have been denounced by international institutions and both national and international laws are in place to guarantee the rights of speakers of different languages, the same protection has not been afforded to speakers of non-standard varieties of a language. Such an oversight, we suggest, can result in a lack of understanding of the serious social and economic effects which linguistic prejudice can have on a country. For example, UNESCO[1] notes that the most pressing problem in Brazil is social inequality, and, with reference to this inequality in developing countries, UNESCO highlights that differences in incomes can be correlated with cultural and linguistic differences. A proposed solution to the latter differences is via a positive awareness and a favourable appreciation of cultural and linguistic diversity, which can lead to economic and social change. However, linguistic diversity is only understood as different languages and not the diversity within the same language. In Brazil, however, despite it being the home to numerous languages, the majority of the population are monolingual Portuguese speakers, and the variable which correlates most strongly with differences in income is not a different autochthonous Latin American culture or language but a particular variety of Portuguese.

Evidence of the deeply ingrained nature of linguistic prejudice towards these popular varieties of Brazilian Portuguese, within some sections of Brazilian society, is attested by the civic response to the introduction of educational measures to foster a non-discriminative approach to non-standard language varieties of Portuguese. These measures, as explained in detail by O'Neill and Massini-Cagliari (2019: 40–44), took the form of a pedagogical textbook,[2] *Por Uma Vida Melhor* 'For a Better Life' (Ramos, 2011), which was aimed at adult learners who were unable to complete their schooling when children or adolescents. The controversial part of the book is the chapter which addresses the differences between writing and speaking, and particularly the lack of nominal, adjectival and verbal agreement in spontaneous spoken language, e.g. saying *os livro ilustrado mais interessante* instead of *os livros ilustrados mais interessantes* 'the most interesting illustrated books' and *os menino pega o peixe* instead of *os meninos pegam o peixe* 'the children catch the fish'. The author classes these constructions as natural forms of the spoken language that are not wrong or debased variants but simply different and makes the point that different variants are appropriate in different contexts. The book also highlights the fact that people who speak this way could be subject to linguistic prejudice. Specifically, the book states the following:

---

[1] http://www.unesco.org/new/en/brasilia/culture/cultural-diversity/

[2] The book was published as part of the *Live and Learn* collection of teaching books aimed at adolescents and adults and developed by a NGO in collaboration with a publishing house. The content of the books is in line with national directives (National O Programa Nacional do Livro e do Material Didático) regarding didactic material that are set out and approved by the Ministry of Education; the books are made available to all Brazilian students.

(1) You could be wondering; 'Can I say 'os livro'? [instead of 'os livros' with the plural marker on the noun as well as the article]. Of course you can. But be careful because, depending on the situation you run the risk of being a victim of linguistic prejudice. Many people say what should and should not be said or written, taking the rules drawn up for the standard as a way of correcting all linguistic forms. The speaker, therefore, has to be able to use the appropriate linguistic variant for each situation.

This textbook became an issue of public debate since a number of media outlets reported on it. The *Jornal Nacional* had the headline that the Ministry of Education was 'defending that students do not need to follow certain grammatical rules to speak correctly[3]' (Batista de Padua, 2014: 15). The public response to the book, as analysed by Leiser Baronas and Cox (2003), was generally negative. It was considered by many as 'outrageous', 'stupid' and 'mad' that the Ministry of Education was endorsing the use of 'bad Portuguese' and the book was characterised as an 'aberration' and 'barbarity', a 'disservice to students' and 'reversal of values', 'the enshrinement of ignorance' and 'academic trash dressed up as cultural avant-garde'; the authors of the textbook were described as 'enemies of good Portuguese', 'murderers of the language' and 'a circle of false intellectuals'. Note the comment in (2) by one member of the public, in imitation to the wording of the book detailed in (1) where the grammatical rules of the standard language are compared with laws against serious crimes. Note, also the comment in (3) by Marcos Vilaça, the former president of the Brazilian Academy of Letters.

(2) The authors of the criminal book could use another example: 'Can I kill someone I don't like? Of course you can. But be careful because, depending on the situation, you run the risk of being a victim of judicial prejudice. Just as killing someone violates a rule, killing the language violates another. To condemn both violations is not prejudice at all. It is a civilizing principle'.

(3) 'One thing is to understand how language, a living organism, evolves but it is another thing to accept and endorse glaring mistakes' says Marcos Vilaça, president of the Brazilian Academy of Letters. 'It's like teaching wrong times- tables. Four times three is always twelve, on the outskirts of towns or in the palace' (Leiser Baronas & Cox, 2003: 85).

What underlies these comments is an extremely aggressive and extreme manifestation of 'standard language' ideology. We characterise it as such since Lippi-Green (2006: 64) defines this ideology as a 'bias towards an abstracted, idealized, non-varying spoken language that is imposed and maintained by dominant institutions'. However, what Marcos Vilaça is expressing in (3) is not merely a bias towards the norm but a steadfast belief that the norm is the only legitimate expression of the Portuguese language and that anything which falls outside this norm is inherently incorrect. The assumption is that just as there is one name for the language, 'Portuguese', so there is one set of grammatical rules. Anything else is situated firmly outside the civilised laws of the language and within the realm of barbarism/ degenerate speech.

---

[3] http://g1.globo.com/jornal-nacional/noticia/2011/05/mec-defende-que-aluno-nao-precisa-seguir-algumas-regras-da-gramatica-para-falar-de-forma-correta.html

The Brazilian reality, however, is that many people use these non-standard forms on a daily basis, as has been shown by in-depth and sophisticated sociolinguistic studies. Scherre and Naro (2014) analysed the three variables discussed in the book in the speech of a community in Rio de Janeiro and concluded that the author of the book, Ramos (2011), 'showed great linguistic sensitivity and presented structures that are genuinely natural in Brazilian Portuguese'. However, such genuine, natural forms of Brazilian Portuguese are not considered legitimate forms by certain sections of the educated elite, which can have serious social implications. For example, within the educational system, linguistic prejudice and discrimination has been identified as a possible contributing factor to the academic failure of students (Soares, 2017) and school drop-out rates (O'Neill & Massini-Cagliari, 2019). Whilst it is true that Brazil is not the only country in the world in which there are significant differences between the speech of the great majority of the population and the language used as a means of instruction and assessment in education, it is considered that the situation in Brazil is aggravated by the severe linguistic prejudice against non-standard forms of the language and the extreme wealth inequalities, which are correlated with linguistic differences.

As for the best ways to combat linguistic prejudice and discrimination, O'Neill (2022) notes that, in Brazil, the strategies are overwhelmingly recognition-based. Here, he is making a distinction, prevalent in social-science literature (e.g. Nancy Fraser, 1995, 2000), between two different types of strategies adopted to address social injustices: recognition-based strategies and redistribution-based strategies. The former involves the recognition of a particular collective (e.g. the working classes, disabled people) as a discrete entity which suffers some type of social injustice/prejudice and attempts to effect social change by foregrounding this injustice and positively valorising the collective. Redistribution-based strategies, on the other hand, do not necessarily reify a particular collective and attempt to change the social attitudes towards this collective; rather their focus is on changing the socio-political and economic structures via the restructuring of systems and the redistribution of economic and political resources. Examples of social movements based on redistribution strategies are the liberal welfare state, means-tested grants, quotas for underrepresented groups for jobs, university places, etc. Much language research nowadays with a social/political dimension adopts recognition-based strategies (see also Block, 2018), as is typical of non-language-based social activism, specifically in the USA (Fraser, 1995). These recognition strategies, however, have been criticised as being limited in achieving real long-term change (Fraser, 1995; Block, 2018).

With specific reference to linguistic prejudice and discrimination in the educational system in Brazil, O'Neill (2022) highlights the prevalence of recognition-based strategies, which often tacitly assume that there are two types of Brazilian Portuguese (Popular Brazilian and Educated Brazilian – Lucchesi, 2002, 2015) and attempt to change the prejudicial opinions towards speakers of the popular varieties and positively valorise this group of speakers and their linguistic features. Most of these recognition strategies, including the one adopted in the textbook described above, are underpinned by a framework, first put forth by the Soares (1986), based on the recognition of differences and the proposal of bidialectalism. This practical approach shows a great sensitivity and understanding of the Brazilian context; it realises that (a) linguistic differences are often conceived as mental or cultural deficiencies and (b) the acquisition of the standard is important for social and economic progress. The strategy, therefore, is to encourage the learning of the standard but to do this in a way which does not denigrate non-standard forms. Specifically, the aim is to recast non-standard forms as mere differences (not deficiencies) that are neither better nor worse than those of the standard but merely just different and to encourage speakers to become bidialectal, which means (a) understanding of the social function and usefulness of the different forms and (b) being able to use them in the appropriate social context.

Such a strategy is typical of previous US-based sociolinguistic studies, notably those on the relationship between language and race, which aspired to achieve social change via a 'principle of error correction', whereby the focus is on academics sharing their 'specialist knowledge' and changing the erroneous beliefs of individuals. This principle has been categorised as being socially naïve and ineffectual (Lewis, 2018) since the focus is on changing beliefs of individuals but not analysing the political, historical and social factors which sustain and reinforce such beliefs and the material structures which endorse and promote them. That is, the focus of these strategies is overly recognition-based, and more attention should be paid to issues often addressed in redistribution-based strategies, e.g. the societal structures which reaffirm and perpetuate injustices. In O'Neill and Massini-Cagliari (2019: 49–52), we have an extensive discussion of the concept of 'error correction' and a review of the recent criticism directed at it. Drawing on numerous sources (most notably Lewis, 2018 and Snell, 2018), we make the point that linguistic prejudice can, at times, not be linguistic at all, in the sense that the prejudices are not related to any specific linguistic features but related to ideologies about classes of people. These people form social hierarchies, and those at the top, due to their material conditions and social positions, are the ones who define what is considered authoritative usage.

A case in point is the socio-historical context which led to the forging of the Brazilian standard. O'Neill (2022) shows how the official standard was intimately linked with social and political preoccupations, prevalent in new Republic, of wanting a country which was focused towards 'Order and Progress' and worried about the effects of racial and social degeneration. The linguistic dimension of the solution, he notes, 'was to establish a standard norm which was spoken naturally by hardly any native Brazilians but which represented a gold standard to aim for and one which was considered to produce positive cognitive benefits' (ibid: 16). Unfortunately, educational provision was deficient and socially and geographically very uneven, which meant that this 'golden norm' was never effectively taught to and therefore adopted by the great majority of speakers, leading to the current chasm between the written standard and the speech of the great majority of the population, and the concomitant prejudice against speakers of certain popular varieties.

We agree that, in order to effectively combat linguistic prejudice in Brazil, there needs to be more emphasis on understanding the historical sources of linguistic prejudice and how it is accepted, reaffirmed and perpetuated in modern-day societies. This should not replace the valiant efforts of colleagues to revalorise prejudicial opinions about popular varieties of spoken Brazilian Portuguese but work alongside them. We suggest there is a need to accept that people make negative value judgements about others based on their use of language, and, in addition to trying to change these judgements, it is necessary also to analyse how they are currently being endorsed, promoted and reinforced within Brazilian society. We therefore analyse linguistic prejudice within the theoretical framework of the French philosopher and sociologist Pierre Bourdieu, and his theory of practice, since, as John Thompson notes in his introduction to Bourdieu's book *Knowledge and Symbolic Power* (Bourdieu, 1991), 'the first step in creating new social relations, alternative ways of organizing social and political life, is to understand the socially instituted limits of the ways of speaking, thinking and acting which are characteristic of our societies today'. We choose this theory since we agree that Bourdieu's 'relentless disclosure of power and privilege in its most varied and subtlest forms, and the respect accorded by his theoretical framework to the agents who make up the social world which he so acutely dissects, give his work an implicit critical potential' (Thompson, 1991: 31). Within this theory the linguistic prejudice against non-standard varieties of Portuguese is conceived as a type of symbolic violence. In what follows we give a brief summary of this theory, give our own interpretation as to the motivations of linguistic prejudice as symbolic violence and suggest how such theorising can contribute to a more effective strategy for combatting linguistic prejudice.

Linguistic Prejudice and Pierre Bourdieu

Bourdieu in a number of various works expounded what has been classified as a grand theory: an 'abstract and normative theory of human nature and conduct' (Skinner, 1985: 1). In the theoretical framework of Bourdieu, society is conceived of as a multidimensional space, consisting of a number of different fields. Fields can be of many different types: the family, the school, the town one lives in, the organisation one works in, etc. Each field and each individual is characterised by its own habitus, which is 'its own taken-for-granted understanding of the world, implicit and explicit rules of behaviour' (Leander, 2017). A habitus is a set of character traits, which are instilled and imprinted upon one in early childhood and which predispose individuals to act and react in particular ways. A habitus is also an understanding of the value that actions, qualities and possessions have. This value is viewed as power within the relative field, is conceptualised in terms of capital, and can take different forms: economic capital (material wealth), social capital (social networks and benefits derived therein) and cultural capital (cultural knowledge and skills). This last type of capital is divided into different sub-constituents:

- Objectified cultural capital: material belongings which have cultural significance, e.g. works of art, sports cars, collections of rare books, stamps, stickers, etc.

- Institutionalised cultural capital: symbols of cultural authority and prestige. For example, credentials and qualifications such as university degrees or even the university one attends.[4]
- Embodied cultural capital: the qualities of your mind and body. These can be skills, tastes in art and literature and, importantly, language.

More powerful social classes differentiate themselves from 'lower' classes by their cultural capital which includes their social tastes and how they look, behave and, of course, speak. One's language or accent, which Bourdieu terms 'articulatory style', not only forms part of one's cultural capital, but it is also an ingrained part of one's linguistic habitus: an intrinsic part of one's bodily functions which has been learnt via imitation and repetition and which one cannot unlearn or supress without extensive training.

This theory of capital attempts to explain the power dynamics in human societies and the concept of social status, for which another type of capital, *symbolic capital,* is important. Symbolic capital is the recognition bestowed upon the sum of the different types of capital within a specific field. For example, within the field of the profession of law, one will have a high status and, therefore, highly valued symbolic capital, not only due to one being skilled at law (embodied cultural capital) but also by being rich (economic capital), well-connected (social capital) having a law degree from a prestigious university (institutionalised cultural capital) and dressing and speaking in what is considered the correct and appropriate way, that is, the extent to which one adheres to the implicit rules and principles of that field, which Bourdieu terms *doxa.* These are not just opinions or common beliefs about how one should act in a particular setting, but they are conceived as unquestioned truths which can produce common behaviours and actions. The individual within a particular field will be evaluated in accordance with their symbolic capital and its accordance with the field's *doxa*; in this way the individual is prescribed a status in the field.

Thus, a *favela* in São Paulo is a very different *field* than that of a swanky apartment block nearby: the people will dress differently, speak differently and act in different ways to social situations which present themselves. The field and its *habitus* are not entirely deterministic; however, rather Bourdieu views it as bestowing upon individuals what he calls *le sens pratique*, an understanding of what is appropriate and in what contexts. Within different fields the value attached to the cultural capital differs. Whereas a person in a pricey São Paulo condominium could be valued as having high symbolic capital due to their collection of the first editions of works of Brazilian literature (objectified cultural capital) and their university degree (institutionalised cultural capital) in a nearby *favela*, the same value may be attributed to having a full collection of posters/programmes of the games of the local football team or the Brazilian national team (objectified cultural capital) and being

---

[4] Skills learnt at university are embodied or learnt cultural capitals, but the institution one attends, e.g. Oxford, Cambridge, Yale and Harvard, constitutes institutionalised cultural capital.

one of the leaders of a Samba association for the carnivals (institutionalised cultural capital).

Regarding language, to be assigned a legitimate place within the relevant field, one would have to speak in accordance with its conventions, which would mean that someone from the *favelas* speaking standard Brazilian Portuguese would be as delegitimised as someone from the condominium speaking in a speech characterised as typical of a *favela*. Each field has its own conventions and ascribes different values to different practices. In this way, people who speak standard forms of a language can also be subject to linguistic prejudice depending on the context. We favour such a theoretical view of society since it portrays the different social classes as equally complex in terms of structures, codes, principles and interactions and does not trivialise or romanticise the lower classes but makes it clear that in the bigger field of the nation/state and in more 'formal' fields, the value attached to different types of capital can favour the middle and upper classes. This theory also captures the fact that language variety like race, religion, ethnicity, sexuality or even haircut style is a human variable and variables are sensitive to being associated with some type of social meaning, entirely independent of the inherent characteristics and qualities of the variable. Within this theory, the meaning is a product of the value of the capital which is entirely determined by the social context.

This differential value of capital depending on the context is conceptualised through an analogy with economies of practices in which actions are guided by interests and therefore fields and society in general are conceptualised as a market, in which people and things have values and are in competition for dominance. Bourdieu considers language not merely as a means of communication but also as 'an instrument of action and power' (Bourdieu, 1991: 37) in which the value and power of speech are highlighted and linguistic interchanges are considered as 'relations of symbolic power in which the power relations between speakers and their respective groups are actualised'.

It is interesting to view linguistic prejudice in this way since it explains why the same linguistic feature can be classed as either standard or sub-standard depending on the country. For example, in Spain aspiration of preconsonantal coda /s/ in words such as *pasta* 'pasta' and *isla* 'island' is considered an incorrect, sub-standard pronunciation found in the speech of Southern speakers and not suitable for the speech of national newsreaders, whilst in Argentina and Uruguay, it is entirely standard. The reason for this difference is that Spain and Argentina constitute different markets and, in Spain, the language variety which dominates the market is that which does not aspirate coda /s/. Bourdieu (1991: 652) notes that 'When one language dominates the market, it becomes the norm against which the prices of the other modes of expression, and with them the values of the various competences, are defined'.

Thus, non-standard forms of a language are given a devalued price, and one's linguistic competence, the ability to adopt different speech forms, functions as linguistic capital in the market of the nation/state. Bourdieu makes the point that discussions and worries around language competence are really about control of the market and social domination. In his view, those who express views about the decline of language standards are concerned with their threatened linguistic capital which is the threatened market that they dominate. The value a standard language derives from the market has no value outside the market. When people try and defend the standard variety as being more 'logical' or 'refined' than other varieties, Bourdieu interprets this as a defence of the market in which their linguistic capital is being threatened. He highlights the importance of the position which the educational system gives to different language varieties since he views the educational institution as having 'the monopoly in the large-scale production of the producers/consumers, and therefore in the reproduction of the market without which the social value of the linguistic competence, its capacity to function as linguistic capital, would cease to exist' (Bourdieu, 1991: 57).

However, the position of the standard language does not merely depend upon the educational system but everyday linguistic interactions in which certain speakers in formal or semi-formal settings either are not exposed to the way that they naturally speak or are corrected and made to feel conscious and insecure about their way of speaking. This inculcation forces the population as a whole, conceptualised as a market, to recognise the place that the standard language plays. In the terms of Bourdieu, people who are 'continuously subjected to the sanctions of the linguistic market, functioning as a system of positive or negative reinforcements, acquire durable dispositions which are the basis of their perception and appreciation of the state of the linguistic market and consequently of their strategies for expression' (Bourdieu, 1977: 654).

According to Bourdieu, this system exists and is perpetuated since it is to the benefit of those who naturally speak the standard and who will naturally pass it on to their children, thus bestowing on them precious cultural capital. In times gone by, it was the economic capital, the actual material wealth, that was passed from dominant generation to dominant generation, to secure and perpetuate their dominance; however, in present times this has become much more difficult due to inheritance laws and taxation. In its stead, modern societies have adopted a policy through which it is assured that the markets highly favour the cultural capital which is passed from the dominant generations: their cultural backgrounds, values, tastes and, of course, their language variety. Bourdieu explicitly states that 'the transmission of cultural capital is no doubt the best hidden form of hereditary transmission of capital, and it therefore receives disproportionately greater weight in the system of reproduction strategies, as the direct, visible forms of transmission tend to be more strongly censored and controlled' (Bourdieu, 1986: 246).

As previously stated, however, in order for a particular type of linguistic capital to be of high value, it must be measured against other types of linguistic capital which must be devalued, and the whole market must be convinced of these relative values, including those who speak the devalued forms. Thus, those who are dominated and discriminated against and are subjects of prejudice partake in their own domination, discrimination and prejudice in assuming unquestioningly and uncritically certain established hierarchies and views about the correct ways of speaking, even though they may reject adopting these forms of speech. In this way, people with non-standard forms of language, generally from lower-class backgrounds, come to share and reinforce a system of evaluation which works against them. Bourdieu terms this *symbolic violence*, not physical violence but an invisible force of suppression, a 'gentle, invisible violence' which those who are subjected to it mistake, or in the terminology of Bourdieu 'misrecognise', as an actual and legitimate force around which society is structured. It is argued, therefore, that nonstandard speakers participate in and are actively complicit in their own subjection and subjugation since the symbolic power of the ruling classes rests upon the foundation of shared beliefs regarding the validity, worth and appropriateness of certain varieties of a language in formal settings and lucrative professions. Individuals are not passively subjected to this violence, like a scalpel to a corpse. Rather, 'symbolic power requires, as a condition of its success, that those subjected to it believe in the legitimacy of power and the legitimacy of those who wield it' (Thompson, 1991: 22–23).

This symbolic violence can result in acts of censorship. In a particular market, if one wishes to be legitimately perceived, one must produce speech which obeys the market's particular criteria regarding grammar, pronunciation, formality and discourse. Not knowing or being unsure of the criteria can result in insecurity and even silencing. Bourdieu illustrates this point by considering some of the typical speech practices of individuals from different class backgrounds when they find themselves in formal or official situations (an interview, a classroom discussion, a public ceremony, etc.) and notes that speakers from upper-class backgrounds distinguish themselves in these contexts and speak with what is considered 'distinction', merely because their natural way of speaking aligns with what is expected and valued in such situations. There is 'a concordance or congruence between their linguistic *habitus* and the demands of formal markets. It is this congruence which underlies the confidence and fluency with which they speak: their confidence merely attests to the fact that the conditions in which they are speaking concur fairly closely with the conditions which endowed them with the capacity to speak, and hence they are able (and know they are able) to reap symbolic benefits by speaking in a way that comes naturally to them' (Bourdieu, 1991: 21).

Contrastively, speakers of other varieties of a language need to make a conscious effort to imitate such a way of speaking which can result in linguistic insecurity and anxiety or even silence for speakers of the lower classes. The speech of this class is often the most different from that of the standard literary language, and therefore they can tend to avoid such situations which can explain school drop-out rates amongst the working-class speakers and their tendency to confine themselves to fields in which their speech is not devalued; thus, they enrol on vocational training courses and seek labour-intensive jobs.

In sum, to couch linguistic prejudice and discrimination in Bordieuan terms would be to define it as a form of symbolic violence, whereby society is structured not only to devalue non-standard speech but also to convince its citizens, including the speakers of non-standard forms, that certain ways of speaking have less worth and are somehow inferior to the speech of others. This shared system of evaluation which works against a certain group of speakers constitutes the subtle but effective form of suppression and control which is symbolic violence.

Our Reservations

Whilst we do agree that linguistic prejudice is indeed a form of symbolic violence, we would like to question what seem to be Bourdieu's beliefs as to the motivations for the existence and perpetuation of symbolic violence. For us, the aforementioned theoretical explanation of linguistic prejudice and symbolic violence bestows an awareness and agency on the ruling classes and supposes that their actions are inspired by some type of interest to protect their linguistic capital or increase the value of their capital, as if they were aware of what was at stake and the intricate ways which societies are structured. Contrastively, the lower classes lack such knowledge and agency and therefore gullibly accept the value system imposed upon them.

We do not believe that the majority of the population are aware that the attitudes about linguistic forms are entirely a product of the societal value attributed to these forms and that these values have been determined politically, socially and historically. Indeed, we reject the notion that this knowledge is what drives the upper classes to protect the system which benefits their way of speech and assures their position at the top of the linguistic hierarchy. Let us take, for example, the comments made by the former head of the Brazilian Academy of Letters in (3) in which he assumes that all varieties of Portuguese obey the same grammar rules and compares these to the times table and thus rejects the recognition of other types of grammar rules. Are these comments motivated by his desire of social domination and of wanting to protect the prestige associated with his form of speech? We think not.

Our view is that individuals from all classes can perpetuate linguistic prejudice since they share the belief that non-standard varieties of a language are less elegant, more chaotic and simply inferior to the standard variety and these beliefs form part of the collective knowledge of the majority of the nation. This collective knowledge is the result of the circular nature of the ideology of standard languages (Lippi-Green, 1997), whereby educated people, who usually speak the standard form of a language, are often considered educated just because they speak the standard language. It is in this way that standard language ideology becomes so entrenched in modern-day societies, to the extent that 'their origin is often forgotten by speakers, and are therefore socially reproduced and end up being "naturalized", or perceived as natural or as common sense, thereby masking the social construction processes at work' (Boudreau & Dubois, 2007: 104). This common-sense way of seeing the world is similar to Bourdieu's notion of *le sens pratique*, referenced above. However, in our interpretation we maintain that it is not reinforced by the upper classes, in general, because they realise that this is the way to protect their position and privilege, rather they merely assume that this is how the world works. Thus, for the majority of individuals who automatically benefit and are advantaged from being born into a field in which the speech approximates to that of the standard, there is not necessarily, in our view, a desire for them to protect and perpetuate their linguistic advantages but merely a shared belief that their form of speech is inherently superior to other forms of speech, due to its similarity to the standard and the ingrained nature of standard language ideologies.

We therefore frame linguistic prejudice within a theoretical framework which merges[5] Bourdieu's theory with the discipline of hermeneutics, which is a method or theory of interpretation. Our view is that individuals that are born into complex societies with various *fields* and their corresponding *doxa* must come to interpret what they experience and make sense of such dynamic societies and linguistic prejudice is born of these experiences and interpretations.

Hermeneutics and Linguistic Prejudice

Originally hermeneutics was concerned with the interpretation of biblical texts, but more recently it has been defined as 'the phenomenon of understanding and of the correct interpretation of what has been understood' (Gadamer, 2013) which, of course, can give rise to different types of understanding. The word derives from associations with the messenger god Hermes, who, on his errands carrying messages between gods or between gods and mortals, would have first to interpret and understand the messages for himself, which could undoubtedly change the meaning, since he acted as a mediator. In the same way, we think individuals born in societies, which may in the past have been formed or contrived with certain ambitions, desires and prejudices in mind, must, in their own way, interpret these societies.

There are two key concepts of hermeneutics which are most compelling to the present discussion: prejudices and horizons. In hermeneutics prejudice is considered extremely natural and part and parcel of what defines humans. In turn, one's prejudices combined with what one has experienced in life (historicity) give an individual (or interpreter) a world view at a particular point in time (Brar, 2016: 38). The limits of these world views are the horizons.

In the philosophical and psychoanalytical literature, there is much debate over this concept of a horizon/horizons and its relation to the authority of traditions and people's worldviews (Gadamer (2013), Habermas and Rehg (1996), Heidegger (1967), Piercey (2004), Wittgenstein and Anscombe (1994), Schatzki (1996), to name but a few). Standing back from the nuances and complexities of the philosophical debate, the basic premise is that people do what makes sense for them to do; they have a general understanding of how the world works and their practices make up their 'horizons of intelligibility'. Within the context of language prejudice, we would argue that the upper classes are not committed to dominate and subjugate the working classes by condemning their language varieties and limiting their field of acceptability and, likewise, the working classes are not docile and submissive in allowing this to happen. Rather, the belief that the standard form of the language is the superior form constitutes their horizon of intelligibility – this is what makes sense to them given their experience of society.

---

[5]The inspiration for this comes from Brar (2016).

Why should this be their interpretation? We suggest that this interpretation follows, on the one hand, from the total lack of representation of non-standard forms in environments which are bestowed with high cultural capital (literature, media, schooling, formal situations, etc.) and, on the other hand, from the erroneous assumption of an inherent and deterministic correlation between language variety, social class and wealth. The idea is that the rich or those who gain wealth speak the standard, and this is directly related to them being socially and economically more successful and having more opportunities. That is, it is believed that those who speak educated Brazilian Portuguese have enhanced mental abilities and enhanced rationality compared with those who speak popular Brazilian Portuguese. The rich are more sophisticated, more cultured and more advanced; in short, they are more civilised. Their way of speaking reflects these aspects and is contrasted with the irrational, spontaneous, illogical, albeit creative, underclass and their speech, which is characterised as being a polluted, debased, denigrated and even a barbaric form of the language (Massini-Cagliari, 2004). This linguistic prejudice is a historic legacy and clearly related to the Latin American preoccupation centred around the concepts of civilisation and barbarism, which in Brazil was articulated around the positivist motto of Order and Progress versus the threat of degeneration and which had very specific linguistic implications (see O'Neill (2022) for a full discussion). Linguistic prejudice is therefore intimately linked with and used as a proxy for other social inequalities involved with race, ethnicity, wealth and social class. In what follows we briefly look at the most effective way to encourage social change and combat linguistic prejudice which, ultimately, we see as a reflection of other societal prejudices.

Possible Solutions

Upon analysis of linguistic prejudice within the theory of Bourdieu, it seems clear that the only way to eradicate the prejudice and discrimination against popular Brazilian is either to eradicate this way of speaking or to allow it to be used in fields which have high cultural value such as the spoken media, TV programmes, politics and even teaching. The first of these options constitutes *linguisticide*, the systematic and pre-meditated eradication of linguistic diversity. Given the lack of respect for the linguistic diversity within languages, this would not be condemned internationally, and its proponents would surely disguise it as a civilising force on the people, having them speak 'correct' Portuguese. The question, however, is whether such a policy would, with sufficient money, be successful in achieving its aim. We think not for two reasons. Firstly, despite the shared belief of popular Brazilian being a sub-standard and inferior form of the language, the speakers of these forms do not consider themselves as barbarous and in need of civilising. Within their communities their forms of speech are markers of identity and viewed positively, and thus these features are reinforced and perpetuated. Secondly, both popular and educated Brazilian Portuguese are nebulous umbrella terms for an ill-defined set of linguistic features. They are not categorically different types of speech; rather they are end points on a continuation of linguistic features. Many of the features traditionally associated with popular Brazilian are, in fact, widespread in Brazil and not only characteristic of the working and uneducated classes. Middle-class educated speakers can and do produce phrases which lack adjectival, nominal and verbal agreement or lack subjunctive forms where the written standard would demand them. Of course, the rate of the appearance of such features is significantly less than that of working class and the poorest in society, but that does not mean that they are not present. In sum the differences between popular and educated Brazilian Portuguese can often be characterised as ones of degree not ones of kind, and, in general, these differences form part of the great variation within Brazilian Portuguese which is generally organised along the following three continua: urban vs rural, written vs spoken and careful monitored language vs informal spontaneous language (Bortoni-Ricardo, 2004).

The second option, which corresponds to having non-standard varieties as a valid language used by positive, likeable and non-poor characters depicted in soaps or the language of political commentators and even newsreaders, seems likewise condemned to failure due to the likelihood of having such measures implemented given the ingrained linguistic prejudices within the Brazilian society. Public opinion would be against having newsreaders not making what are considered the necessary nominal and verbal agreements. There would be the worry that such use of language could spread and even be picked up by other children who do not naturally speak that way. In short, there would be a public outcry much similar, but on a larger scale, to that recorded for the pedagogical textbook discussed above. Brazilians in general believe that certain non-standard forms, especially those which lack standard morphosyntactic agreement, are bad and barbarous forms of Portuguese, and they would sound cacophonous as a means for delivering the news.

However, that these linguistic forms should sound disagreeable and unacceptable is akin to when in the past some people in the USA considered it inappropriate to have black people eat in the same restaurants as white people or drink from the same water fountains, since the sight of them or thought of touching something that a black person had touched made some white people nauseous. Reid (2014: 59) relates the problems which the *mulatto* André Rebouças, celebrated Brazilian economist and engineer and friend of Dom Pedro II, faced trying to secure entrance into the New York Grand Opera House and even securing accommodation in New York in 1873 on account of his skin colour. Although denied entry to the Opera, the distinguished Brazilian was eventually offered board in a third-class hotel, on the condition that he ate in his room and never in the restaurant. What underlies both the linguistic and racial prejudices is an irrational dislike not based on experience but on beliefs which are a product of a skewed social system which sees and treats linguistic forms or skin colour as inherently bad to the extent they become repulsive. Thus, not wanting newsreaders, political commentators, teachers or other people in important social roles to speak without the standard morphosyntactic agreements is related to the fact that such a role legitimises these forms of speech and thus there is a risk that others will adopt these forms. Consequently, these forms could even be adopted by one's own social circle and family. The arguments and fears were under-lyingly the same in the USA with the introduction of newsreaders of colour – the role legitimised people of colour in such professional positions and within educated society – and there was therefore the risk of people of colour entering such elite circles and even marrying into families. The fear and rejection of people of colour in the past and people speaking non-standard forms of a language in the present are due to such human variables (speech and skin colour) being inherently considered by the past and/or present ruling elites as bad.

However, the ruling elites did not have this belief due to any intrinsic qualities pertaining to them (the ruling elite) but because of the lack of people of colour/people speaking non-standard forms in their social milieus and the value system of society which devalued and even denigrated different ways of speaking and/or non-white skin colour. This brings us to the core of the problem with combating linguistic prejudice and discrimination. The most effective solution is to change (a) the social structures and value systems which generate negative opinions about non-standard forms and (b) the social pressures whereby people feel the need to change their speech to be accepted or perceived as successful. However, changing these social structures can meet fierce opposition from the opinions of society which are the very product of the social structures.

Although it would be untrue to claim that in modern Brazil racial prejudice and discrimination is not a problem today, it is true that historically the situation has improved greatly and that Brazil has arguably carved out an identity by accepting and celebrating its cultural heritage and racial mixture. Michael Reid (2014) notes how 'the works of Giberto Freyre and Sérgio Buarque…. urged Brazilians to lose their inferiority complex in relation to Europe and embrace their racial mixture as the core of their national identity'. To this one should also add the modernist anthro-pophagic movement inspired by Oswald de Andrade (for its relation to language and prejudice, see O'Neill, 2020). Not all Brazilians are black or mixed-race or particularly like *samba*, *feijoada*, *capoeira*, *bossa nova*, *candomblé* or the films of Carmen Miranda, but most Brazilians accept them and even celebrate them as being part of the complex mosaic of what it means to be Brazilian. We suggest that if the Brazilian society could do the same with spoken language and allow the linguisti-cally legitimate natural forms of speech of a great proportion of Brazilian society to have visibility within the state in contexts with high social value, then these forms can cease to be discriminated against. They can be recognised and celebrated as authentic and legitimate forms of Brazilian Portuguese, which, as with modern English, came about as a result of its complex history and the expansion in its num-ber of speakers.

Can this be achieved? Of course it can. Much of human society, including Brazil, is witnessing a special and transitory moment in their history, a moment of reason and tolerance of the difference of others, as elaborated on by Steven Pinker (2011, 2018), We propose that this moment needs to be taken advantage of to change old prejudices relating to the character and nature of the Brazilian people and their non-standard forms of speech. However, as Einstein noted, it is easier to disintegrate an atom than a prejudice, and thus we recommend that linguistic prejudice and measures to tackle it be put on the national agenda of future governments. It is necessary for national governments, the international community and, more importantly, individuals to realise that linguistic prejudice and discrimination towards non-standard varieties of a language is a reality, that language can often be used as a substitute for other types of prejudices and that this type of linguistic discrimination does pose a challenge and obstacle to social and economic development.

Amongst Brazilians it is a common narrative that God endowed Brazil with a land resembling paradise with regard its natural resources and climate but that God then condemned the country by bestowing on it the Brazilian people. The Brazilian society needs to realise that one of the greatest sources of wealth of a country comes from its population, and in order to harness their support and efforts in national projects of development, they need to be supported and respected and given the opportunity to flourish. This means accepting and celebrating their linguistic differences whilst at the same time maintaining a written standard (not necessarily the present one) and the unity of the Brazilian language and Brazilian people.

Acknowledgements The authors would like to thank the Brazilian Federal Agency for Support and Evaluation of Graduate Education [Coordenação de Aperfeiçoamento de Pessoal de Nível Superior – CAPES], in the scope of the Program CAPES-PrInt (process number 88887.310463/2018-00). Gladis Massini-Cagliari also wishes to thank the Brazilian National Council for Scientific and Technological Development (Conselho Nacional de Desenvolvimento Científico e Tecnológico – CNPq, 302648/2019-4).

References

Batista de Padua, D. (2014). *A polêmica em torno do livro didático "por uma vida melhor": (des) construindo sentidos.* Masters (Mestre em Estudos de Linguagem) – Estudos de Linguagem, Universidade Federal de Mato Grosso.

Block, D. (2018). The political economy of language education research (or the lack thereof): Nancy Fraser and the case of translanguaging. *Critical Inquiry in Language Studies, 15*(4), 237–257.

Bortoni-Ricardo, S. M. (2004). *Educação em língua materna: a sociolinguística na sala de aula.* Parábola.

Boudreau, A., & Dubois, L. (2007). Competing discourses on language preservation along the shores of the Baie Saint-Marie. In A. Duchêne & M. Heller (Eds.), *Discourses of endangerment: Ideology and interest in the defence of languages* (pp. 99–120). Continuum.

Bourdieu, P. (1977). *Outline of a theory of practice.* Cambridge University Press.

Bourdieu, P. (1986). The forms of capital. In J. G. Richardson (Ed.), *Handbook of theory and research for the sociology of education.* Greenwood Press.

Bourdieu, P. (1991). *Language and symbolic power.* Polity/Basil Blackwell.

Brar, V. (2016). *Using Bourdieu's theory of practice to understand academic under achievement among Inner-City students in British Columbia: A conceptual study.* (Doctor of education) – Faculty of Education, Simon Fraser University.

Fraser, N. (1995). From redistribution to recognition? Dilemmas of justice in a 'Post-Socialist' age. *New Left Review, 212,* 68.

Fraser, N. (2000). Rethinking recognition. *New left review, NLR3,* 107.

Gadamer, H.-G. (2013). *Truth and method.* Revised second edition/translation revised by Joel Weinsheimer and Donald G. Marshall. Bloomsbury.

Habermas, J., & Rehg, W. (1996). Between facts and norms: Contributions to a discourse theory of law and democracy. *Polity*.

Heidegger, M. (1967). *Being and time*. Blackwell.

Hofstadter, D., & Sander, E. (2013). *Surfaces and essences analogy as the fuel and fire of thinking*. Basic Books.

Leander, A. (2017). Habitus and field. *Oxford Research Encyclopedia of International Studies*. https://oxfordre.com/internationalstudies

Leiser Baronas, R., & Cox, M. I. P. (2003). Por uma vida melhor na mídia: discurso, aforização e polêmica. *Linguagem em Discurso, 13*(1), 65–93.

Lewis, M. C. (2018). A critique of the principle of error correction as a theory of social change. *Language and Society, 47*(3), 325–346.

Lippi-Green, R. (1997). *English with an accent: Language, ideology, and discrimination in the United States (2nd ed.)*. Routledge.

Lippi-Green, R. (2006). Language ideology and language prejudice. In E. Finegan & J. R. Rickford (Eds.), *Language in the USA* (pp. 289–304). Cambridge University Press.

Lucchesi, D. (2002). Norma linguística e realidade social. In M. Bagno (Ed.), *Linguística da norma* (pp. 63–90). Loyola.

Lucchesi, D. (2015). *Língua e Sociedade Partidas. A polarização sociolinguística do Brasil*. Contexto.

Massini-Cagliari, G. (2004). Language policy in Brazil: Monolingualism and linguistic prejudice. *Language Policy, 3*(1), 3–23.

O'Neill, P. (2020). Racial and linguistic prejudice in Brazil: Comparisons, contrasts and possible solutions to the linguistic problem. *Falange Miúda: Variação, mudança e preconceito linguístico: fenômenos da língua portuguesa atual e antiga, 5*(2). http://www.falangemiuda.com.br/index.php/refami/article/view/303/437

O'Neill, P. (2022). Language and education in Brazil: Linguistic structural problems and their historical origins. In N. Bermingham, P. O'Neill, & A. Timbane (Eds.), *Language and education in the Lusophone countries: Theory and practice*. Liverpool University Press. https://www.modernlanguagesopen.org/articles/10.3828/mlo.v0i0.422/

O'Neill, P., & Massini-Cagliari, G. (2019). Linguistic prejudice and discrimination in Brazilian Portuguese and beyond: Suggestions and recommendations. *Journal of Language and Discrimination, 3*(1), 32–62.

Piercey, R. (2004). Ricoeur's account of tradition and the Gadamer: Habermas debate. *Human Studie, 27*(3), 259–280.

Pinker, S. (2011). *The better angels of our nature: The decline of violence in history and its causes*. Allen Lane.

Pinker, S. (2018). *Enlightenment now: A manifesto for science, reason, humanism, and progress*. Allen Lane.

Ramos, H. S. (2011). Escrever é diferente de falar. *Por uma vida melhor [Coleção Viver e aprender]*. (pp. 11–27). Global.

Reid, M. (2014). *Brazil: The troubled rise of a global power*. Yale University Press.

Schatzki, T. (1996). *Social practices: A Wittgensteinian approach to human activity and the social*. Cambridge University Press.

Scherre, M. M. P., & Naro, A. J. (2014). Sociolinguistic correlates of negative evaluation: Variable concord in Rio de Janeiro. *Language Variation and Change, 26*(3), 331–357.

Skinner, Q. (1985). *The return of grand theory in the human sciences*. Cambridge University Press.

Snell, J. (2018). Critical reflections on the role of the sociolinguist in UK language debates. *Language in Society, 47*(3), 368–374.

Soares, M. (1986). *Linguagem e escola: uma perspectiva social*. Contexto.

Soares, M. (2017). O fracasso da/na escola: uma escola para o povo ou contra o povo? http://blog.editoracontexto.com.br/magda-soares-o-fracasso-da-escola/

Thompson, J. B. (1991). Editor's introduction. In P. Bourdieu (Ed.), *Language and symbolic power*. Polity/Basil Blackwell.

Wittgenstein, L., & Anscombe, G. E. M. (1994). *Philosophical investigations* (3rd, reprint of English text with index. ed.). Basil Blackwell.

Chapter 3
Literacy and the Problem of Linguistic Prejudice

Luiz Carlos Cagliari (iD)

Oral Language Acquisition

We may consider the period of alphabetization a very important time in the children's life (Cagliari, 1989). What is learnt then will have great consequences towards their entire life. With reading and writing, they will learn how to live. The literacy experience must support their progress in all school experiences until the end. On the other hand, a native speaker's life starts when the individual was born well before he initiates his life at school. It is astonishing how a 2-year-old baby participates in conversation, saying what they think, and at the same time is able to understand what people say to him (da Costa Silva et al., 2017). When a 3-year-old child hears a story with unknown words, expressions or passive syntactic structures, he/she may follow the general meaning or ask for explanations, reflecting upon the language system. He/she may also comment on what had heard and add his/her own point of view.

When watching programmes on television, a child may start to compare how he/she speaks the language with what he/she hears from different personages. The television speech becomes someone else's speech. At home, the family speech overlaps the speech the child hears on television and from different people. Therefore, within 3 or 4 years, a child had already experienced the use of language marked by linguistic differences. Not everybody speaks like him/her. Comments on people's linguistic varieties occur among elder people. But the children listen and think about it. As usual the discrimination focuses on individuals and their status in society. When the focus is on the language, the evaluation is an idiosyncratic behaviour. When it aims the speaker, the discrimination is stablished. The sum of the two is linguistic prejudice. For example, some people criticize individuals who speak

L. C. Cagliari (✉)
Unesp – Sao Paulo State University, Araraquara, Sao Paulo, Brazil
e-mail: luiz.cagliari@unesp.br

© The Author(s), under exclusive license to Springer Nature Switzerland AG 2023   29
G. Massini-Cagliari et al. (eds.), *Understanding Linguistic Prejudice*,
https://doi.org/10.1007/978-3-031-25806-0_3

differently from the normative grammar; if someone uses the grammatical interpretation to take the conclusion that the other is ignorant, with low-class education, this is discrimination of the individual by the way he speaks, this is linguistic prejudice (Cagliari, 2000a). The dialect variation per se characterizes social groups, which is clearly recognizable. For example, lawyers have a proper dialect, also doctors, priests, etc. However, when the language comes with evaluation of socioeconomic status, education and ideologies, even children face and play linguistic prejudice. Suddenly, the socioeconomic difference becomes the reason by which people speak according to special education behaviour and some people sound bad from the point of view of a determined society. That association between the linguistic value of the dialectal variations and the socioeconomic value will determine who is who in many things in the life of a society (Cagliari, 2000b).

Therefore, when a child is 5 years old, he/she not only is a competent native speaker who knows how to use his/her language perfectly in all communication and special use of language, but also he/she can understand several linguistic varieties of her language and became aware of linguistic discrimination. And he/she starts to pay attention to the way everybody speaks (Cagliari & Gnerre, 1985a, b). However, the notion of linguistic prejudice needs to be founded not in the language system, but in a social behaviour that he/she does not yet understand well. In spite of one's familiar background, a child is inclined to think that everyone should have the same opportunities and share the same good life. At that age, the human being starts to fight the rest of his life against all sorts of prejudice. It is very convenient for the society to discriminate against people because this is an easy way to stratify the society, showing who will succeed and who will fail. All prejudice is a tree which is very strong but produces many rotten fruits.

At School

It is desirable to have some sort of school education for children from 5 years old. When possible, a kindergarten helps the parents who need to work. In Brazil, the fact that poor children may attend the school presupposes that they will have food besides basic education. Most important is the opportunity to interact with mates of the same age outside the familiar environment. Being together in the same room, doing the same thing, configures the good scenery for a better interaction. So, it is time to learn how to read and write. When older, for instance, at 7 or more years old, the innocence and ingenuity of the infancy have gone, and the social relationship between young people presents many behaviour problems, including bad language. The school must be a pleasant place to stay in order to be a good place to study. The discovery of literacy follows the acquisition of better social education.

In the first year, there are activities of different kinds: the students hear stories, sing traditional tunes and keep alive folklore histories and carols (see my website <alfabetizandoonline.com.br>). They also play games, paint and make sculptures. In some schools, there is a vegetable garden and flowers. The ideal school takes care of the whole education of the citizens. This objective must be present along all school years of science, art and education with different approaches.

The most important activity among all important realizations is to learn how to read and write, i.e. the alphabetization process. For still not well-known reasons, in a quick and easy process, the human being learns how to use one language with the same facility he/she learns how to live and to survive. Given the fact that the language is a highly complex system, the acquisition of speaking is something magic. On the other hand, when a child learns how to read and write, there is a quite different situation: the process is not easy, and it seems confusing, even complicated and long-lasting. After all this effort, when the person already knows how to read and to write, these abilities are recognized as very simple, produced automatically, as the acquisition of speaking occurred, and the language is used for all purposes. As a matter of fact, literacy is one of the most complicated processes of learning for the one who teaches and for the students. But literacy is a basic study for all subsequent activities in school and in life. Not knowing how to read and write, the studies at school are over, since everything depends on reading and writing (Cagliari, 1997).

In addition to the difficulties in social adaptation at school, children will also need linguistic adaptation. They face two problematic situations: existence forces people to talk to each other, revealing the speakers' dialect with their similarities and not similarities. Speech differences create expectation of fear; besides that, children will face a formal study situation with a particular variety spoken by the teacher in order to facilitate the learning of the relationship between letters and sounds, as possible aiming the spelling. This approach leaves aside many problems that may be avoidable when the children start to learn how to read (Cagliari, 2001). In this game, the whole class is united by the same pronunciation; reading will be favoured, but writing starts to show all the incongruences of the spelling system. The two processes may appear mirrored or parallel, but they are not.

In a normal situation, every reader deciphers what is written and translates what he sees into a spoken variety of his own. That is the reason by which individual reading is comfortable because the reader does not need to speak out loud what he processed in his mind (Cagliari, 2002). This mental reading usually is quite different from the dialect of the text author. We do not mentally read Shakespeare processing a speech exactly as Shakespeare had spoken his dialect. If the reader must say what he got from reading, the problem can be bigger depending on the speaker's dialect and his interlocutor. In a neutral situation, one expects that the reading will be performed sounding a school variety which is commonly accepted by the local society as the standard norm. When reading, the children depart from orthographic representation of words, without dialectal variations that may be interpreted as an undesirable way to speech by many. Children see that the spelling represents no one speech, so that everyone can appropriate the semantic of the text and process it in their mind, following the normal process to speak. The language as a whole remains in the mind. When language is going out of the mouth, the mind needs to adapt the language to the circumstances.

On the other hand, at school, the student must master something highly problematic for him. The student needs to observe his own speech, a task that is not easy at first sight. After that, he needs to choose the appropriate letters to represent the sounds of his pronunciation. The process of writing is quite different from a phonetic transcription by linguists who have a special alphabet where each symbol refers to a unique sound and vice versa. This transcription has no ambiguities, which produce exact representations of speech. The IPA (International Phonetic Alphabet) contemplates all articulatory possibilities of human beings used to produce all sounds of all languages. However, that is not the case of using the IPA to teach children how to read and write. To properly use the IPA, the children should be well-trained linguists.

At school the student must perform several steps (Cagliari, 1998) to segment the speech chain into words so that they result in morphological words in isolation that are officially represented by the spelling system, i.e. (1) words separated by a void space. (2) As a word is identified, it is necessary to choose which letters are appropriate to compound the spelling representation of the word. (3) Since there are many rules associating letters and sound, the choice must check all possibilities. (4) If the student already knows the spelling, he can write correctly; if not he must search in a vocabulary or ask someone who may help him. Sometimes, he will decide by guessing the best result, but he may fail. (5) When the attempt fails, the student has to start all over again. (6) Without a solution, the student stops the process (Cagliari, 2011a). Memorizing the spelling of the most common words used at primary school, the student will have less difficulties in reading and writing.

The explanation above shows that the student has one way to read and another way to write (Cagliari, 1998). Writing and reading are different linguistic activities: writing is rigid, but reading may lead the speech to different realizations, depending on the linguistic variety the speaker uses. For example, who reads a sentence like *os homens fizeram outro* ('the men did another [one]') may speak differently according to the reader's variety: [uz ómeĭs fizérãu outru], [uz ómi fizéru otru], [uz ómi feiz otru], a Carioca speaker would say: [uiz ómeĭsh] *os homens* ('the men'), etc. However, who speaks that sentence and searches how to write it will face different levels of difficulty to write it orthographically. This game is played comfortably by the adult who are already alphabetized. But to the children who are beginning their activities at school, alphabetization is the greatest challenge they will have in school life (Cagliari, 1997).

The Difference That Produce Discrimination That Produce Linguistic Prejudice

The student in the alphabetization process is like someone who decided to live abroad. As a click of the eyes, everything seems good, nice but different. As time passes by, the person discovers that there are also some peculiar difficulties. The most terrifying one is the correct use of the language. Although the person has studied the language, he/she is not a native speaker; instead, he/she knows only the standard variety of scholar speech. When abroad, there is the feeling that soon everyone will learn the language and speak like a native speaker. However, this is a false conclusion. After the strangeness in the first conversations, native speakers expect that the foreigners learn and use the language as the common local citizens. Soon, the strangeness generates small discriminations, which become greater with time. All kinds of meetings are avoided because of oral communication. The foreigner feels like an alien, discriminated against and humiliated. He/she avoids speaking, and when it is necessary, his/her language and voice often get confused, which makes things worse. A speaker is humiliated when he/she does not speak like the others in the community.

Some children find themselves in an analogous situation when they start studying in the first year at school learning to read and write. The difference between how people use the language at home and at school can be amazing. The social relationship among the children can induce silence because of the way other people consider the pronunciation they hear. The children also observe how different the teacher, the staff and some schoolmates speak. Of course, they notice the differences. Consequently, this situation may constrain some children inducing them to avoid conversation with the school's staff, including the teacher, and also with their colleagues. The teacher must intervene, and talk to all students about linguistic variations and socioeconomic situation in society, poverty and richness, showing that everyone learn how to speak a language everywhere in the world when they are still infants, that in family there is no discrimination because the social environment is the same to all, that the kids play with their friends without linguistic discrimination, with no concern with speech, and finally that the school will not destroy the language system everyone speaks at school mainly inside the classroom. But the school is a place where people acquire new knowledge to improve their future life. Aiming at that ideal, a more educated variety of the language will be taught to all, regardless of the level of the use of the school standard pronunciation they have. As a matter of fact, the school does not need to teach anyone to speak. Everybody knows it. This talk needs to be performed just at the beginning of the scholar year.

It helps a lot, whether the teacher reads stories for kids where the problem of speech appears or watch television documentaries, films, etc. This approach allows good discussion and good teaching. Every time the problem of discrimination by the way one speaks appears, to turn back to the basic ideas is absolutely necessary (Cagliari, 1989).

Over time if a student is not able to use the standard variety of speaking at school, he will be in serious trouble. The interpretation of speech leads to interpretation of value, and the summed-up result is bad behaviour and difficulty in learning. Children learnt one standard dialect at home, and the primes of reading and writing will have less troubles at school. It is not true that they have less difficulties to learn; they are ahead in a run. They bring from home some knowledge other students need to acquire at the beginning. As usual, the classrooms are heterogeneous in many ways. The good teacher will adapt his programme to serve all kinds of students. The difference in learning requires different approaches in order for everyone to advance

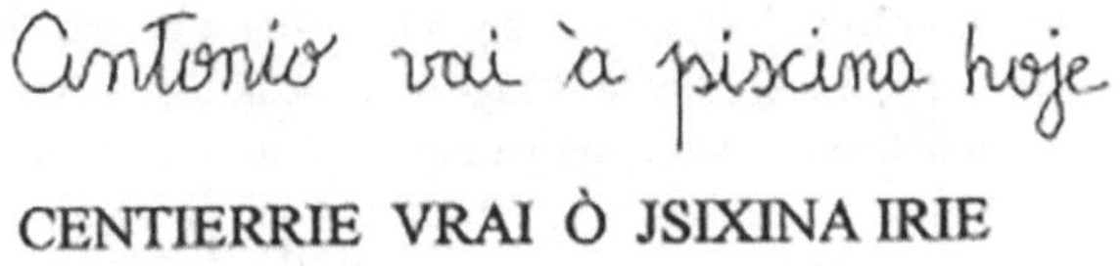

Fig. 3.1 *Antônio vai à*
piscina. Misinterpretation
in copying from
handwriting

Antônio vai à piscina hoje

CENTIERRIE VRAI Ò JSIXINA IRIE

from where they are, so that in a few months all students in the classroom find themselves at a similar level (Cagliari, 1998).

There is a good reason to start teaching reading and writing with the reading process. To make clear what is all about, the first step is to use capital letters, in order to avoid confusion generated by other fonts of letters (Fig. 3.1). The student must be absolutely sure about which letters appear before the eyes (Massini-Cagliari & Cagliari, 1999). Concatenated style of writing such as handwriting is the worst.

After that it is necessary to analyse the speech in comparison with writing, making the alphabetic correspondence with the sounds of speech. But this is not sufficient: when writing, it is necessary to find the exact letter that is required by the spelling system to write the word correctly. Other types of exercises bring direct and indirect facilities to the beginner, such as the use of pencils to trace lines, to make drawings and even to trace letters.

On the other hand, learners have a terrible problem when departing from speech to writing. This activity is extremely difficult. As explained previously, it is easier to learn how to read a word in its spelling representation, because the reader will start discovering what is written using his own dialect and guessing the word. The process sounds familiar as when he/she sees something and names it. The spelling representation of words makes the student's dialect occult, since it represents nobody's speech; instead it allows everybody to interpret which word is written and what happens in the reader's mind as if he had recognized an object in the real world.

On the other hand, doing school activities, the students will bring up features of their speech. The question is harder when the students need to write without copying but observing how they speak. Depending on the student's background, the difficulty may be immense, and it is found at every moment. For instance, a student who says [uz ómi trabaia] *os homens trabalham* ('the men work') needs to translate what he/she speaks into a standard pronunciation inside his/her mind, and remember which letters are appropriate, check up the spelling and only after all these exercises write down the words *os homens trabalham* ('the men work'). A suggestion for the teachers is that he/she writes on the blackboard the words the students do not know how the spelling forms are. It is worthwhile to remember that the activity of copying is an old method to teach reading and writing (Cagliari, 1998, 2009: 17–52).

Out in the playground, interacting with other children all forms of discrimination, bullying, etc. may happen, even bad words (Alvarez, 2020; Anselmo, 2017). The school has to intervene to not allow those unacceptable behaviours. Respect might be seen as an ethical action, but it is also an educative action (Cury, 2020). The school is the place where respect and education are priority. Indiscipline usually grows where there is no respect nor education. The school has to have a friendly environment, a place where it is rewarding to attend for all students and the staff.

The Discrimination of Bad Spelling

Our writing system is alphabetic. This system was created applying an acrophonic principle which generated what we call *alphabetic principle*. It means that all sound of a language is represented by one letter: the sound [a] is written A, and if it is written A, this letter indicates the sound [a]. Taken like this, the *alphabetic principle* is what linguists call *a phonetic transcription* (Cagliari, 2009). Since the languages have dialect variations, the correspondence between sounds and letters will necessarily be variable as shown before (one says [fizéru], others say [fizérãu], and the spelling form is *fizeram* 'they did [it]'). The letter A may be pronounced with the sound [u] or the sound [ãu]; the letter E must be prononced with [é] and not [e].

When we see some mistakes, it is clear that the school emphasizes the use of the *alphabetic principle*, hoping that through this way, one will reach the spelling form. But some people leave the school without this aim. Out of school or even as a student, some people need to write, but they don't know the exact letters to employ. Then, they think in the *alphabetic principle* and use a kind of phonetic transcription (Cagliari & Gnerre, 1985b). Of course, doing this, the probability of occurring spelling mistakes is very high. For example, on one board outside a restaurant, it was written *selv serfice* (English: 'self-service'). On another board it was written *vendese calvão bujã (vende-se carvão butijão)* ('coal gas canisters are sold'). The children also find difficulties of the kind when starting to write without copying. At school, the odd results are different as follows: *dixi*, 'disse' ('said'); *prisipe*, 'príncipe' ('prince'); *qaza*, 'casa' ('house'); etc. (Perez, 2021). In both cases, the writers hope to be understood. However, this expectation is undesirable at school. No writing system can vary the spelling of words according to an individual's desire.

The question pointed out above shows that it is difficult to teach how to read and write. Knowing the spelling form of words by heart takes time, and many things must happen before it. Because the *orthographic principle* directs all variants of all speakers towards a unique word spelling representation, thinking of the *alphabetic principle*, we find many and confused rules (Cagliari, 2009). For example, in Portuguese, letter X has at least five different uses according to the Paulista dialect: [sh] *xícara* ('cup'), [ks] *tórax* ('chest'), [z] *exame* ('examination'), [s] *texto* ('text') and [zero] *exceto* ('except') (no sound pronounced). If we take into consideration different dialects of Brazilian Portuguese, we find examples for written letter A as follows: [ɑ] *maus* ('bad') is different from [a] in *mais* ('plus'); [ɐ] *cama* ('bed'); [u] *acharu*, 'acharam' ('found'); [i] *lâmpida, lâmpada*, (lamp); and [e] *achemu*, *achamos* ('we found'). The last two words are typical from Caipira dialect (a discriminated variety of Brazilian Portuguese). Even using the standard pronunciation, the relationship between speech and spelling is quite complicated. It is inevitable that some students will commit more errors than others (Cagliari, 2011b). The difference in the results provokes the discrimination and favours the prejudice among the students in a classroom. The next thing will be bullying, bad behaviour, violence and revenge. A smart teacher will minimize the student's errors, avoiding that they become object of discrimination.

The spelling problems extrapolate the literacy room and hit the students of other years. It is never too late to return to basic ideas. The students who commit too many errors of spelling need to be informed and do special exercises under special supervision. The use of a dictionary is very important.

If the school succeeds making the students understand, since the literacy programme, that spelling errors are occasional and therefore nobody has the right do judge more than a simple spelling error, the life in a poor country like Brazil, with plenty of problems of education, will be more bearable, and the people can live as they want (Cagliari, 2011b).

The School, the Family and the Society

To many Brazilian students, the fact that they can go to school is already a great privilege and a tense situation. The school needs to relieve the natural tension to disarm it and create a happy environment for all. A comfortable environment can define a great deal of what must happen along the year, whether in terms of social and linguistic discrimination or about learning.

Bad behaviour such as the use of bad words and offenses happens frequently in a kid's life when they play together. The conflicts are occasional, and they are forgotten, and everything returns to normal. But inside the school, some types of offenses are really destructive and may last for many years, as sad memories of school times.

Another problem is what happens to the linguistic relationship between the parents and the kids at home, after the children have mastered the standard variation and acquired other school habits. Different linguistic habits may create a confrontation and lead the sons or daughters to question the mental capacity of their parents in their adult life. The next step is the disrespect towards everything the parents point out discording from the children. The parents receive the same kind of discrimination their sons and daughters had when they started the studies at school. A person does not need to be alphabetized to be wise and have an adequate comprehension of life. The standard speech is not a prerequisite for wisdom. Any kind of association of that kind reveals linguistic and intellectual prejudice. Moreover, combating the linguistic discrimination and prejudice has many faces; it may correct the way people think about the language, and by the same token, it may transform victims into aggressors.

Conclusion

When one searches for the origin of linguistic prejudice considering the discrimination of individuals based on different speaking of any kind, we find many causes and reasons. Although education helps eradicate socioeconomic and linguistic discrimination since the beginning of schooling and promotes a better place for people in society, the better knowledge empowers one against the others. Even coming from a stigmatized situation, because of good education, one person may become one that produces stigmatization, discriminating who is what he was before. Despite this, it is important to bet on good education since literacy, to conscientize society in regard of all evil things a prejudice can cause to life. Ultimately, everything depends on the way this matter is treated by the teacher. There must be in the teaching programme a special moment when the prejudice and the discrimination will be discussed.

Considering linguistic prejudice as some sort of bullying, the theme must be talked with the students in clear terms and with scientific approach. Unfortunately, the knowledge of the language is too poor at school because of a lack of scientific understanding in government programmes and in didactic books.

Before finishing this paper, it would be interesting and even necessary to remember that linguistic prejudice also comes from teachers, programmes, books and didactic materials (Cagliari, 1997). Because of some inertia in the behaviour in the society and at school, old habits act continuously without showing bad traditions. The intolerance towards some students because of spelling errors in writing must be dealt with by teaching in a better way the basic notions of the writing systems and promoting special classes to teach orthography. When the teacher incentivizes spontaneous production of text, the students will tell good stories but with many spelling mistakes (Cagliari & Giovani, 2015). A brief study of the most common spelling mistakes will guide the class towards memorization of the correct spelling of the most common words. This attitude beyond the didactic benefices instructs all people (students, teachers, staff, government programmers, authors of didactic books, the parents, etc.) to deal more gently with spelling errors, at school, at home and in society.

Acknowledgements The author would like to thank the National Council for Scientific and Technological Development CNPq (302024/2020-4).

References

Alvarez, B. (2020). Linguistic discrimination still lingers in many classrooms. In: *Nea Today*. https://www.nea.org/advocating-for-change/new-from-nea/linguistic-discrimination-still-lingers-many-classrooms. Accessed 19 May 2020.

Anselmo, T. (2017). *Diga não ao preconceito linguístico*. https://redes.moderna.com.br/2017/06/29/preconceito-linguistico-combate/. Accessed 29 June 2017.

Cagliari, L. C. (1989). *Alfabetização & Lingüística*. Editora Scipione.

Cagliari, L. C. (1997). O príncipe que virou sapo: considerações a respeito da dificuldade de aprendizagem das crianças na alfabetização. In *Introdução à psicologia escolar*. Org. Maria Helena Souza Pato (3ª ed., pp. 193–224). Casa da do Psicólogo.

Cagliari, L. C. (1998). *Alfabetizando sem o BA BE BI BO BU*. Scipione.

Cagliari, L. C. (2000a). Avaliação e promoção. *Línguas e Letras*. UNIOESTE, Curso de Letras. Centro de Educação, Comunicação e Artes, *1*(1), 143–156.

Cagliari, L. C. (2000b). *Variação e preconceito. Textura. Revista do Centro de Educação, Ciências Humanas e Letras* (pp. 15–22). ULBRA.

Cagliari, L. C. (2001). Como alfabetizar: 20 anos em busca de soluções. *Letras de Hoje – Anais do 5° Encontro nacional sobre aquisição da linguagem (ENAL) e do 1° Encontro internacional sobre aquisição da linguagem*. Org. Regina Lamprecht and Sérgio Menuzzi. Porto Alegre: Centro de estudos sobre a aquisição e aprendizagem da linguagem – PUCRS, Vol. 36, n. 3. pp. 47–66.

Cagliari, L. C. (2002). Alfabetização e ortografia. *Educar em Revista: Dossiê Linguagem e Ensino: temas e perspectivas*, 20. Editora da UFPR. (20), 43–58.

Cagliari, L. C. (2009). Aspectos teóricos da ortografia. In *Ortografia da Língua Portuguesa*. Maurício Silva (Org.) (pp. 17–52). Ed. Contexto.

Cagliari, L. C. (2011a). Alfabetização: o que fazer quando não der certo *Formação de Professores Didática dos Conteúdos*. Cultura Acadêmica. 2.1, 72–95.

Cagliari, L. C. (2011b). Uma grande dificuldade na alfabetização. *Alfabetização e cognição*. 1. EDIPUCRS. 127–137.

Cagliari, L. C., & Giovani, F. (2015). *Letras e textos*. Paulistana.

Cagliari, L. C., & Gnerre, M. B. M. A. (1985a). Textos espontâneos na primeira série: evidências da utilização pela criança de sua percepção fonética da fala ao representar e segmentar a escrita. *Recuperando a Alegria de Ler e Escrever – Cadernos CEDES, 14*. Cortez Editora, 25–29.

Cagliari, L. C., & Gnerre, M. B. M. A. (1985b). Leitura e escrita na vida e na escola. *Leitura: Teoria e Prática, 6*. ALB, 15–26.

Cury, A. (2020). Como evitar o preconceito linguístico na escola? In: *Escola da Inteligência. Educação socioemocional*. https://escoladainteligencia.com.br/blog/preconceito-linguistico/. Accessed 16 Nov 2020.

da Costa Silva, C. L., Del Ré, A., & Cavalcante, M. C. B. (2017). *A criança na/com a linguagem: saberes em contraponto*. UFRGS, Editora do Instituto de Letras.

Massini-Cagliari, G., & Cagliari, L. C. (1999). *Diante das letras: a escrita na alfabetização*. Editora Mercado de Letras.

Perez, L. C. A. (2021). Variações linguísticas e o preconceito linguístico – português. https://www.portugues.com.br/redacao/variacoes-linguisticas-preconceito-linguistico.html. Acessed 24 Nov 2021.

Chapter 4
"What Deeply Irritates You": Subjective Evaluation and Societal Evidence of (Socio) Linguistic Phenomena

Marcus Garcia Sene (iD)**, Caroline Carnielli Biazolli** (iD)**, and Silvia Maria Brandão** (iD)

Initial Considerations

> The actual reality of language-speech is not the abstract system of linguistic forms, not the isolated monologic utterances, and not the psychophysiological act of its implementation, but the social event of verbal interaction implemented in an utterance or utterances. Thus, verbal interaction is the basic reality of language. (Vološinov, 1973, p. 94)

Language is a social phenomenon that does not exist without its speakers. The quote by Vološinov (1973), regarding this, breaks the homogeneous view of language and endorses the importance of verbal interaction in the constitution of linguistic reality. Once language is a social object, it is subject to the subjective evaluation of its users, and, therefore, the object of study of sociolinguistics is not only linguistic materiality in itself but also the social community and subjective evaluations that are recurrently manifested by its speakers.

During verbal interaction performed through utterance or utterances (Vološinov, 1973), linguistic forms in use are always the target of subjective evaluations, once speakers believe that "languages exist in standardized forms, and this kind of belief affects the way in which they think about their own language and 'language' in general" (Milroy, 2011, p. 49). Due to this standardization ideology, along with the

M. G. Sene (✉)
Newton Paiva University, Unesp - São Paulo State University, Araraquara, São Paulo, Brazil

C. C. Biazolli
Federal University of São Carlos, São Carlos, São Paulo, Brazil
e-mail: caroline.biazolli@ufscar.br

S. M. Brandão
Unesp - São Paulo State University, Araraquara, São Paulo, Brazil

© The Author(s), under exclusive license to Springer Nature Switzerland AG 2023
G. Massini-Cagliari et al. (eds.), *Understanding Linguistic Prejudice*,
https://doi.org/10.1007/978-3-031-25806-0_4

overvaluation of standard language,[1] so clearly spread across different social contexts, the linguistic uses that escape this supposed standard consequently cause some type of reaction in people, that is, an evaluation, which, when negative, may result in linguistic prejudice and, when positive, may generate acceptance, reinforcing identity matters and linguistic security (Calvet, 2002).

The subjective evaluation of variant forms becomes recurrent in the everyday life of speakers, since, according to Bourdieu (2008), language is praxis. That is to say, language is much more than an instrument of communication, and it is also an instrument of power; after all, "we do not seek to be only understood, but also obeyed, believed, respected, distinguished" (Bourdieu, 2008, p. 5). Therefore, since it mediates human relationships, language is subject to forces of ideology and historically constructed values, and the conflict between the said forces is the beginning of the emergence and consolidation of linguistic prejudice.

The ideas that underlie the term *prejudice* are not new. Until the Enlightenment, the concept of prejudice did not convey any kind of negative connotation. Only after Enlightenment criticism did this notion start to suffer a limitation; that is, it stopped representing a supposedly neutral view to take on the notion of "unfounded judgment." For this reason, from the philosophical point of view, "prejudice is a phenomenon observed when an individual discriminates or excludes another, based on misconceptions that come from habits, customs, feelings or impressions" (Leite, 2008, p. 27). Such judgments are unfounded (or mistaken) precisely because they do not reflect any scientific explanation; on the contrary, they are based on beliefs that, when it comes to language, there is only one way of saying something, which is regulated by the grammar of the language, while other ways are not.

The aforementioned judgments are established when a particular linguistic norm – in this case, the standard – becomes the reference for correct speaking and writing. Bourdieu (2008, p. 11), in this regard, clarifies that:

> the integration into the same "linguistic community" (equipped with the coercive instruments necessary to impose universal recognition of the dominant language: schools, grammarians etc.) of hierarchized groups, driven by different interests, is the condition for the establishment of relations of linguistic domination. When one language dominates the market, it becomes the norm against which the prices of other modes of expression and the values of the various competences are defined.

Once the standard is supposedly the norm that presents the highest value in the linguistic market (Bourdieu, 2008), it becomes the scale which will bear the value judgments and labels attributed to the uses that distance themselves from an expected linguistic standard. Thus, such value judgments are manifested in linguistic prejudice, which, according to Bagno (2005, p. 64), in the case of Portuguese:

> [...] is based on the belief that there is [...] only one Portuguese language worthy of this name, which would be the language taught in schools, explained in grammars and cataloged in dictionaries. Any linguistic manifestation that escapes this school-grammar-dictionary triangle is considered, under the view of linguistic prejudice, "wrong, ugly, crippled, rudimentary, deficient."

---

[1] Standard language is a "sociohistorical construct that serves as reference to stimulate a standardization process" (Faraco, 2008, p. 75).

This belief that there is only one Portuguese language, as well as only one way to say something, is a mistaken idea created throughout history (unfortunately, it persists in some contexts), according to which it was believed (or is still believed) that language and grammar were (are) the same thing. Furthermore, language is still understood by many as something invariable, which may create derogatory views and judgments about it and its uses. The said judgments are materialized in societal evidence (Garrett et al., 2003) that may or may not result in violence, be it symbolic or not (Bourdieu, 2008).

For Garrett et al. (2003), the general population presents insights and stereotyped associations regarding linguistic concepts that constitute societal evidence – and such evidence composes the *corpus* analyzed in this chapter. Still concerning societal evidence, it is worth mentioning that any content (governmental, educational, from the media, advertising etc.) that presents a view on language or linguistic variety is an important piece of societal evidence for sociolinguistic investigation. This occurs because the knowledge about the variation process and the social meaning associated with linguistic forms are obtained not only by knowing how people effectively use the language but also by identifying how they evaluate and react to variable linguistic uses.

With that in mind, this text presents a set of societal evidence which expresses stereotyped subjective evaluations regarding variable linguistic uses of the Portuguese language, collected from a virtual environment (Facebook). Such pieces of evidence not only represent what speakers effectively think about some linguistic uses but are also frequently used to discriminate the way another person speaks, generating linguistic prejudice. The data presented herein were extracted from part of the research "Linguistic prejudice online and offline: phenomena categorization, social profiles and subjective evaluation" (Sene et al., 2019; Brandão et al., 2020).

Besides these introductory words, the conclusions, and the references, this chapter is divided into three other sections. The first one proposes a deep theoretical exploration concerning subjective evaluation in sociolinguistic research, directly focusing on the treatment of variable phenomena of different degrees of salience and sociolinguistic awareness. The second section describes the methodological procedures used in this study, which, in order to discuss societal evidence regarding language, collected and analyzed subjective evaluations expressed in a virtual context of interaction between users of the Portuguese language. Finally, the evidence is interpreted in the third section, also considering other facts that occurred in society and reinforce it, such as derogatory metalinguistic discourses broadcast in the media.

Subjective Evaluation: The Starting Point to Understanding Societal Evidence

In the study of the relationships between language and society, especially considering how the former varies to adapt to different social and/or stylistic contexts or even to reveal different social and/or stylistic meanings, many are the analytical approaches that surfaced over 60 years of sociolinguistics. Such different analytical views did not develop consecutively in the history of sociolinguistics but overlapped throughout time, meaning one did not emerge to substitute the other. In the words of Eckert (2005), these different ways of working with linguistic variation may be called "waves of sociolinguistics".[2]

Pioneering sociolinguistic studies became known for mainly focusing on exploring the use of language in large urban centers, concentrating on linguistic variation patterns that emerged from the comparison between speakers from different social groups and their different speech styles, as well as focusing on the comprehension of the spread of linguistic change across society. Two studies that have marked this type of analytical approach were *The Social Stratification of English in New York City*, by Labov (1966), and *The Social Differentiation of English in Norwich*, by Trudgill (1974).

These studies became known due to the fact that the speakers participating in the researches, who were part of a speech community, were grouped into broader social categories, such as gender, age, social status, and education, for instance. Based on this, the researches of the field started to present a sociolinguistic picture of the communities involved, by unveiling variation patterns that emerged from statistical analyses.

With the development of sociolinguistic research, new concerns appeared, especially because language ceased to be solely a reflection of a system used to convey referential meanings, and began to be interpreted as a social practice that reveals different social meanings and identities. Regarding such concerns, discussions about the subjective evaluation of linguistic uses, ideologies, and linguistic perceptions and beliefs have become extremely important, once sociolinguistic investigation needs to include, besides the understanding of the language in use (linguistic production) and how people speak, the way people evaluate, perceive, and interpret what is being said (Campbell-Kibler, 2006, 2009; Oushiro, 2015; Berlinck et al., 2020).

In order to understand the sociolinguistic approach, it is necessary to grasp the correlations between linguistic and social factors, which generate variation patterns – duly explored in several studies – as well as the positioning of speakers in the social world and also how they build and rebuild the world from variable linguistic uses (Campbell-Kibler, 2009; Eckert, 2012). Such positioning is a complete process that has many aspects within itself – among which is the subjective evaluation of linguistic uses.

Evaluation is a recurrent practice in several contexts in society and falls upon the multiple social behaviors (Sene, 2019). In this respect, language cannot be left out, since it is a social practice and is subject to the evaluation of those who speak and listen to it. These evaluations are at times materialized in positive or negative societal evidence (Garrett et al., 2003), which represent how a variety, variant, or linguistic item is evaluated, as previously described.

---

[2] For further knowledge on the three waves proposed by the author, check Eckert (2005, 2012).

Subjective evaluation occupies a privileged place in the sociolinguistics scene, once it is one of the five empirical foundations for the investigation of linguistic change.[3] According to Weinreich et al. (2006 [1968]), knowing the subjective correlates speakers manifest regarding linguistic varieties and/or variants is essential to identify the spread or interruption of a specific form that composes a sociolinguistic phenomenon. Thus, any variety or variant is an object of sociolinguistic evaluation.

Conscious or unconscious evaluation of varieties and/or variants is linked to the cognitive capacity of the speaker and, at the same time, to values that are socially imposed. For Calvet (2002, p. 65), "[...] there is a whole set of attitudes and feelings of speakers toward their languages, language varieties and those who use them [...]." Consequently, the evaluation process is, above all, social and political; the target of evaluation is not only speech, what is being said, but also who says it and where.

Concerning linguistic features that are evaluated based on their level of social appreciation, it is necessary to investigate the fact that some pieces of societal evidence appear more frequently in the discourse of speakers about the use of language than others. This happens due to the degree of salience that affects a specific phenomenon. Regarding that, Freitag (2021a) identifies four groups of social evaluation in which sociolinguistic phenomena may be placed. Such groups show different degrees of salience and sociolinguistic awareness of the phenomena investigated.

The first group is called *variable phenomena to which people do not react*. In this group, for instance, it is possible to find phenomena such as the verbal alternation in conditional constructions (Brandão, 2018) and the expression of null subjects (Mendonça & Nascimento, 2015):

(1)

(a) *Aí tem a fadiga, se você soltá(r) seu poder cê **gasta [vai gastá(r)]** a fadiga....* (Brandão, 2018)
    Then there's the fatigue, if you let go of your power you **spend [will spend]** the fatigue....

(b) *[eu] Espero que você entenda nosso ponto de vista, [nós] esperamos muito que [nós] possamos curtir essa viagem juntos.* (Mendonça & Nascimento, 2015)
    [I] Hope you understand our point of view, [we] really **hope [we] can** enjoy this trip together.

Such phenomena, which are variable, are hardly identified as linguistic uses that vary in the language. Lay people, for example, do not seem to react positively or negatively to them. These cases are different from linguistic uses that distinguish the social or dialectal origin of the speaker, which, according to Freitag (2021a), fit in the second group, called *variable phenomena that are dialectally salient*. This matter is well exemplified by the variation between *tu* and *você* (the expression of the second person singular) (Rumeu, 2008; Machado, 2006; Lopes, 2009), besides the commonly known lexical variation between the terms *mexerica* and *bergamota* ("tangerine"), for instance. It is possible to dialectally pinpoint the speaker once, according to the Brazilian region being analyzed, one form or the other is more

---

[3] For further knowledge on the five empirical foundations, check Weinreich et al. (2006 [1968]).

widely used – that is, *tu* or *você*, regarding pronominal forms of reference to the second person, and *mexerica* or *bergamota*, lexical items to refer to an orange-colored citrus fruit. When it comes to these phenomena, people are able to react and express subjective reactions to them, as opposed to the others previously mentioned (verbal alternation in conditional constructions and expression of null subjects). That occurs because such uses are situated in a higher level of the sociolinguistic awareness of the speaker, once they are sociolinguistically conditioned by linguistic, pragmatic, historical, geographical, and social factors (Lopes et al., 2016).

By closely examining the notion of non-linguistic conditioning of particular phenomena, it is possible to identify that certain forms may also be appreciated based on aspects that make them socially salient, as is the case of some linguistic uses that vary depending on formality, context, and generation/age group (Freitag, 2021a). Social evaluation of variation in the use of *senhor/a*, *você*, and *tu* is not motivated by the linguistic forms themselves, once their spelling is correct, but by social (extralinguistic) aspects that are related to formality and the context where they would be used. Freitag (2021a) called such cases *variable phenomena that are socially salient*, constituting the third group of social evaluation in which sociolinguistic phenomena may be placed.

Finally, according to the author, some phenomena are recurrently displayed in different spaces and, due to prescriptivism, are responsible for the materialization of several pieces of societal evidence. For Freitag (2021a), linguistic uses that are subject to correction, and whose "correct" uses are valued, refer to the fourth and last group, *variable phenomena that are salient due to prescriptivism*. In such cases, not only is the linguistic form itself under evaluation but also who uses it and where and when it is used. This prescription occurs recurrently on television and social media, where the focus is only on the "mistake" and the "correction." In general, language features that are subject to correction are also the ones associated with a speech "style" and are at the highest level of sociolinguistic awareness, once speakers talk about them and label those who use them, that is, it is a piece of linguistic data subject to correction, a form subject to public discussion (Labov, 2001).

One example is the case of *eu* x *mim* pronominal variation, in which the uses of *mim* with verbs in the infinitive (*para mim fazer*) are always under the spotlight of prescription/correction. Moreover, the use of this linguistic item is frequently associated with the indigenous way of speaking, which feeds a misleading stereotype about the indigenous population that inhabits the Brazilian land. Once it is very salient and belongs to the shared social imaginary of language users, the use mentioned is always being fought through correction practices and memes on the Internet, which largely reveal a discriminatory tone.

Another phenomenon that is also salient due to prescription is, for example, the use of *a gente* x *agente*. Though very recurrent in writing, the case of hyposegmentation related to these two terms is frequently pointed out as a "mistake" to be "fought." Such phenomenon is interesting since, in speech, there is no difference between the pronunciation of *a gente* ("we") and *agente* ("agent"). There is no pause in speech to ensure the distinction between the two forms; thus, context will define the use of one form or another. In writing, *a gente* x *agente* is salient and easily recognized by speakers, as is *mim + verb in the infinitive*. This easiness of recognition does not happen due to their morphosyntactic or phonetic-phonological nature, but because of excessive prescriptivism, even resulting in the circulation of memes with such phenomena (as seen in Fig. 4.1), which also become responsible for retaining these uses in the sociolinguistic awareness of speakers.

Even though memes are used for humor purposes, they go beyond what is funny; they use linguistic prescriptions to materialize "jokes," despite the fact that this content may cause embarrassment for people who use the linguistic forms in question. Regarding this matter, it is worth mentioning that the problem with this type of meme is that it starts being used as a manner to discriminate against the way some people speak, showing a lack of linguistic respect. In this regard, beyond a simple instrument, "language is a social practice that produces and organizes ways of life, forms of action and forms of knowledge" (Marcuschi & Dionisio, 2007, p. 14), and, for that reason, the correction of linguistic uses outside a context of humanizing education ends up endorsing a model of exclusion for those who do not master linguistic norms that are necessary in the most diverse social environments.

To the division of the four groups, which encompass different levels of social evaluation toward variable phenomena, it becomes essential to add the discussion regarding the fact that one phenomenon, depending on the context, may not completely fit into only one group. If considered in diverse linguistic contexts, as in the following sentences, variation in pronominal collocation (Biazolli, 2018), for instance, may pass as a phenomenon to which people do not react (2a) or may be classified as salient due to prescriptivism (2b).

Fig. 4.1 Memes related to the use of *mim + verb in the infinitive* and *agente* x *a gente*. (Left figure: Then the person writes: "add me." Then I reply: Me no add. Me be bad Indian. Right figure: You are not FBI. Stop writing agent!). *In:* Elaborated by the authors. (The memes were elaborated from illustrations available at the website *Storyset*. All illustrations from this website are free for personal and professional use. The only requirement is that the link for each one of them is made available. The illustration in the meme on the left was extracted from the link https://storyset.com/illustration/feeling-angry/pana; the illustration in the meme on the right, from the link: https://storyset.com/illustration/feeling-angry/bro)

(2)

(a). *O* delator do esquema *se irritou [irritou-se] hoje com os jornalistas que estão em frente à casa dele.* (Biazolli, 2018)

The whistleblower of the scheme got irritated today with the journalists that are in front of his house.

(b). *[Se trata] Trata-se de forte conteúdo de preconceito.* (Biazolli, 2018)

It is strong prejudice content.

In 2a, the proclisis or enclisis after the subject does not seem to be subject to any evaluation, if they are present in oral or written texts, even though prescription determines the use of enclisis, when the subject comes immediately after the verb, in affirmative or interrogative clauses. However, the same cannot be said about 2b. For Biazolli (2018, p. 95, highlighted by the author):

> […] though isolated, there is at least one context in which it is possible to evidently notice the negative evaluation of speakers toward the use of one of the variants [of the pronominal collocation phenomenon]: proclisis to only one verb or to a verbal complex at the beginning of a clause, in written texts (especially in more formal ones), may bother language users, especially by those considered "educated," literate, urban. This probably happens because the placement of the pronoun before the verb in this context is the most **fought** issue in all language standardization instruments, among all the rules prescribed for pronoun collocation.

Construction of the Scope of the Study

The construction of this study is based on the widely spread idea that, nowadays, Internet users are comfortable expressing their opinions and value judgments on multiple themes online. Among other possible reasons, this happens due to the fact that screens become a shield to many, encouraging them to say things they would not always say in person. These users have, at their disposal, the possibility of being protected behind devices, safe from physical reactions, and, if needed, kept in anonymity (Cabral & de Lima, 2018).

Evaluations regarding linguistic uses do not escape this movement. Therefore, opinions and value judgments related to the use of the Portuguese language were collected on Facebook, from a post published by a member of the LDRV – Taubaté New Global Era group in 2019 (Fig. 4.2). At the moment these data were collected for this study, the group had approximately 436,000 members.

Subjective evaluations present in comments on Facebook were chosen once this social network is a part of the daily lives of over 130 million Brazilians,[4] who come from various social strata and regions of Brazil.

When the data were collected, 2500 comments were available. From this total, 577 tokens were selected. It is necessary to clarify that this amount (577) refers to the number of "irritating mistakes" collected from 334 members who replied to the

---

[4] Available at https://www.tecmundo.com.br/redes-sociais/139130-brasil-terceiro-pais-usuarios-facebook.htm. Accessed on 09 Mar. 2019.

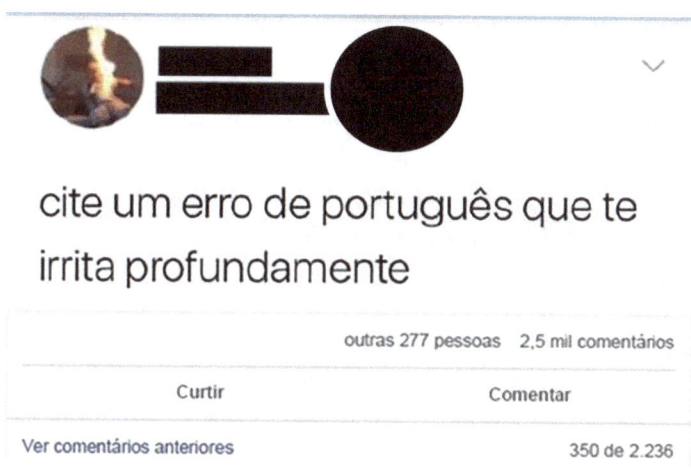

cite um erro de português que te irrita profundamente

	outras 277 pessoas	2,5 mil comentários
Curtir		Comentar
Ver comentários anteriores		350 de 2.236

Fig. 4.2 Source for data extraction. *In*: Brandão et al. (2020, p. 229). (Image translation: Mention a Portuguese mistake that deeply irritates you.)

post. The quantity of members who pointed out more than one "irritating mistake" was recurrent, which resulted in a larger amount of data. Regarding the 334 members, this number was the result of a sampling calculation performed to obtain an approximate reference of how many "members" would need to be collected in order to have a representative sample. This calculation was performed considering a standard deviation of 1.96 and a confidence level of 95%, which would allow for a margin of error of only 5%.[5]

After they were collected, the data – that is, the "Portuguese mistakes that deeply irritate you" – were placed and systematized on electronic tables created using the *Microsoft Excel* software. Beyond the recording of the piece of data itself (the "mistake"), categorized according to its phonetic-phonological, morphophonemic, morphosyntactic, semantic, or even orthographic nature, other variables were also assessed, such as age, gender, education, city of birth, city of residence, and occupation of the Internet user who replied to the post, responsible for evaluating a certain linguistic use as an "irritating mistake." These variables have been used to analyze and interpret the social profiles of such users, providing the information necessary for the other branch of the research "Linguistic prejudice online and offline: phenomena categorization, social profiles and subjective evaluation" (Sene et al., 2019; Brandão et al., 2020), which escapes the scope of this chapter.[6]

---

[5] Further information on the sampling calculation may be found at the following link: https://pt.surveymonkey.com/mp/sample-size-calculator/

[6] The research "Linguistic prejudice online and offline: phenomena categorization, social profiles and subjective evaluation" (Sene et al., 2019; Brandão et al., 2020) analyzes (i) data from the

The analysis of pieces of societal evidence that manifest stereotyped subjective evaluations regarding variable linguistic uses of the Portuguese language is proposed here, in consonance with the objective of this text, after having identified the "irritating mistakes" and counting which were mentioned the most.

Analyses: Societal Evidence of the Variable Linguistic Phenomena

The most frequent "irritating mistakes," that is, the ones most mentioned by users that reacted to the post, are shown in a word cloud (Fig. 4.3). It is important to mention that not all variable linguistic forms are presented as "irritating," and, even if they are not mentioned as linguistic features to be fought, this does not mean they are esteemed by society.

As can be seen in Fig. 4.3, among the "most irritating mistakes" is the prominent mention of the use of *mim* **("me") + verb in the infinitive** (*para mim fazer*) – categorized as one of morphosyntactic nature – followed by the use of *mais* ("plus") instead of *mas* ("but") (from the phonetic-phonological level). There is also a recurrence of *agente* ("agent") in place of *a gente* ("we"), representing a combination of words of phonetic-phonological nature. Furthermore, the word cloud shows a reference to the verb *ir* ("to go") in contexts of periphrasis. Due to the fact that *ir* has been grammaticalizing in Portuguese (Gibbon, 2000), this particle was only mentioned by Internet users when the full verb was also *ir*, in cases such as *vou ir*.

Once such forms are on the radar of the sociolinguistic awareness of speakers, the stigmatization falls upon themselves and not upon a specific phenomenon to which they are attached. In other words, it is not the variation between personal pronouns and their respective functions, diphthongization, hyposegmentation, and verbal periphrases that irritate Internet users. It is, in fact, the use of *mim* as a subject, *mais* instead of a coordinating conjunction (*mas*), *agente* in place of *a gente* (*we*), and the use of *ir* **[auxiliary verb] + *ir* [main verb]** which are the targets of stigma by language users. This happens because, when the linguistic difference is noticed, all speakers are able to distinguish and attribute meaning to it. Therefore, such specific uses receive negative evaluations for being associated with culturally fixed social meanings and for suffering normative prescription in and out of the media. The association between a culturally fixed social meaning and prescription does not always work the same way or with the same intensity, which implies recognizing that there is not only one formula for the realization, understanding, and evaluation of any language facts.

---

cyberspace to understand the nature of stigmatized phenomena in Brazilian Portuguese, (ii) social profiles of Internet users responsible for the stigmatization of such phenomena, and (iii) subjective evaluations underlying these phenomena, when presented through tests to freshmen of the languages and literature course at an Institution of Higher Education. The R software (Core Team, 2019) was used for these three steps.

Fig. 4.3 Most recurrent "irritating mistakes" in the comments. (Translation of the words that make up the word cloud: *mais* – "more"; *menos* – "less"; *vir* – "to come"; *nada* – "nothing"; *comigo* – "with me"; *causa* – "cause"; *ver* – "see"; *mim + verbo* – "me + verb"; *por* – "to put"; *ir* – "to go"; *agente* – "agent"; *estar* – "to be"). *In:* Brandão et al. (2020, p. 235)

The reference to some variable linguistic uses and not to others shows that subjective evaluations emerge as the speakers become aware of such uses. As for awareness, phenomena which vary may be above or below its level. In the case of this study, pieces of societal evidence extracted from Facebook comments are above the level of awareness of speakers, once they are a product of linguistic ideologies that, in the words of Silverstein (1979, p. 193), represent "any sets of beliefs about language articulated by the users as a rationalization or justification of perceived language structure and use."

For Silverstein (1979), language users are able to produce conscious explanations about some linguistic uses and, thus, clarify which are the social meanings associated with the linguistic forms in use. These conscious explanations are, in fact, subjective evaluations that emerge when the speakers have contact with linguistic variation. The fact that Internet users can point out some specific pieces of evidence, as is the case of the words displayed in Fig. 4.3, does not imply saying language users are fully aware of its linguistic functioning and that, for this reason, they are able to make such observations.

What makes these "mistakes," and not others, be pointed out is related, firstly, to the fact that there are some variable phenomena that are salient due to prescriptivism (Freitag, 2021a) and, also, to the type of social meaning associated with them. Therefore, by mapping the most frequent "mistakes" pointed out as "irritating," it is possible to understand what people think about some variable linguistic uses and, above all, what is behind the way people perceive and process variation (Fig. 4.4).

Prescriptions promote the recognition of some variable uses, once language users are alert to uses that escape the standard defined by traditional grammar, as a result of constantly feeling subject to them and having to "correct what is wrong." This type of prescription centers on the set of "normative metalinguistic practices, focusing on the value of correction, on the 'correct' use, according to the norm encoded in grammars" (Freitag, 2021b, p. 3). In Fig. 4.4, explanations and tips – grammar rules – are shown for the "correct" use of the phenomena featured here.

In some cases, such as with ***para mim* + verb in the infinitive** e *a gente* x *agente,* prescription comes followed by stereotypes that are frequently associated with these uses, as is the case of the stereotyped representation of the "Indian" (Fig. 4.4), a derogatory term that represents a process of not recognizing the indigenous peoples who lived here before Portuguese colonization.[7] This is a cruel tautology: if indigenous people use **para *mim* + verb in the infinitive**, and using ***para mim* + verb in the infinitive** is a "mistake," therefore, indigenous people are wrong. In Fig. 4.4, the image of the white boy in an "Indian" costume further contributes to the creation of this scenario of colonial, racist, and ethnocidal stereotypes.

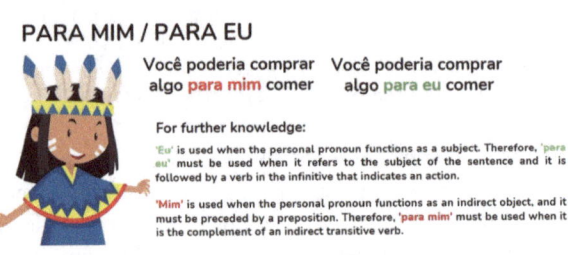

PARA MIM / PARA EU

Você poderia comprar algo para mim comer

Você poderia comprar algo para eu comer

For further knowledge:

'Eu' is used when the personal pronoun functions as a subject. Therefore, 'para eu' must be used when it refers to the subject of the sentence and it is followed by a verb in the infinitive that indicates an action.

'Mim' is used when the personal pronoun functions as an indirect object, and it must be preceded by a preposition. Therefore, 'para mim' must be used when it is the complement of an indirect transitive verb.

Do you know the difference?
AGENTE X A GENTE

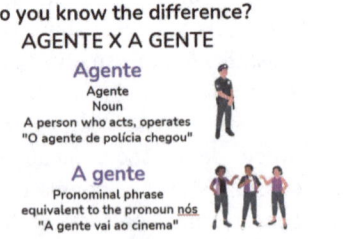

Agente
Agente
Noun
A person who acts, operates
"O agente de polícia chegou"

A gente
Pronominal phrase
equivalent to the pronoun nós
"A gente vai ao cinema"

Dicas de Português

MAS X MAIS

MAS
Adversative conjunction
Indicates opposition

It may substitute "porém"
"Eu posso ir com você, mas tenho que voltar cedo"

MAIS
Adverb of intensity or indefinite adverb
The opposite of "menos"

"Adorei o encontro, vamos marcar mais vezes"

Fig. 4.4 "Irritating mistakes" – normative prescriptions. *In:* Elaborated by the authors. (The memes were created from illustrations available at the website *Freepik*. All illustrations from this website are free for personal and professional use. The only requirement is that the link for each one of them is made available. The illustration in the meme with the image of an "Indian" is available on the following link: https://bityli.com/jCASe. The illustration of the police office can be found on the https://bityli.com/sjJjx, and the one of the group of youngster on this one: https://bityli.com/hMIbI)

---

[7]Available at https://almapreta.com/sessao/cotidiano/resistencia-indigena-entenda-porque-o-termo-indio-e-considerado-pejorativo. Accessed on 13 Feb. 2022.

Having this knowledge, speakers feel authorized to correct other people, besides using this correction as a way to spread linguistic prejudice. In this context, among the collected data, it is possible to observe that Internet users not only mentioned the "mistake" *para mim* + **verb [in the infinitive or some other verb form/tense]** but also made stereotypical comments regarding such use (Fig. 4.5), as discussed based on Fig. 4.4.

Even though sociolinguistics have unveiled an important part of the complex linguistic reality (Faraco, 2011), that is, though many studies on sociolinguistic production have performed a systemic mapping of Portuguese spoken in Brazil, little is known about how language users think and how their perceptions, evaluations, and ideologies compose a specific social imaginary. The identification of this societal evidence is one of the ways to recognize such social imaginary shared between speakers, once some "irritating uses" identified here compose, due to prescriptivism, "a powerful set of images that give meanings to society and each one of the social facts" (Faraco, 2011, p. 263).

The fight against linguistic prejudice and the promotion of linguistic respect become disconnected without the comprehension of how the collective imaginary is formed, since identifying what is or is not linguistic prejudice is not sufficient. Along with this, it is also necessary to identify its roots and which ideologies support them. After this identification, it is possible to offer joint actions to not only fight against linguistically prejudiced practices but also against the ideologies behind such practices. After all, there is an array of stereotypes and ideologies that surround a language, and, many times, these factors are more powerful than a logic-rational and empirical argumentation of the facts of this language, once, before boosting the stigmatization of linguistic uses, the social imaginary is responsible for the ordering and organization that provide meaning to the social world. This makes such imaginary more real than reality itself (Castoriadis, 1982).

The reality that does not represent what is real is the same one that rejects the scientific discourse that defends linguistic variation as systematic and distorts some discourses that fight prejudice and discrimination practices. For a large part of society, adhering to linguistic variation is equivalent to degrading the Portuguese

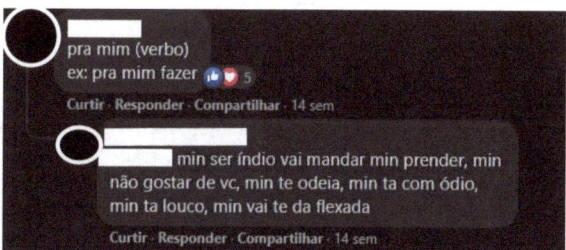

Fig. 4.5 Societal evidence on the use of mim + verb. (Translation of comments: The first one: for me (verb). Ex: so me can do. The second one: me be Indian will arrest me, me no like you, me hate you, me is angry, me is crazy, me will shoot arrow at you). *In:* Facebook: LDRV – Taubaté New Global Era

language. Nevertheless, when linguistic prejudice is not fought, immeasurable consequences may be observed, as seen in the situation in which a doctor mocked his patient for not knowing how to say pneumonia as well as other words "correctly" (Fig. 4.6). This attitude, for instance, is a case that illustrates not only the discrediting of a linguistic use but also the invalidation of a social identity.

This case reported by G1 is one among many that demonstrates the fact that the practice of prescribing norms is recurrent due to the shared illusion that there is only one linguistic standard, only one way to use the Portuguese language, and, above all, due to the lack of knowledge that not all people have had equal access to education. For this reason, it is established and proven that linguistic prejudice is the means through which other prejudices are materialized within the collective social imaginary, and that is why linguistic prejudice is also a social prejudice (Bagno, 2005; Scherre, 2005; Leite, 2008).

Another factor that promotes the appearance and materialization of societal evidence, represented here as "most irritating mistakes," is the media itself and social networks, which not only display information but also objectify certain language uses, making them the target of attention and metacomments. In this respect, it is mostly in social media where speakers share their ideologies about language that a knowledge disconnected from the linguistic reality is noticed. Such lack of knowledge consequently expresses prejudice and linguistic discrimination. One example of this, widely spread on the Internet, is the videos by YouTuber Marcela Tavares, entitled "Não Seja Burro!" ("Don't be stupid!").[8] In these videos, the YouTuber discusses all the "mistakes" that are common online and offline and need to be, in her words, annihilated.

The YouTuber approaches some "mistakes" that appear in different environments and, in a comic way – within her view of what is comical, belittles variable uses such as the ones previously analyzed (*mim* x *eu*, *agente* x *a gente*, *mais* x *mas*), promulgating the fight against them as if they needed to be exterminated instead of being understood from a scientific point of view. The performance of the YouTuber

29/07/2016 12h56 - Atualizado em 30/07/2016 10h43

Médico debocha de paciente na internet: 'Não existe peleumonia'

Médico e duas funcionárias foram afastados após postagem em rede social.
Guilherme Capel disse que não teve intenção de ofender e pediu desculpas.

Fig. 4.6 Piece of news about a doctor that mocks a patient for not "speaking correctly". (The news headline translates to "Doctor mocks patient on the Internet: 'there is no peleumonia'," referring to a "mispronunciation" of the word "pneumonia." The subtitle reads "Doctor and two employees were suspended after post on social media. Guilherme Capel says he did not have the intention of offending and apologized"). *In*: G1 – Globo. (Available at https://g1.globo.com/sp/campinas-regiao/noticia/2016/07/medico-debocha-de-paciente-na-internet-nao-existe-peleumonia.html. Accessed on 01 Apr. 2022.)

---

[8] Available at https://www.youtube.com/watch?v=Uy_0zzOdgXo&t=109s&ab_channel=Marcela Tavares. Accessed on 01 Apr. 2022.

is extensively shared on different social networks, once, besides her supposedly funny way to "teach Portuguese," she employs other semiotic resources to cause humor: the crooked glasses on her face, emulating a clumsy "teacher"; the fact that she screams every time she is going to fight a "mistake"; etc. The problem with this type of material is that linguistic prejudice ends up marginalizing people in the name of "good" grammar rules. Concerning this matter, Scherre (2005, p. 43, highlighted by the author) emphasizes that:

> In the name of *good language*, social injustice is practiced, frequently humiliating the human being by not accepting one of its most divine cultural assets: the unconscious and complete command of a communication system specific to the community around it. And worse than this: the schools and society – of which schools are an active reflection – make cruel associations, with no structural linguistic support, between the command of specific linguistic forms and beauty or ugliness; between the command of specific linguistic forms and elegance or inelegance; between the command of specific linguistic forms and competence or incompetence; between the command of specific linguistic forms and intelligence or stupidity [...].

Therefore, the phenomena identified here as those which "irritate the most" are reflections of a disapproving society that, in the name of a "good language," does not recognize linguistic variation as a phenomenon inherent in natural languages. Thus, they become targets of prescriptivism, resulting in a more salient evaluation of some linguistic uses than of others. The identification of the pieces of societal evidence, as well as the ideology that pervades them, is important so that people do not disregard others due to the way they speak once again, as did the Greek who called "*barbarians* all of those that did not speak Greek" (Ilari & Basso, 2006, p. 195).

It is also important to highlight that the societal evidence and ideologies analyzed here add a new matter to the study of linguistic prejudice: connected to the social domain recurrently intertwined with prejudiced manifestations is the strength of normative prescriptivism which affects a certain linguistic use. After all, not all "irritating mistakes" found in the sample indicate specific social types, as emphasized in the case of ***mim* + verb in the infinitive** being associated with the "Indian" way of speaking. The other "mistakes," on the other hand, are pointed out as "irritating" and even used in prejudiced manifestations, but not all of them vehemently indicate particular social types.

Final Considerations

Conscious or unconscious evaluation of a certain linguistic phenomenon is linked to the cognitive capacity of the speaker and, at the same time, to values that are socially imposed on a linguistic form. With this in mind, the present study gathered societal evidence extracted from a post on Facebook. Such evidence represents the "mistakes" that Facebook users judged to be the "most irritating" ones. Among the phenomena presented as "irritating," it is possible to find the uses of ***mim* + verb in the infinitive** (*para mim fazer*), *agente* instead of *a gente*, and *mais* rather than *mas*. These linguistic forms were the most frequently found in the *corpus* and are on the radar of the sociolinguistic awareness of speakers once they are phenomena that are affected by prescriptivism.

In this respect, this study, therefore, concludes that, as a phenomenon becomes the target of normative prescription because it escapes the grammatical standard, it also becomes the target of linguistic ideologies responsible for indexing a social meaning Y to a linguistic form X. This is the case, for instance, of the use of *mim + verb*, which, as discussed in the analysis section, is associated with the stereotyped representation that this linguistic use comes from the indigenous way of speaking, together with the value of correction. In other words, Facebook users not only pointed out the "mistakes" that were "the most irritating" for them but also indicated to which social meanings said "mistake" was linked. These reflections contribute to the discussion regarding the possibility that the social meaning of variation may not be related to the variable itself, but to a certain variant.

Furthermore, these data were analyzed according to the linguistic ideologies and subjective evaluations expressed by speakers and compared with memes, pieces of news, and grammar prescriptions that concern the phenomena collected from the Facebook post and systematized. Such results reveal there is a collective imaginary that is stronger than a logic-rational and empirical argumentation about the linguistic uses. In order to properly fight this, it is necessary to recognize that these same uses are utilized to promote linguistic prejudice and that they consequently favor the exclusion and discrimination of a specific linguistic form (or way of speaking) in the name of "good" grammar rules.

Finally, this research points to the need of promoting the recognition of variable linguistic uses as legitimate and inherent in natural languages. Moreover, this study boosts the appreciation of linguistic diversity instead of calling *barbarians* all those who do not speak the idealized standard of the language, since the appreciation of variable uses is not equivalent to the degradation of the Portuguese language, but to one of the ways of ensuring linguistic respect to all speakers of the language.

Acknowledgments and Information This study was conducted with the support of Coordenação de Aperfeiçoamento de Pessoal de Nível Superior (CAPES), Brazil – Finance Code 001.

This study was developed within the scope of the project "Diversidade linguística, Avaliação subjetiva e Respeito linguístico" (Div.AR) and with financial resources by the Newton Paiva University Center.

References

Bagno, M. (2005). *Preconceito linguístico: o que é, como se faz*. Loyola.
Berlinck, R. A., Brandão, S. M., & Sene, M. G. (2020). Desafios e caminhos na compreensão da variação sintática: design de um teste de percepção. In C. dos Santos Carvalho, N. da Silva Lopes, & A. Rodrigues (Eds.), *Sociolinguística e Funcionalismo: vertentes e interfaces* (pp. 23–52). EDUNEB.
Biazolli, C. C. (2018). *Inter-relações de estilo, gênero, modalidade e norma na variação da posição de clíticos pronominais*. Cultura Acadêmica.
Bourdieu, P. (2008). *A economia das trocas linguísticas: o que falar quer dizer* (2nd ed.). Edusp.

Brandão, S. M. (2018). *Alternância verbal em construções condicionais: um fenômeno variável?* Dissertation. São Paulo State University.

Brandão, S. M., Biazolli, C. C., & Sene, M. G. (2020). Preconceito linguístico dentro e fora da rede. *Falange Miúda, 5*(2), 222–243.

Cabral, A. L. T., & de Lima, N. V. (2018). Interações conflituosas e violência verbal nas redes sociais: polêmica em comentários no Facebook. *Revista (Con)textos linguísticos, 12*(22), 39–58. https://periodicos.ufes.br/contextoslinguisticos/article/view/20626. Accessed 13 February 2022

Calvet, L.-J. (2002). *Sociolinguística: uma introdução crítica.* Parábola.

Campbell-Kibler, K. (2006). *Listener perceptions of sociolinguistic variables*: The case of (ING). Dissertation. Stanford University.

Campbell-Kibler, K. (2009). The nature of sociolinguistic perception. *Language Variation and Change., 21,* 135.

Castoriadis, C. (1982). *A instituição imaginária da sociedade.* Paz e Terra.

Core Team, R. (2019). *R: A language and environment for statistical computing.* R Foundation for Statistical Computing.

Rumeu, M. C. B. (2008). *A implementação do 'Você' no Português Brasileiro Oitocentista e Novecentista:* Um Estudo de Painel. Dissertation. Federal University of Rio de Janeiro.

Sene, M. G. (2019). Percepções sociolinguísticas, avaliações subjetivas e atitudes linguísticas: três domínios complementares. *Revista Todas as letras – Mackenzie., 21,* 304–323.

Sene, M. G., Brandão, S. M., & Biazolli, C. C. (2019). *Preconceito linguístico na rede e fora dela: categorização, perfis sociais e avaliação subjetiva.* Open Science Framework. https://osf.io/6ymrv/. Accessed 09 June 2022.

Eckert, P. (2005). *Variation, meaning, and social change.* Annual Meeting of the Linguistic Society of America.

Eckert, P. (2012). Three waves of variation study: The emergence of meaning in the study of sociolinguistic variation. *Annual Review of Anthropology, 41,* 87–100.

Faraco, C. A. (2008). *Norma culta brasileira – desatando alguns nós.* Parábola.

Faraco, C. A. (2011). O Brasil entre a norma culta e a norma curta. In X. Lagares & M. Bagno (Eds.), *Políticas da norma e conflitos linguísticos* (pp. 259–275). Parábola.

Freitag, R. M. K. (2021a). *Gramática Viva ao Vivo.* https://rkofreitag.github.io/gramatica.html/. Acesso em 02 de fev. 2022.

Freitag, R. M. K. (2021b). O desenvolvimento da consciência sociolinguística e o sucesso no desempenho em leitura. *ALFA: REVISTA DE LINGUÍSTICA, 65,* e13027. https://doi.org/10.1590/1981-5794-e13027

Garrett, P., Coupland, N., & Williams, A. (2003). Investigating language attitudes: Social meanings of dialect, ethnicity and performance. *International Journal of Applied Linguistics, 15,* 411. https://doi.org/10.1111/j.1473-4192.2005.00100d.x

Gibbon, A. O. (2000). *A expressão do tempo futuro na língua falada de Florianópolis: gramaticalização e variação.* Dissertation. Federal University of Santa Catarina.

Ilari, R., & Basso, R. (2006). *O português da gente.* Contexto.

Labov, W. (1966). *The social stratification of English in new York City.* Center for Applied Linguistics.

Labov, W. (2001). *Principles of linguistic change.* Vol. 2: Social Factors. Blackwell Publishers.

Leite, M. Q. (2008). *Preconceito e intolerância na linguagem.* Contexto.

Lopes, C. R. S. (2009). Retratos da mudança no sistema pronominal: o tratamento carioca nas primeiras décadas do século XX. In A. Cortina & S. M. G. da Conceição Nasser (Eds.), *Sujeito e Linguagem: Séries Trilhas Linguísticas* (Vol. 17, pp. 47–74). Cultura Acadêmica.

Lopes, C. R. S., de Oliveira, T. L., & de Carvalho, B. B. A. (2016). A Expressão da 2ª Pessoa do Singular: Variação e Percepção numa Abordagem Experimental. *Revista Todas as Letras – Mackenzie, 18,* 117–132.

Machado, A. C. M. (2006). A implementação de "você" no quadro pronominal: as estratégias de referência ao interlocutor em peças teatrais no século XX. Dissertation – Federal University of Rio de Janeiro.

Marcuschi, L. A., & Dionisio, Â. P. (Eds.). (2007). *Fala e escrita*. Autêntica.

Mendonça, J. J., & Nascimento, J. S. (2015). Expressão do sujeito nulo em redações de alunos do Ensino Fundamental. *Cadernos de Letras da UFF., 25*, 201–215.

Milroy, J. (2011). Ideologias linguísticas e as consequências da padronização. In X. Lagares & M. Bagno (Eds.), *Políticas da norma e conflitos linguísticos* (pp. 49–87). Parábola Editorial.

Oushiro, L. (2015). Identidade na pluralidade: avaliação, produção e percepção linguística na cidade de São Paulo. Dissertation. University of São Paulo.

Scherre, M. M. P. (2005). *Doa-se lindos filhotes de poodle: variação linguística, mídia e preconceito*. Parábola.

Silverstein, M. (1979). Language structure and linguistic ideology. In P. R. Clyne, W. F. Hanks, & C. L. Hofbauer (Eds.), *The elements* (pp. 193–248). Chicago Linguistics Society.

Trudgill, P. (1974). *The social differentiation of English in Norwich*. CUP.

Vološinov, V. N. (1973). *Marxism and the philosophy of language*. Seminar Press.

Weinreich, U., Labov, W., & Herzog, M. (2006[1968]). *Fundamentos empíricos para uma teoria da mudança linguística*. Parábola.

Chapter 5
Rhotacism and Lambdacism in Portuguese: The Process of Orthographic Standardization and Liquid Consonants

Débora Aparecida dos Reis Justo Barreto ⓘ and **Gladis Massini-Cagliari** ⓘ

The objective of this work is to study the variation between <l > and < r > in the writing of medieval Galician-Portuguese songs, composed in the thirteenth to fourteenth centuries, but surviving in manuscripts dating from different periods, from the thirteenth to the sixteenth century (Massini-Cagliari, 2007). Cases of variation in specific words will be analyzed, which can be characterized as occurrences of the processes of rhotacism and lambdacism. The methodological procedure adopted is the observation of the graphic variation, from facsimile editions, and the reflection on the meaning of the alternation verified at that time, compared to the non-variation in the current writing of Brazilian Portuguese (BP), due to the orthographic standardization, in the light of the concepts of prejudice and linguistic intolerance (Bagno, 1999; Leite, 2008; O'Neill & Massini-Cagliari, 2019).

Massini-Cagliari (2012) claims that the study carried out by researchers working with historical linguistics is a kind of archeology of the language, since it aims to unravel past facts that may contribute to clarifying the linguistic current, through certain remaining clues, many of them almost hidden. Thus, by discovering the historical course of specific linguistic processes, we seek to reconstruct how the Portuguese language would have sounded in the past and how the organization of its phonological grammar would have been. It should be noted that studies in this area, nowadays, seek not to assume positive or negative attitudes toward change, not understanding the phenomenon as either an advance or a degeneration (Aitchinson, 2006). According to Massini-Cagliari (2012), the search for the historical reason of current events can promote relevant subsidies for language teaching and for understanding (and combating) the linguistic prejudice present in Brazilian society.

Bagno (1999: 9) explains that linguistic prejudice is linked to the confusion created, in the course of history, between language and normative grammar. Although,

D. A. dos Reis Justo Barreto · G. Massini-Cagliari (✉)
Unesp – Sao Paulo State University, Araraquara, Sao Paulo, Brazil
e-mail: debora.barreto@unesp.br; gladis.massini-cagliari@unesp.br

nowadays, it is possible to observe a tendency to fight against the different types of prejudice, showing that they have no rational basis and are just the result of igno- rance, this tendency does not affect linguistic discrimination, which, on the con- trary, is fed in different media, in manuals that aim to teach what is correct and what is incorrect and in traditional educational instruments (didactic books and norma- tive grammars). According to the author, linguistic prejudice is based on the belief that there is only one language, which would be the one taught in schools, explained in grammars, and cataloged in dictionaries. Therefore, any manifestation that escapes this school-grammar-dictionary triangle is considered, from the point of view of linguistic prejudice, wrong, ugly, and rudimentary (Bagno, 1999: 40). As Bagno (1999) ponders, linguistic prejudice has reigned in the mentality of society for a long time and is the result of the combination between the overvaluation of the graphic representation of the language and the aversion to the variety spoken by certain social classes and in certain regions, such as the characteristic speech from the Northeast region of Brazil.

In the troubadour period of the language, which is between the thirteenth and fifteenth centuries (Mattos e Silva, 2006), Archaic Portuguese (AP) still did not have a standard orthography established by law, which made the language exist independently of grammarians and schools, since in the archaic phase Latin was the language taught to the minority that had access to education. As an orthographic standardization of the AP had not yet been established, variation dominated the written documentation of that period, which fluctuated in spelling, morphology, and syntax. According to Mattos e Silva (2006), the existing variations in the texts pro- duced in the Middle Ages are indicators for the changes that came to occur, and that, from the standardization, the written materials began to oppress the diversity, since only a part of the variants used is chosen to integrate the orthographic system. The remaining works of the AP, therefore, constitute an important resource for the knowledge of the Portuguese used in the Iberian Peninsula, despite the limitations imposed throughout the process of representing the oral in writing.

The present reflection turns to the poetic productions of the focused period, con- sidering that the medieval documents were written in an alphabetical writing system (without any attention to the prosodic phenomena). Therefore, in prose composi- tions, it is not possible to obtain information about the pronunciation of the past. In poetic texts, on the contrary, there are indications of the segmental and supraseg- mental elements of the AP, a fact that makes it possible to arrive at inferences about the accent and rhythmic patterns of that stage of the language.

The Galician-Portuguese lyric is composed of two strands: one religious and one profane. The first comprises the *Cantigas de Santa Maria* (henceforth, CSM), a col- lection in praise of the Virgin Mary carried out in the second half of the thirteenth century, whose authorship is attributed to Dom Alfonso X, the Wise, of León and Castile. The second includes songs of love, friend, mockery, and cursing, produced by about 160 writers, who are responsible for more than 1700 works in the interval between the end of the twelfth century and the middle of the fourteenth century.

One of the recurring variations in the archaic phase was the exchange of <r > for <l > and vice versa, a fact recorded in the remaining poetic sources. When the exchange takes place in the direction of the lateral to the rhotic, there is the phenomenon of rhotacism. Costa (2013: 179) defines rhotacism only as "the exchange of a lateral sound for a rhotic sound"; Freitag et al. (2010: 18) relate this phenomenon to the constitution of the syllable: "in the linguistic literature, rhotacism is the neutralization of a lateral liquid by a vibrant liquid in CCV-type syllables, such as 'brusa' for 'blusa' [blouse]." Lambdacism, on the other hand, corresponds to "the phenomenon opposite to rhotacism, in which the speaker produces a lateral where a rhotic would be expected, such as the realization of 'plato' for 'prato' [plate]."

In the Middle Ages, *groriosa* ("glorious") and *miragre* ("miracle") were forms widely used in written productions, as well as *paravla* ("word") and *regla* ("rule"), with no devaluation of these uses, as only songs performed by the court managed to survive until modern times. Therefore, these words were most likely used by the aristocracy, a prestigious portion of troubadour society. We propose, therefore, a reflection focused on the phenomena of rhotacism and lambdacism in Archaic Portuguese (AP) and current Brazilian Portuguese (BP), seeking to establish relationships between the standardization process and the difference in the degree of valuation in the exchange of the vibrant liquid consonant for the lateral, or the opposite, in these two stages of the historical constitution of the Portuguese language.

According to Conde Silvestre (2007), when we investigate cases of variation in a diachronic way, it is necessary to consider that the analyzed material survived by chance and, possibly, portrays a small portion of the whole. Furthermore, the scholar will find, in the ancient documentation, data relating to literate individuals (men, in general) of society, belonging to the middle and upper classes, in certain styles and registers. Labov (1994) states that the linguistic forms represented in the texts of the past are commonly distinct from the authors' vernacular, as they reflected efforts to apprehend a normative dialect that was never anyone's native language. As a result, many works are marked by overcorrections, mixing of dialects and errors made by the scribes in the making of the copy.

Because the AP does not have an official orthography, different writers spelled the same term differently. In fact, this even happened with the same author, who wrote the same word in different ways (Massini-Cagliari, 1998; Chagas, 2008), which can be seen in Fig. 5.1, taken from CSM **67**. In it, we find the *groriosa/gloriosa* ("glorious") alternation within a single stanza, which was copied by only one hand, that is, its writing was surely written by the same person. It is worth remembering that vibrant and lateral share phonetic properties and behaviors in many languages. In Portuguese, they are the only possible units in the second position of a consonantal group.

Faraco (2008) argues that the profile of the feudal community (marked by political decentralization, by an essentially agrarian economy, and by few communication relations beyond its regional limits) resulted, in terms of language, in a vast diversification. In response to the varied linguistic map of the locality, a standardizing project emerged. As can be seen, through normative instruments, a standard of language capable of attenuating all the regional and social diversity inherited from the medieval experience was sought. As a general rule, the language standard created in order to standardize the speeches was based on the variety adopted by the

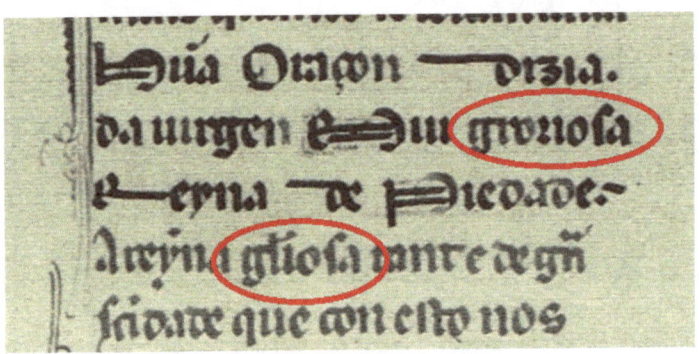

Fig. 5.1 *Cantigas de Santa Maria* **67**. Groriosa/gloriosa ("glorious") variation. (Facsimile edition of Códice Escorial Músicos, edited by Anglés (1964: 86v))

nobility; however, the standard norm designed by the authorities of the period is virtually impossible to find in the reality of uses, as it is an ideal language, abstract, and elitist, based on myths without practical support, inspired by certain archaic models of social organization (Bagno, 2003: 75–76). This form of language is until today seen as an eternal and immutable truth, which creates the (wrong) notion that there is only one correct way to speak, which would be that set of rules detailed in grammars. That said, variation, when it appears, is simply seen as a synonym for error (Bagno & de Oliveira Rangel, 2005).

Milroy (2011) comments that the standardization process acts by promoting invariance or uniformity in the language structure. As we explained, it is an imposed regime and never fully achieved in actual use. One effect of standardization is the development of awareness among the user group of a right way to speak the language. Milroy (2011) calls this phenomenon standard language ideology *[ideologia da língua padrão]*, and a categorical aspect of it is the belief in correctness. This conviction shows that, when there are two or more variants of some word or construction, only one of them can be correct. If we think about the present, only *gloriosa* ("glorious") is considered to be right, because there is a high degree of stigma associated with the *groriosa* variant. However, the two forms appear in AP without any distinction of value. What if, during the troubadour era, both variants were prestigious uses? The analysis of the cases allows us to recognize that the valuation of occurrences takes place at the social level, since the varieties of the language do not have prestige in themselves; they gain notoriety when their speakers have a high reputation.

In Figs. 5.2 and 5.3, we show another example of variation found in the songs but now in the secular aspect of Galician-Portuguese lyricism. The passage in question is part of a *cantiga de amigo* ("friend song"), by Airas Nunes, which is located in two *cancioneiros* ("songbooks"): from the *Biblioteca Nacional de Lisboa* (CBN) and from *Vaticana* (CV). In the first, there is no variation. In the second, in turn, the substitution of <l> for <r> (and the reverse) can be seen within the same word but in different contexts. *Floridas/frolidas* ("flowery"), as well as *groriosa/gloriosa*

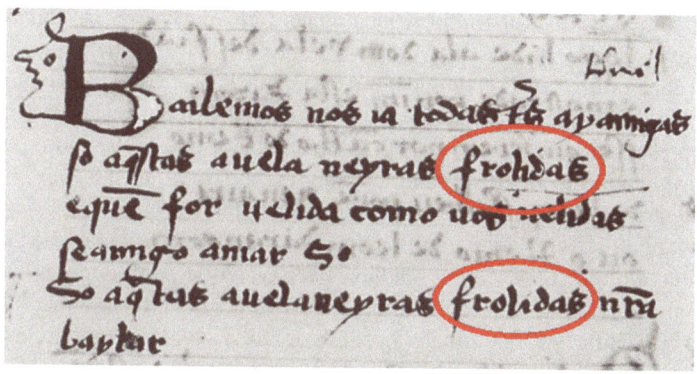

Fig. 5.2 *Cantiga de amigo* ("friend song"): *"Bailemos nós já todas três, ai amigas"* [*Let's dance, all three of us, oh my friends*]. (Facsimile edition of Códice da Biblioteca Nacional de Lisboa – Colocci-Brancuti (1982: 879))

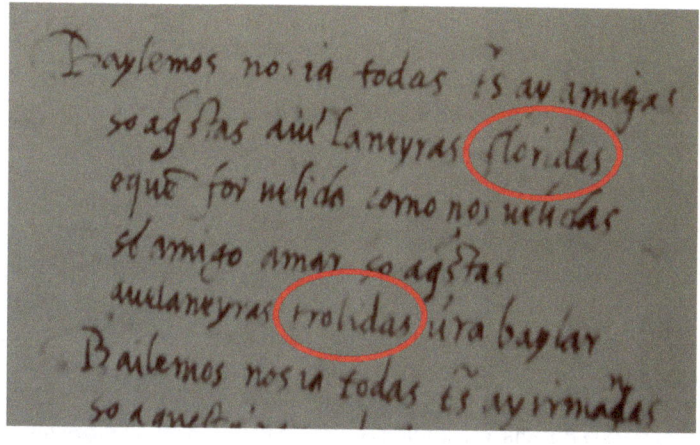

Fig. 5.3 *Cantiga de amigo* ("friend song"): *"Bailemos nós já todas três, ai amigas"* [*Let's dance, all three of us, oh my friends*]. *Floridas/frolidas* variation. (Facsimile edition of the Cancioneiro Português da Biblioteca Vaticana (1973: 462))

("glorious"), occupy the interior of the same poetic text, demonstrating not only the enormous lexical richness of the archaic production but also a possible equity between the variants at that moment of the Portuguese language, in which it is not possible to affirm certainly if a change in writing was a reflection of a change in phonetic realization (Chagas, 2008: 144).

Contrarily to Chagas (2008), Mattos e Silva (2006: 37) feel more confident in relation to the phonetic realization clues brought by the medieval Galician-Portuguese songs, as she considers that, as they are poems in generally isosyllabic and rhyming verses, this makes them fundamental for the knowledge of phonetic facts of this period, such as, questions regarding the encounters between vowels (hiatus/diphthongs), vowel timbre (opening and closing), vowels, and nasal/oral diphthongs.

Gomes and Souza (2003) comment that the identification of variable phenomena presupposes that, for a certain category of language, there are at least two possibilities of representation. It also implies that the choice of one of the forms is not random, but is related to linguistic and extralinguistic issues. In this way, the social environment is decisive in the construction of the prestige or stigma value of each of the variables. The development of a standard norm for Portuguese has led to the devaluation of linguistic varieties that have been widely used throughout the history of the language. The standard norm, therefore, instituted the thought that other ways of saying or writing are illegitimate, because only the standard is genuine.

As is well known, the language is in continuous transformation, as it adapts its system to the speakers' social interaction needs, which change over time. Portuguese is an example of this: although it retains several characteristics of the archaic period, it has undergone many changes in lexicon, syntax, prosody, semantics, morphology, and other levels of analysis. In view of this, Faraco (1991) emphasizes that the world's languages comprise heterogeneous realities and that changes emerge from diversity. From this position arises the fact that not all variation implies change, but all change presupposes variation. Modification is a constant in languages, not affecting their structural integrity, since it always affects certain parts, never the linguistic totality.

When we think about the *groriosa/gloriosa* ("glorious") variation, we realize that this type of change still occurs today throughout the Brazilian territory (da Costa, 2011). In addition, we know, as speakers, that *groriosa* presents a great degree of stigma, being the target of linguistic prejudice. Thus, at some point in history, the two forms ceased to be a process of change and became a condition of stable variation (Gomes and Souza, 2003; 76). Thus, both terms went through a period of variation that, for social reasons, never materialized in a change. It is possible to consider that the high degree of discredit associated with the form with <r > has acted and still acts as a kind of blockade in the use of this variant. However, the question that remains is as follows: in what period of the constitution of the Portuguese language did the exchange of the lateral consonant for the vibrant one, and vice versa, acquire social stigma (O'Neill & Massini-Cagliari, 2019), becoming the object of linguistic prejudice?

Bagno (2003) emphasizes that the social prestige of the linguistic varieties practiced by the most favored classes of the community is not related to intrinsic qualities, that is, with some kind of beauty, logic and specific, and natural elegance to these ways of using the language. Social prestige comprises an ideological construction (O'Neill & Massini-Cagliari, 2019), given that, for historical, political, or economic reasons, certain classes of society assumed power, gained value, or even attributed prestige to themselves. The process of rotation in BP used nowadays, for example, is usually linked to the most disadvantaged classes of the population, who suffer extremely negative judgments by the dominant social groups. According to Bagno (2003), when prestigious individuals from a certain society stop reacting against certain linguistic productions, ceasing to analyze them as *deviations*, it is because the ideal of a *correct* language has already changed, in a phenomenon of natural self-regulation and intrinsic to groups, which does not depend on the prescription of official instances. In relation to rhotacism, this has not yet happened, as the stigma associated with the <r > variant inhibits its use by the higher strata of the Brazilian social body.

It should be noted that the impulse toward orthographic standardization had economic and social ends and that the process took place gradually throughout history (Cagliari, 1995). If we carry out a quick assessment of the standardization of Portuguese, we realize that it is never finished, since the standard actually used is always changing as the language adapts to the new needs of individuals. The standardization of the language began with the emergence of the first reflections on the language, which date from the years 1536 and 1540 and are *Gramática da linguagem portuguesa* ["Portuguese language grammar"], by Fernão de Oliveira, and *Gramática da língua portuguesa* ["Portuguese language grammar"], by João de Barros. According to Mattos and Silva (2006), these discussions were responsible for the beginning of the establishment of an invariable writing for the Portuguese language.

Milroy (2011) states that the doctrine of correction was common among medievalists, which consisted of rectifying the mistakes made by the original scribes, aiming to make their writing more uniform. So, even in AP, where there was still no official orthography, the view that there was a right way to use the language was already rooted in the mentality of the feudal population. However, how to know if the corrections were made in order to fix the work done by the copyists or if they were practiced by the copyists themselves? Furthermore, it is necessary to consider the possibility that the revision took place in the original document, that is, it was undertaken by the troubadour in the first version of the song. In Fig. 5.4, we show a repair case found in CBN. In the aforementioned song by Nuno Fernandes Torneol, the grapheme <h > was added at a later time to the representation of *tol(h)estes*. It can symbolize a behavior operated at the same moment of copying the poem (due to an error in the copying process), or it can portray a future event in relation to the moment of the first copy, authored by the same individual or under the responsibility of another person (in this case, the addition appears to be written by the same hand that copied the song).

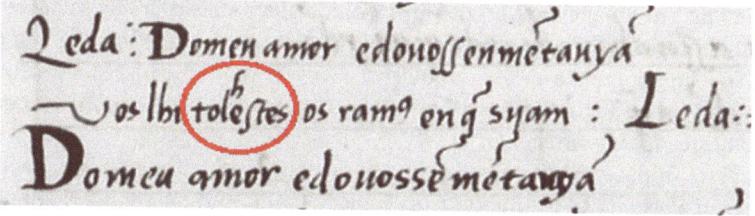

Fig. 5.4 *Cantiga de amigo* ("friend song") "Levad', amigo, que dormides as manhanas frias" ["Rise, friend, because you slept the cold mornings"]. Example of graphic amendment present in the profane version of Galician-Portuguese lyricism. (Facsimile edition of Códice da Biblioteca Nacional de Lisboa – Colocci-Brancuti (1982: 641))

Cambraia (2005) considers that the texts set back in time were modified by third parties, without authorization or prior knowledge of the author. Part of these changes occurred voluntarily, that is, by the will of those who reproduced the document, and, possibly, did not agree with the ideology defended by the troubadour. Therefore, whoever was editing the material censored what seemed inappropriate. However, some changes were due to lapses, also called copy errors. The variants, very recurrent in the codices of the archaic period, are attributed to the scribes by modern researchers, who also share the opinion that the composers of the period followed certain criteria in the elaboration of the texts. That said, even in the face of a wide variety of forms, copyists and writers of that phase adopted certain parameters, which were determined by a collective conscience about the writing system of the chosen language. This statement reiterates Faraco's (1991) sayings, given that languages are in constant transformation and change, but without ever losing their systematicity and semiotic potential.

It is important to point out that the medieval songbooks that reached the present day are not original records but first copies or copies of copies (Massini-Cagliari, 2007). Castro (1991) emphasizes that the identity of the scribes is not generally known and that the dates, places, and circumstances in which the transcription of the songs was undertaken are unknown and doubtful. The graphic alterations between simple and duplicated segments of AP are the result, for Williams (1975[1938]), of the copyists' difficulty in recognizing the difference in the sound of the graphemes reproduced. It should be noted that numerous factors may have motivated the use of one form and not another, including the style defined by the scribe with the aim of refining his craft through innovations in literary language.

When questioning whether a particular correction was directed to the copyist's work or whether it was carried out by him, we realize the complexity of the debates proposed here. Returning to the first example, we can conjecture whether *gloriosa* ("glorious") would have been a correction made by the copyist to the troubadour, which would have spelled *groriosa*. By admitting this hypothesis, we focus on a temporal demarcation, since the scribes of the profane side date from the fifteenth and sixteenth centuries and the songs, from much earlier. The defense of this possibility would indicate that the *groriosa/gloriosa* variation prevailed throughout the AP and that, for various reasons, *groriosa* came to be gradually replaced by *gloriosa* over time, until it was fixed as the only appropriate disposition. The equity between the variants in the Middle Ages would have been shaken by social aspects, since the form with <r> acquired a lack of prestige and became the target of prejudice. The stigma related to the use of *groriosa* was reinforced by standardization, which prescribed the existence of only one correct way to use the language: the doctrinal standard norm.

The brief reflections presented here demonstrate the importance of a diachronic analysis of Portuguese in order to truly understand its current configuration. Every language can be considered as a cultural object, being performed in countless situational and social contexts by people of different genders, socioeconomic levels, educational levels, and age groups, among other characteristics. The process of orthography standardization put an idea in the mind of Brazilians: that language is

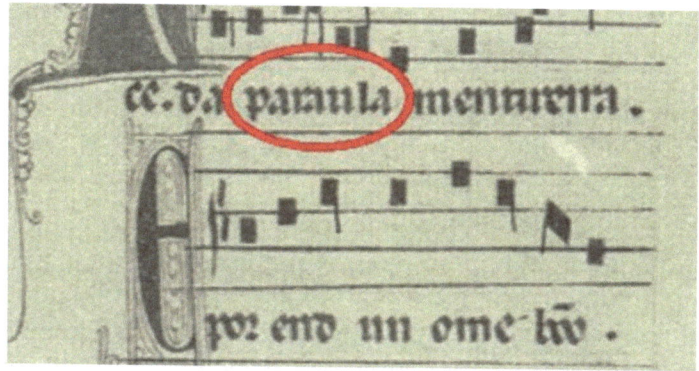

Fig. 5.5 Cantiga de Santa Maria **43**. Paravla (for "palavra" – "word"). (Facsimile edition of Códice Escorial Músicos, edited by Anglés (1964:.65r))

the standard norm, that is, that perfectly delimited and stable variety, which, in reality, is never really produced in speech by anyone. As discussed in this study, the normalization of the Portuguese language led to the devaluation of other varieties, which began to suffer linguistic discrimination.

As can be seen, it is the society of each epoch that determines the value of the forms of language. The degree of prestige or stigma of a given variant changes according to the speaker's social and economic environment (Gnerre, 1991). In the archaic period of the language, it can be interpreted that the diversity of spellings was legitimized by the poets, who adopted alternating forms within the same text. As the compositions that have come down to us are the result of work carried out at the court, by the noblest part of the population, it can be considered that there was no devaluation in the use of rhotacism and lambdacism, phenomena highly stigmatized today. Figure 5.5 shows the representation of the two processes occurring simultaneously within the same word. The example was found in CSM **43**.

The use of *paravla* ("word") in today's daily life would be the target of linguistic prejudice, since, in BP, the exchange between liquids is the target of great discredit. As Bagno (2003) explains, when individuals from certain social classes stop reacting negatively to certain realizations, ceasing to see them as wrong, the model of the *correct* language has already changed. So, most likely the form *miragre* ("miracle"), instead of *milagre*, would be perfectly accepted today if a specific layer of society, with prestige, started to use it.

Conclusion

From the analysis of specific cases of rhotacism and lambdacism, this work aimed to show that the historical study of language, more than a curiosity about our linguistic origin and even than hedonism, in the eager reading of the very interesting poetic texts that remain from the medieval period, brings subsidies for the teaching of the Portuguese language today and for the understanding of the existence and nature of linguistic prejudice and the fight against it, insofar as it reveals that structures that are currently discriminated against and considered as wrong they are, in fact, the result of the natural historical drift of the language, of trends of changes present in our past since our Latin origin, and that, therefore, have nothing of *ignorance* or the result of *cognitive deficit*. This becomes quite clear when one notices that forms such as *groriosa*, in that period, corresponded to the representation of the speech of a monarch, since the song in which it was mapped is attributed to a king, Alfonso X, and, more than that, to the *wisest* among kings.

Acknowledgments The authors would like to thank São Paulo Research Foundation FAPESP (Grant 2018/24793-3 – Debora Aparecida dos Reis Justo Barreto) and the National Council for Scientific and Technological Development CNPq (302648/2019-4 – Gladis Massini-Cagliari).

References

Aitchinson, J. (2006). *Language change: Progress ou decay?* (3rd ed.. 5th printing). Cambridge University Press.

Anglés, H. (1964). *La música de las Cantigas de Santa María del Rey Alfonso el sabio: facsímil, transcripción y estudio critico por Higinio Anglés*. Diputación Provincial de Barcelona; Biblioteca Central; Publicaciones de la Sección de Música.

Bagno, M. (1999). *Preconceito Linguístico: o que é, como se faz*. Edições Loyola.

Bagno, M. (2003). Norma lingüística & preconceito social: questões de terminologia. *Veredas*. Juiz de Fora, *5*(2), 71–83, ju./dez. 2003.

Bagno, M., & de Oliveira Rangel, E. (2005). Tarefas da educação lingüística no Brasil. *Revista Brasileira de Linguística Aplicada, 5*(1), 63–81.

Cagliari, L. C. (1995). Algumas reflexões sobre o início da ortografia da Língua Portuguesa. *Cadernos de Estudos Lingüísticos* (UNICAMP), Campinas, *27*, 103–111.

Cambraia, C. N. (2005). *Introdução à crítica textual*. Martins Fontes.

CANCIONEIRO da Biblioteca Nacional (Colocci-Brancuti): Cód. 10991. (1982). Reprodução fac-similada. Biblioteca Nacional, Imprensa Nacional – Casa da Moeda.

CANCIONEIRO Português da Biblioteca Vaticana (Cód. 4803): Reprodução fac-similada com introdução de L. F. Lindley Cintra. (1973). Centro de Estudos Filológicos, Instituto de Alta Cultura.

Castro, I. (1991). *Curso de história da língua portuguesa*. Universidade Aberta.

Chagas, P. (2008). A mudança lingüística. In *Introdução à Lingüística*. José Luiz Fiorin (Org.) (5th ed., pp. 141–163). Contexto.

Conde Silvestre, J. C. (2007). Problemas y Principios. In *Sociolingüística Histórica* (pp. 19–72). Gredos.

da Costa, L. T. (2011). *Abordagem dinâmica do rotacismo*. Tese de Doutorado. Universidade Federal do Paraná.

da Costa, L. T. (2013). Fenômenos variáveis e variantes líquidas produzidas no ataque complexo. *Acta Scientiarum. Language and Culture*. Maringá, *35*(2), 179–186.

Faraco, C. A. (1991). *Lingüística Histórica: uma introdução ao estudo da história das línguas*. Ática.

Faraco, C. A. (2008). *Norma culta brasileira: desatando alguns nós*. Parábola.

Freitag, R. M. K., Araújo, A. S., Barreto, E. A., & dos Santos Silva Carvalho, E. (2010). "Vamos prantar frores no grobo da terra": Estudando o rotacismo nas séries iniciais da rede municipal de ensino de Moita Bonita/SE. *RevLet – Revista Virtual de Letras, 2*(02/2010), 17–31.

Gnerre, M. (1991). *Linguagem, escrita e poder.* Martins Fontes.

Gomes, C. A., & de Souza, C. N. R. (2003). Variáveis fonológicas. In *Introdução à Sociolinguística: o tratamento da variação.* Maria Cecilia Mollica and Maria Luiza Braga (Orgs.) (pp. 73–80). Contexto.

Labov, W. (1994). *Principles of linguistic change.* Vol. 1: Internal Factors. Blackwell Publishers.

Leite, M. Q. (2008). *Preconceito e intolerância na linguagem.* Contexto.

Massini-Cagliari, G. (1998). Escrita do Cancioneiro da Biblioteca Nacional de Lisboa: fonética ou ortográfica? *Filologia e Lingüística Portuguesa, 2*, 159–178. Humanitas – FFLCH/USP.

Massini-Cagliari, G. (2007). *Cancioneiros Medievais Galego-Portugueses. Fontes, edições e estrutura.* WMF Martins Fontes.

Massini-Cagliari, G. (2012). O que é fazer pesquisa em Linguística Histórica? In *Ciências da Linguagem: o fazer científico?.* Adair Vieira Gonçalves and Marcos Lúcio de Sousa Góis. (Orgs.) (Vol. 1, pp. 267–292). Mercado das Letras.

Mattos e Silva, R. V. (2006). *O português arcaico: fonologia, morfologia e sintaxe.* Contexto.

Milroy, J. (2011). Ideologias linguísticas e as consequências da padronização. In *Políticas da norma e conflitos linguísticos.* Xoán Lagares and Marcos Bagno (Orgs.). Parábola.

O'Neill, P., & Massini-Cagliari, G. (2019). Linguistic prejudice and discrimination in Brazilian Portuguese and beyond: Suggestions and recommendations. *Journal of Language and Discrimination, 3*(1), 32–62.

Williams, E. B. (1975). *Do latim ao português* (3ª ed.). Tempo Brasileiro. [1ª ed.: 1938].

Chapter 6
Neology and Group Identification in Brazilian Funk Lyrics

Daniel Soares da Costa ⓘ and **Geisibel Cristina Andrade Nascimento** ⓘ

Introduction

The objective of this chapter is to analyze some uses of neologisms in lyrics of Brazilian funk.

The Brazilian funk movement had its origins in the North American black music of the 1960s, being a musical genre arising from the mix between soul music, jazz, and rhythm and blues (R & B). According to de Amorim (2009), in recent decades, this music genre, whose most active space in Brazil is the outskirts of Rio de Janeiro, has gained stronger beats and a certain eroticism, manifested mainly through dance.

As a musical genre linked to social issues – such as daily life in ghettos, in favelas, violence, drugs, exacerbation of sexuality, our hypothesis is that the lyrics present some characteristics of speech which can be interpreted as marks of a social identification. We noticed a frequent occurrence of neologisms, which can be classified as slang for identifying a particular social group. We will make an introduction about neologisms and the speech community; then, we will discuss the variation related to the identification of social group (mainly slangs); and we will highlight some aspects about the origin and some characteristics of Brazilian funk and analyze ten neologisms found in song lyrics of this musical style.

D. S. da Costa
Unesp – Sao Paulo State University, Araraquara, Sao Paulo, Brazil

G. C. A. Nascimento (✉)
Unesp Sao Paulo State University, Belo Horizonte, Brazil

© The Author(s), under exclusive license to Springer Nature Switzerland AG 2023
G. Massini-Cagliari et al. (eds.), *Understanding Linguistic Prejudice*,
https://doi.org/10.1007/978-3-031-25806-0_6

69

Neologisms and Speech Community

Language is alive and is in a constant process of construction and change. And this possibility of mutation is what allows its renewal and conservation over time. Language is the result of the society in which it is inserted, and, therefore, it is natural that it follows its dynamism. This movement of transformation of societies over time is also accompanied by the emergence of new words. The evolution of the world and thinking, the advances, and transformations of society are reflected in the lexicon, transforming it into an open system, in which, continually, new meanings demand new signifiers (Pilla, 2002). This process of linguistic creation and renewal is called neology.

According to Alves (1990), it is possible to classify the neological processes into phonological, semantic, syntactic, and borrowings. The phonological neologisms are defined by the unprecedented combination of phonemes in the language, originating a new word; the semantic neologisms are those which are characterized as the attribution of a new meaning to existing words; the syntactic neologisms are formed by the combination of elements that already belong to the linguistic system, through processes such as prefix or suffix derivation or composition; and the linguistic borrowing occurs when a new word, from another language, enters our vocabulary, becoming part of the usage of the linguistic community.

Neology, however, is not limited to linguistic knowledge. It reflects linguistic creativity, considering the means of production, the community, and the speaker.

Linguistic changes take place, initially, in speech and, mostly, in informal contexts, where monitoring is quite reduced (or even consciously non-existent) and the proximity of speakers is greater. In this daily context of language use, the speaker has the possibility to access and explore the potential of their linguistic system, create new words, or develop new uses to those that already exist, aiming to improve communication or to create a linguistic identity for that group or speech community.

The speech community is a social unit that provides a reasoned base to explain the social distribution of linguistic similarities and differences, the reasons why certain groups of speakers share linguistic traits which distinguish them from others, as well as providing a theoretical reason for uniting idiolects from individual speakers (which are the linguistic objects that can be observed) into larger objects, the languages (which are abstract constructions).

In speech communities, the linguistic features are shared. It means that words, sounds, or grammatical constructions which are used inside the community are not used outside of it; the density of internal communication is very high, and that means people in a group talk to each other more frequently than talking to other people outside the group; and rules are shared, and members have common attitudes about the language use, rules in common about the direction of stylistic variation, and social evaluations about linguistic variables. The participation as a member of a speech community is defined by the use of specific traits in that community: when using them you are presented as a member, and not using them shows you are an outsider (Guy, 2000).

In other words, according to Guy (2000), a person speaks in the same way as people they talk to. A simple exposure to a linguistic trait is not enough to acquire and accommodate it. The model for speech communities is organized just like Russian dolls, one inside the other.

They have, among themselves, degrees of linguistic differences and similarities at different levels. A local speech community may have differences from another local community, but it has similarities in an upward level in a regional dialect and then belonging to a national speech community and still being part of an international speech community that shares the same language.

Other communities may also be interconnected and join speakers in overlapping and intersecting ways: these are subcommunities, defined by neighborhood and networks, contacts and communication, religion, social class, ethnicity, and occupation, among others.

Linguistic Variation and Slangs as Forms of Identification of a Social Group

The term "slang" refers to a typically oral and informal vocabulary, often restricted to social groups. Horton and Hunt (1980) define social group as the set of people who share awareness of membership and interaction, no matter the size of the group. Therefore, we can say that a social group is built with people who share interests and tastes in common and interact with each other to expose thoughts and information considering topics of common interest.

In addition to being part of a group, in some cases, people feel the need to identify themselves as belonging to that group. In order to achieve this purpose, some characteristics are established and may refer to the way of dressing (e.g., people who are members of a motorcycle club usually wear black leather jackets, jeans, and boots), products that people consume – or not (people who are vegetarians or vegans, e.g., don't eat meat), the music they listen to (e.g., people who call themselves "rockers" because they just listen to rock music and watch or go to rock concerts), and, among many others, the way they speak, which can be characterized as a dialect of the members, as well as jargons, in the case of people who have the same profession, and the slangs that, unlike jargons, are not related to professions, but are specific words, which identify a certain social group. It's also important to mention that these characteristics can be used together to identify the same group (way of dressing + way of speaking + way of walking, etc.).

In language, specifically, we call a group slang the vocabulary used by restricted social groups in which the behavior of their members is different from the majority either because of the unusual (interests in some sports or university group, music) or because the conflictual – the conflict they have with society (groups linked to the world of crime, prostitution, people who live in prison). When the language and the behavior are no longer linked just to restricted social groups, when they have already spread to society, the group sign is lost, being incorporated into popular language, becoming a common slang (Preti, 2008).

Nowadays, with the speed of dissemination of information and social media, slangs are popularized very quickly, just as quickly as they become extinct and new ones emerge. This ephemerality is one of the most striking features of the slang vocabulary, which reflects the speed that things change in contemporary society.

Concerning the semantic path, the slang usually arises from a change in the meaning of a word that already exists in the language. According to Preti (2008, p. 3), when a slang word of a group becomes known, it's necessary to replace it. So, there are three possibilities: "(1) it returns to the common vocabulary; (2) it disappears, becoming a slang archaism; and (3) it is linked to others group vocabularies, with a modification of meaning." As an example, the author mentions the word *bárbaro* (a Portuguese word that means "barbaric"). Initially, this word has the meaning of "cruel," "inhuman," and "gross." In the 1960s, this word, in Portuguese, started to be used by the Jovem Guarda[1] group to express something great, very beautiful. Over time, the slang was incorporated into popular speech, losing its group sign, and becoming a popular slang. The word lost its secret meaning and became a slang archaism.

Still on the semantic path of the slang word, these words are used as a resource to express feelings such as criticism, irony, humor (sometimes dark humor; in Brazilian Portuguese, the word *presunto* ["ham"] is sometimes used to refer to a corpse), denunciation, and opposition to traditional values. The slangs are often related to the speaker's view of the world in which they live. It's the way he expresses this vision he has of everything around him. It's the feeling he has about the environment, critical judgment, and the representation of the world.

Embarking on the history of slang means to embark on the world of marginality, groups excluded from society – whether because of their economic condition (poverty) or the activity they perform (sometimes illegal) – which started to create their own vocabulary as a way of defending their communities.

It doesn't mean that social groups which are part of economically higher classes do not create or have their own slang. However, we believe they are much less frequent than those related to social groups of economically lower classes mainly because of their identification and protection features for the members of the social group. These social groups – from lower economic classes – are the ones which are always looking for their places and, because of this, are often in conflict with society.

From the historical point of view, the presence of slang in written texts is very restricted and reinforces the idea of the low social prestige of this vocabulary.

According to Preti (2008), the condition of security, of cryptological words, ended up placing the slang as an opposition to the common language and linking

---

[1] Jovem Guarda was a movement that emerged in the second half of the 1960s and mixed music, behavior, and fashion. It started as a TV show which was exhibited by Rede Record in 1965. The members of this movement were influenced by beatrock, especially by The Beatles. (http://www.arte.seed.pr.gov.br/modules/galeria/detalhe.php?foto=265&evento=3 – Accessed 21 January 2022 – In Portuguese).

this vocabulary to classes which conflict with society. Over the centuries, a tendency of excluding the slangs from what is considered "the good language" was built in order to see it as a kind of word marked by the feeling of aggressiveness, opposition, and what can be seen not only in technical vocabulary (such as those which name activities from a restricted social group) but also their expressive resources (e.g., the processes of metaphors that express their judgment of the world) from less favored social groups in society.

The origin of slang vocabulary linked to social groups rejected by society ended up associating slang with the economically lower classes of the population, which have less income and schooling and are considered "less enlightened." Thus, this language is considered the language of the people.

In writing, slangs are used to indicate the fidelity of a transcription, to bring the writer closer to his reader, or to explain the use in disagreement with the vocabulary used by people with a higher level of education. According to Preti (2000), this absence in written texts (a modality of language that is more planned than speech) and the restrictions of use in many situations of oral communication prove a linguistic attitude of rejection on the part of those who speaks or write and make the slang a branded vocabulary, and its use faces prejudice in societies (in some more, in others less).

This scenario, however, has changed in the last years when the popular language started to lose its pejorative feature, although the slangs are still considered a lexical substandard condition (Preti, 2008). The attenuation of prejudice against slangs is because they have been used more and more expressively by the journalistic media, modern writers, and TV shows and appear more often in music, cinema, and, of course, social media.

The Brazilian Funk

Brazilian funk has origins in blues and soul music from the United States, in the late 1950s and early 1960s, with a change in their beats, which became stronger, and the addition of a certain eroticism, mainly because of the dance that accompanies the song. According to de Amorim (2009), the roots of the movement go back to the North American black music of the 1960s, from the blues laments, in the most remote period, to rhythm and blues, which presents a stronger rhythmic part, and soul music, which incorporates melodies from American gospel music.

In the 1950s, the American pianist Horace Silver was already talking about "funkstyle" when he combined jazz and soul music to create a more danceable style. In the 1960s, Miles Davis and the band Kool & The Gang were already playing funk, a mixture of jazz, soul music, and rhythm and blues (R & B). James Brown made the new style internationally known, adding the swing, a dance style originated in Harlem – New York. So, it's possible to say that funk has its origins in a mixture of rhythms that emerged in the center of black movement in the United States. Because it is composed of many music styles, funk continued to change during the 1970s, when hip-hop and breaking dance appeared, mainly in Bronx – New York.

Funk arrived in Brazil around 1969, initially with songs which were brought from the United States and with Brazilian classic songs performed in this new beat. In the 1970s, the first funk parties took place and became more frequent in the next decade. The main features were the faster beats and the more eroticized lyrics, in addition to the presence of DJs.

In the 1990s, funk carioca, inspired by Miami bass beats and with the increasing number of songs recorded in Portuguese, began to gain its own identity. The songs reflected the daily life in communities and became increasingly popular at the parties. At the end of the decade, funk started to gain more space outside the favelas of Rio de Janeiro, and the artists were performing in high-rated TV shows. In the 2000s, funk gained space at the national level, received international recognition, and became more frequent on TV shows, at parties in favelas, and outside of them, and many Brazilians fell in love with the new style of music and not just in Rio de Janeiro but also all over the country.

According to Vianna (1988), funk, since its origins, goes far beyond just being a musical style. Funk is also a style of behavior, a way of dressing, talking, and walking, haircut, and many other things.

The development of funk as a musical style brings with it the mixing technique (mixing of sounds, superposition of melodies and rhythms, use of electronics for musical production) and scratch, which consists of producing noise, obeying a certain rhythm, through reversing the rotation of the vinyl record by hand, and differentiating this style from others. The lyrics address the violence and poverty of favelas and the exploitation of Africans in western culture (as well as other themes), making funk a musical style engaged with the social situation, specially related to marginalization of those who are underprivileged economically.

However, as we have already mentioned before, funk is not just a musical style. It is possible to perceive, in this context, the formation of a well-defined group: the *funkeiros*. Nevertheless, *funkeiro* is not the one who creates and who composes the funk songs; those are the MCs (MC = master of ceremony). *Funkeiros* are those who like to listen to the songs, go to funk parties, wear certain types of clothes and accessories, and live this lifestyle. The main responsible for this diffusion of funk – in some types of media – are the MCs, who tend to dress and behave in a specific way: they usually wear a wide brimmed cap with a higher height on the top, shirts much larger than their size, shoes and sneakers often from famous and expensive brands, and oversized jewelry and accessories (such as necklace and rings made with gold), in addition to often having many tattoos and walking in a very specific way, with a certain waddle. Thus, people start to dress and behave in the same way, whether they are from the favelas or not.

The peculiar *funkeiros'* style goes beyond the sphere of behavior and fashion. It also involves a particular way of using the language and the use of slang, very common in funk music.

Our hypothesis is that some characteristics in lyrics in Brazilian funk represent not just an aesthetic work with words but the typical speech from people who live in favelas. The use of specific words points to an identification of this social group through slangs which are, according to Patriota (2009), "linguistic forms and expressions that, motivated by some facts, such as age, gender, occupation, social condition, schooling, emerge as variations proper to groups that share a particular form of communication."[2]

In the following pages, we will present the analysis of some neological words that appear in lyrics of Brazilian funk, which can be considered slang for social identification of the group.

Neologisms in Brazilian Funk Lyrics

For data analysis, we selected ten neologisms found in Brazilian funk songs from Rio de Janeiro and São Paulo, since these cities are the two main producing centers of this musical style, especially in ghettos. The selected words were *bonde* ("streetcar"), *nave* ("ship"), *plaque* ("common metal coated with a thin layer of gold or silver"), *periguete* ("dangerous, provocative woman"), *picadilha* ("style"), *lance* ("act or effect of throwing; impetus, occasion, risk, danger, adventure, hard case, situation, event"), *treta* ("trick" or "ruse"), *revoada* ("flock of birds that fly together"), and *sofrência* ("act of suffering"). First, we introduce the word, the name of the song, and the composer, as well as the passage where this neologism appears in the lyrics. Then, we check if the word is registered in a dictionary, and what its meaning is to see if there has been any change. We also present a structural morphological analysis, in case of syntactic neologisms. When the word is registered in the dictionary, we will present its meaning translated into English to make the reading process easier. However, the link presented in the footnotes is the link of the dictionary in Portuguese.

We are going to start with the word "bonde," present in the lyrics of the song "Na Atividade" ("On Activity"), by MC Guimê. First, let's look at the verse where it appears to determine the meaning through the context:

> *Eles ficam atacados e começam a reclamar*
> *Porque o **bonde** chega e sai bem de qualquer lugar....*[3]

According to Priberam Online Dictionary of Portuguese Language (2022), the word "bonde" (in English, "streetcar") means, in general, a type of vehicle ("Urban vehicle used to transport passengers, generally with only one composition, powered by electricity and running on iron rails").[4]

---

[2] From the original: "formas e expressões linguísticas que, motivadas por fatores como idade, sexo, profissão, condição social, escolaridade, surgem como variações próprias de grupos que compartilham uma forma particular de comunicação."

[3] Translation: "They get attacked and start complaining/Because the streetcar arrives and departs well from anywhere...." The expression "get attacked" in this case means "get irritated."

[4] https://dicionario.priberam.org/bonde – Accessed 24 January 2022.

However, in these lyrics, the meaning of *bonde* is "a group of friends who are always together." It is a semantic neologism, since there is no change in the form of the word, just in its meaning.

The second word is "nave" (in English, "ship" or "spaceship"), found in the lyrics of the song "Plaquê de 100"[5] ("100 Plaque"), by MC Guimé. Let's take a look at the excerpt where the neologism appears:

*E como de costume, toca a **nave** no rasante*
De Sonata, de Azera, as mais gata sempre pira....[6]

According to the dictionary, "nave" is "vehicle designated for space travel beyond the Earth's atmosphere."[7] However, the presence of names "Sonata" and "Azera" denotes that, in the context of the lyrics, "nave" means "an expensive car, large and modern car," because these names are for two luxury cars from Hyundai. Again, we have a semantic neologism.

In this song, we also have the neologism "plaquê." Let's look at the verse where it appears:

*Contando os **plaquê** de 100, dentro de um Citroën.*[8]

According to Priberam Dictionary (2022), "plaquê" means a "common metal coated with a thin layer of gold or silver."[9] Nevertheless, in the lyric's context, we can see that the meaning of this word is "set or bundle of bills (money)," in this case, 100 reais bill. This is also a semantic neologism.

We also found an example of syntactic neologism. This means that it is originated from one of Portuguese word formation processes. The word is "periguete," present in the song "Beijinho no Ombro"[10] ("Little Kiss on the Shoulders"), by Gaiola das Popozudas ("fat bottomed girls' cage"). Let's look at the verse where the neologism is found:

*O meu sensor de **periguete** explodiu*
Pega sua Inveja e vai pra...(Rala sua Mandada).[11]

There is no definition for this word in any dictionary. However, there is a definition in an informal, virtual dictionary, web address https://www.significados.com.br. According to this website, "periguete" or "piriguete" is "a slang in Portuguese,

---

[5] https://www.youtube.com/watch?v=gyXkaO0DxB8 – Accessed 24 January 2022.

[6] Translation: "And as usual, put the spaceship in low-flying/By Sonata, by Azera, the most beautiful girls always get crazy...."

[7] https://dicionario.priberam.org/nave – Accessed 24 January 2022.

[8] Translation: "Counting the 100 bills, inside of a Citroën."

[9] https://dicionario.priberam.org/plaqu%C3%AA – Accessed 24 January 2022.

[10] https://www.youtube.com/watch?v=73sbW7gjBeo – Accessed 24 January 2022.

[11] Translation: "My sensor of dangerous girl exploded/Get your envy and go to... (get out, submissive woman)."

considered as a pejorative term, used to describe a provocative woman who shows interest in other people, even if they are in a relationship."[12]

Our hypothesis about the formation of this word is that it is a noun derived from the noun "perigo" (in English, "danger"), through the addition of the suffix "-ete," which would result in the following structure:

$$\left[\left[Perigo\right]_{noun} + \left[ete\right]_{suffix}\right]_{noun}$$

The basis for derivation is the word "perigo," which generates a relation of meaning proposed for "periguete," which would be, in a way, a woman who is dangerous (in this case, in Portuguese, "oferece perigo") to other women in terms of their love relationship, their boyfriend. According to Alves (2010), the suffix -ete, originated from the Latin diminutive suffix -ittum and -ittam, creates several derivatives that express smallness, often with a pejorative, laudatory, hypocoristic value.

Another very interesting word is "picadilha," that appears in the song "Picadilha de Boy"[13] ("Playboy Style"), by MC Galo. There is no definition for this word in dictionaries. Nevertheless, according to Morais (2015), it is a noun with a meaning of attitude, action, or expectation. Let's look at the verse where the neologism is found:

Olha o bonde passando
Olha o bonde passando
***Picadilha** de boy*
Coração de malandro.[14]

In the lyric's context, we can see that, beyond the definition given by Morais (2015), "picadilha" can also mean "style," related to the way of dressing. It means that, despite having a "playboy style," he still has a rogue's heart.

There is the word "lance," as well, that can be found in the lyrics of "Ela é Top Top"[15] ("She is Top Top"), by MC Bola. According to Priberam Dictionary (2022), "lance" is a word formed by the process of back-formation, coming from the verb "lançar" and means "act or effect of throwing; impetus, occasion, risk, danger, adventure, hard case, situation, event."[16] Let's look at the verse where the neologism is found:

Encanta com seu jeitinho ela não é de ninguém
*Mas é chegada num **lancinho**.*[17]

---

[12] https://www.significados.com.br/piriguete/ – Accessed 24 January 2022.

[13] https://www.youtube.com/watch?v=B0lmBuX8Kf4 – Accessed 24 January 2022.

[14] Translation: "Look at the streetcar passing by/Look at the streetcar passing by/Man's style/ Vagabond's heart."

[15] https://www.youtube.com/watch?v=t3zer7gq_Kg – Accessed 24 January 2022.

[16] https://dicionario.priberam.org/lance – Accessed 24 January 2022.

[17] Translation: "She enchants with her way/But she likes a loving bid."

The word appears in the diminutive form in the lyrics, and we have, again, an example of a semantic neologism, since the meaning of this word in the context of the song is "dating without commitment or 'being' with someone in funk parties."

The neologism "treta" was found in the lyrics of two songs: "Bipolar,"[18] by MCs Don Juan, Davi, and Pedrinho, and "Vou Chamar Ela Pra Treta"[19] ("I Will Call Her for a Trick or a Ruse"), by MC Pedrinho.

According to Priberam Dictionary (2022), the possible meanings for this word are as follows: (1) ruse (general used in fights) to win the opponent; (2) trick, stratagem, malice, artfulness; (3) false story, lie; and (4) conversation, which is not important, or a conversation used to deceive.[20]

It is possible to see that, in the context in which this word appears in lyrics, the meaning is "sexual relation" (sex act). This is a semantic neologism, as we can see in the following verses:

> *Minha paz não tem preço, e é isso que eu prezo*
> *Eu não posso ser preso, por isso fico quieto*
> *Na hora da **treta**, cê acorda o prédio*
> *Na hora da foda, nóis fode até o teto.[21]*
> *(BIPOLAR – Mcs Don Juan, Davi e Pedrinho)*

> *Eu vou chamar ela pra **treta***
> *Eu vou comer sua b'*
> *Ela adora problema.[22]*
> *(Vou Chamar Ela Pra Treta – Mc Pedrinho)*

Still in the song "Vou Chamar Ela Pra Treta," we also found the word "revoada" which, according to the dictionary, means "(1) act or effect of flying, (2) flock of birds that fly together, and (3) opportunity." Let's see the verse where this word is found:

> *Uma brejinha gelada*
> *Uns amigos de confiança*
> ***Revoada** monstrona*
> *Tocando funk e samba.[23]*

From the context in which the word is used, it is possible to infer that the meaning, in these lyrics, is close to meaning 2 in the dictionary (flock of birds that fly together), because the expression "revoada monstrona" refers to "reliable friends." It is a noun derived from the participle form of the verb "revoar," by the process of improper derivation or conversion in Portuguese.

---

[18] https://www.youtube.com/watch?v=12-3ZAsO_xA – Accessed 24 January 2022.

[19] https://www.youtube.com/watch?v=BE8w_9reHwg – Accessed 24 January 2022.

[20] https://dicionario.priberam.org/treta – Accessed 24 January 2022.

[21] Translation: "My peace is priceless, and that is what I value/I can't be arrested, so I keep quiet/ When there is sex, you wake up the building/When it comes the fuck, we fuck to the ceiling."

[22] Translation: "I'm going to call her to sex/I am going to eat her p'/She loves trouble."

[23] Translation: "A cold beer/Some trusted friends/A monstrous flock/Playing funk and samba."

Another noun we found, also formed by the process of improper derivation or conversion, is "o corre," derived from the verb "correr" (to run, in English). This word was found in two songs, "Loucura Que Ela Fez Comigo,"[24] by MC Zaquin and MC Rick, and "Favela No Topo,"[25] by Hungria Hip-Hop, Kawe, and N.O.G., and has the meaning of "crime, criminal life, work in crime":

> Ela é atrevida, gosta dos cara **do corre**
> > Vou aplicar bebida, aplico o chá, depois o golpe
> > Vou aplicar bebida, aplico o chá, depois o golpe
> > Fetiche dela: Eu de Glock e de Lacoste.[26]
> (Loucura Que Ela Fez Comigo – Mc Zaquin and Mc Rick)

> Tamo botando a favela no topo
> > Fique de frente com a fome e o sufoco
> > Perdi amigos **no corre** por pouco
> > Marca de bala em muro sem reboco.[27]
> (Favela No Topo – Hungria Hip-Hop, Kawe, and N.O.G.)

In Priberam Dictionary, all the meanings listed for this word are derived from the verb "correr,"[28] (to run), making no reference to criminal life. In the first song lyrics, it is possible to understand that "os caras do corre" (the guys on the run) would be "criminal workers, drug dealers, robbers, among others." In the second song lyrics, the speaker refers to friends he lost because they were killed while leading a criminal life.

The last word of our list is "sofrência" found in the lyrics of the song "Coração Gelado 3,"[29] by MCs Joãozinho VT, Ryan SP, Kako, V7, Leozinho ZS, IG, and Letto. This word is not registered in the dictionary.

At first, we thought this is a case of suffix derivation, from the verb "sofrer," with the addition of the suffix "-ncia," as in the word "tender > tendência." However, due the fact that there is already a noun derived from the verb "sofrer," with the addition of "-mento" (sofrer > sofrimento), we discarded this hypothesis. Interestingly, this word is very common in musical environments nowadays, especially in a musical style named "sertanejo universitário," in songs that are about love suffering caused by the couple's separation. Let's look at the verse in which this word appears:

> Eu pelos bololô e o coração na solidão
> > Eu pelas madrugada implorando por compaixão
> > Coração tá gelado, gelo boia no copão
> > E a cada golada, **sofrência** de uma paixão.[30]

---

[24] https://www.youtube.com/watch?v=SX5xZDqYm-M – Accessed 24 January 2022.

[25] https://www.youtube.com/watch?v=Va1LAgBdhUI – Accessed 24 January 2022.

[26] Translation: "She is sassy, she likes the guys on the run/I'll apply the drink, apply the tea, then the blow/I'll apply the drink, apply the tea, then the blow/Her fetish: me in Glock and Lacoste."

[27] Translation: "We are putting the favela at the top/Face the hunger and suffocation/I lost friends on the run for almost nothing/Bullet mark on the unplastered wall."

[28] https://dicionario.priberam.org/corre – Accessed 24 January 2022.

[29] https://www.youtube.com/watch?v=2PkxaVyVLpE – Accessed 24 January 2022.

[30] Translation: "I am in the crowd and the heart in solitude/Me at down begging for compassion/Heart is frozen, ice blows in a big glass/And in each sip, the suffering for a passion."

Our hypothesis is that this word is a case of composition by agglutination with the words "sofrimento" (suffering) and "carência" (lack), amalgamating the first part of the word "sofrimento" and the second part of the word "carência," originating, as a global meaning, the sum of meanings of these two words.

Conclusions

Considering the presented data, we were able to verify that most of the neologisms found in lyrics of Brazilian funk songs are semantic neologisms. It means the use of an existing word, in a certain context, in which its meaning changes to a new one that is not attested in the dictionary. The examples of semantic neologisms found were bonde, nave, paquê, lance, treta, and revoada.

We found just one neologism created by derivation that was "periguete." We understand that it is a suffix derivation from the noun "perigo" and the addition of the suffix "-ete," originating a new noun that means "uma mulher que oferece perigo" (a dangerous woman).

We also found a single case of composition, the word "sofrência," originated from the junction of the words "sofrimento" (suffering) and "carência" (lack), and a single case of improper derivation, with the word "o corre," derived from the verb "correr," but having the meaning of "criminal life."

The only word that is not registered in the dictionary and that is not possible to describe its process of formation is "picadilha," which means "estilo" (style).

The creation of neologisms in song lyrics is very common. We were able to find this phenomenon in lyrics created by many different artists in Brazilian music, from different musical genres. Normally, the occurrence of neologisms in song lyrics has a stylistic purpose and refers to a composer's wordplay, based on many possibilities of lexical construction, in so many levels of language: phonological, morphological, syntactic, and semantic.

Funk, in this aspect, is different because the neologisms that appear in its lyrics do not represent a stylistic purpose by the composer. They portray a language variety used by this social group that is gaining another status, a lifestyle, and behavior approach, being disseminated to other regions of the country and not being restricted to the ghettos of Rio de Janeiro and São Paulo anymore.

References

Alves, I. M. (1990). *Neologismo: criação lexical*. Ática.
Alves, I. M. (2010). O sufixo -ete no português brasileiro contemporâneo. In. *Actas Semiotica et Linguística*. http://periodicos.ufpb.br/ojs/index.php/actas/article/viewFile/14657/8309. Acessed 30 May 2019.
de Amorim, M. F. (2009). *O discurso da e sobre a mulher no funk brasileiro de cunho erótico*: uma proposta de análise do universo sexual feminino. Thesis. Unicamp.

Dicionário Online Priberam da Língua Portuguesa. https://dicionario.priberam.org/. Acessed 24 January 2022.

Guy, G. (2000). A Identidade lingüística da comunidade de fala: paralelismo interdialetal nos padrões de variação linguística. *Organon, 14,* 17–32.

Horton, P., & Hunt, C. L. (1980). *Sociology.* McGraw-Hill.

Morais, F. L. (2015). *Funk, a linguagem proibida*: um ponto de vista sociolinguístico. Dissertation, Pontifícia Universidade Católica.

Patriota, L. M. (2009). *A gíria comum na interação em sala de aula.* Cortez.

Pilla, É. H. (2002). *Os neologismos do português e a face social da língua.* Age.

Preti, D. F. (2000). A gíria na língua falada e na escrita: uma longa história de preconceito social. In D. F. Preti (Ed.), *Fala e escrita em questão* (pp. 241–257). Humanitas/FFLCH/USP.

Preti, D. (2008). *O léxico na linguagem popular*: a gíria. https://simelp.fflch.usp.br/sites/simelp.fflch.usp.br/files/inline-files/S1802.pdf. Acessed 02 January 2022.

Vianna, H. (1988). *O mundo funk carioca.* Jorge Zahar Editor.

Part II
Diversity, Variation and Modalities

Chapter 7
Confronting Grammatical Ideology with Usage: Toward a Socially Realistic Account of Spoken Portuguese

Milena Aparecida Almeida (ID), Rosane Andrade Berlinck (ID), and Stephen Levey (ID)

Introduction

Much energy has been invested in combatting prejudice and discrimination relating to race, class, sexuality, and religion, but the province of language is one where many ill-founded stereotypes continue to abound unchecked, fueled by the strong ideological component of the prescriptive grammatical tradition. Bolstered by advances in literacy and mass education, public opinion in Brazil, as in many other countries, generally views the standard written language as the model of linguistic correctness. In the popular conception, the most legitimate and revered variety of the language is believed to be embodied in grammar books and dictionaries rather than in the *speech* of millions of individuals who use the language on a daily basis (Milroy & Milroy, 2012:22). The ideology of the standard, predicated on the suppression of optional variability in language (Milroy & Milroy, 2012:6), has perpetuated many simplifications and distortions relating to everyday colloquial usage. Value-laden judgments pervade public discussions of linguistic variation and change and are typically articulated from a perspective that endorses certain usages as "correct," while censoring others as "wrong," "inappropriate," or "inelegant," irrespective of whether the offending forms in question are firmly rooted in speech (Lippi-Green, 2012; see also Bagno, 2000, Britto, 2002, Mattos e Silva, 2004). Witness, for example, the public furore that erupted in Brazil in 2011, following the publication of educational material, approved by the Ministry of Education and Culture, recognizing *variable* subject-verb and noun phrase concord as a natural

M. A. Almeida · R. A. Berlinck (✉)
Unesp - São Paulo State University, Araraquara, São Paulo, Brazil
e-mail: milena.aparecida@unesp.br; rosane.berlinck@unesp.br

S. Levey
University of Ottawa (UOttawa), Ottawa, ON, Canada
e-mail: slevey@uottawa.ca

© The Author(s), under exclusive license to Springer Nature Switzerland AG 2023
G. Massini-Cagliari et al. (eds.), *Understanding Linguistic Prejudice*,
https://doi.org/10.1007/978-3-031-25806-0_7

feature of vernacular Portuguese (Ramos, 2011:14–16). Despite its laudable sensitivity to authentic and robust speech patterns (Scherre & Naro, 2013:188), this material was sensationally depicted in the Brazilian media as an assault on "good" Portuguese, a bid to "consecrate ignorance," as well as an outright attempt to "assassinate" the language (see Baronas & Cox, 2013:80).

Among the major social institutions responsible for diffusing prescriptive ideologies, the school plays a key role in promoting a highly idealized and largely invariant standard variety as the language as "it should be," often divorced from the realities of actual speech (Bagno, 2002; Scherre, 2005; Zilles & Faraco, 2015). So widely are these ideologies embraced that departures from standard norms are frequently denounced as the province of the uneducated, the lower social classes, or other marginalized and under-privileged groups. With their capacity to generate social biases and prejudice, the tenacity of such ideologies has important implications for speakers belonging to disfavored social groups, potentially impacting their employment prospects as well as other opportunities for social advancement (O'Neill & Massini-Cagliari, 2019).

In sharp contrast with the prescriptive enterprise, the discipline of sociolinguistics has been collecting, analyzing, and interpreting community-based speech data to demonstrate that the language used in everyday social contexts is inherently variable, rule-governed, and structured (Weinreich et al., 1968; Labov, 1972; Silva & Scherre, 1996; Vandresen, 2002; Paiva & Duarte, 2003; Paiva & Gomes, 2014; Martins & Abraçado, 2015). Cumulative advances in sociolinguistics over the past several decades have amply confirmed that many of the rule-governed patterns of speech lie so far below the level of conscious awareness that they cannot be readily intuited by native speakers or inferred from casual observation (Poplack & Cacoullos, 2015:272). Little surprise, then, that most people, even those who deal with language in a professional capacity, lack a scientifically informed perspective on the underlying systematicity of informal speech (Milroy & Milroy, 2012:116; Cyranka, 2014). And supported by a rigid apparatus of grammatical prohibitions and sanctions, the prescriptive tradition continues to remain immune to actual usage norms, often equating productive vernacular features with decay or corruption, rather than recognizing them as variable components of structured systems regularly employed by native speakers.

It is in this context that we situate the present study. Our goal in this paper is to contribute to the body of scholarship elucidating the variable and patterned nature of colloquial Brazilian Portuguese. We exemplify with an investigation of the variable expression of locative relativization, a relatively understudied domain of spoken Brazilian Portuguese (but see, e.g., Kersch, 1996; Braga & Manfili, 2004) as well as fertile territory for further cross-linguistic investigation (Ballarè & Inglese, 2022:221). A fundamental motivation for targeting relativization in colloquial Brazilian Portuguese derives from the well-documented fact (e.g., Tarallo, 1983) that this grammatical sub-sector accommodates rampant variation between standard and non-standard variants. This study therefore affords opportunities to investigate possible disjunctions between prescriptive accounts of variable relativization strategies on the one hand and actual usage norms on the other. This kind of endeavor can, in turn, lead to a clearer appreciation of the structural possibilities and spectrum of variation found in spoken language data (Cheshire & Stein, 1997:5) while also helping to refine our understanding of non-canonical relativization strategies that are often neglected in traditional typological studies (Murelli, 2011:17).

Observing that an adequate understanding of locative relativization cannot be achieved without corpus-based analysis, we apply a quantitative methodology to our data in order to explore the motivations for variant selection in the locative relativization system. A cornerstone of the method employed here is the importance we attach to the analysis of all exponents of locative relativization, in accordance with the principle of accountability (Labov, 1969:738).

Our major research objectives are twofold: (i) to investigate the social and linguistic mechanisms which constrain the selection of locative relativizers in natural speech data and (ii) to assess the extent to which structured variation in this system is congruent with prescriptive accounts.

Although our primary focus is on a specific linguistic variable, our results are intended to contribute to a larger body of empirical research characterizing the structured heterogeneity of spoken Portuguese (see Bagno, 2001; Silva & Scherre, 1996; Vandresen, 2002; Paiva & Duarte, 2003; Castilho, 2006; Paiva & Gomes, 2014; Martins & Abraçado, 2015). Additional impetus for this line of inquiry derives from Labov's (1982) recommendation that linguists should, where possible, capitalize on the wider social applications of their research findings to enable communities to benefit from them in a humanistic and emancipatory way (Sankoff, 1988:144; Scherre & Naro, 2013:189). A key practical application of sociolinguistic research lies in its capacity to engage with, challenge, and perhaps even influence public debate and policy on language matters. This is of particular importance in cases where official discourse on language (e.g., in educational directives) is at variance with the findings of linguistic science (see, e.g., Labov, 1982; Cheshire & Edwards, 1993; Rickford, 1997; Bagno, 2002; Callou & Lopes, 2004; Scherre, 2005; Görski & Coelho, 2006; Vieira & Brandão, 2007; Milroy & Milroy, 2012; Zilles & Faraco, 2015; Cheshire & Fox, 2016).

The remainder of this article is structured as follows: we first situate the targeted grammatical variable in its wider research context before addressing the theoretical framework in which our investigation is embedded and describing our data and methods. After presenting our quantitative findings, we discuss their pertinence to addressing our research objectives. We conclude with directions for future investigation.

Relativization Strategies in Spoken Brazilian Portuguese

Over the past several decades, relative clauses have received extensive consideration in the theoretical, typological, psycholinguistic, and language acquisition literature (Chomsky, 1956; Keenan & Comrie, 1977, 1979; De Villiers et al., 1979; De Vries, 2002; Guasti & Cardinaletti, 2003; Flynn et al., 2004; Diessel & Tomasello,

2005; Roland et al., 2007; Camacho, 2013a; Figueiredo-Silva, 2019). Sociolinguistic studies of relativization, though somewhat rarer, have gained a good deal of traction among scholars of Brazilian Portuguese since the early 1980s (see, e.g., Tarallo, 1983, 1985; Braga & Manfili, 2004; Bispo, 2007, 2009; Ribeiro, 2009; Silva, 2011, 2018, to name but a few).

There has been increasing recognition by scholars of Brazilian Portuguese—and Romance languages more generally—that finite relative clauses in spontaneous (adult) speech may diverge from the canonical relative constructions that are described in prescriptive grammars or characterized on the basis of linguist intro-spection (Assmann & Rinke, 2017:9). Among the Romance languages, many codi-fied standard varieties exhibit a mixed paradigm of relative clause marking, comprising pronominal relativizers that may agree with the head noun in terms of animacy (e.g., Portuguese *quem*, Italian *chi* (for human referents), gender and num-ber (e.g., Portuguese *o qual/os quais; a qual/as quais; cujo(s)/cuja(s)*), as well as invariable relative markers that are homophonous in most cases with the regular complementizer(s) used in the languages concerned (Stark, 2016:1029). In pre-scribed usage, pronominal relativizers tend to be assigned to oblique or genitive relative clauses (i.e., syntactic positions lower down the Accessibility Hierarchy; Keenan & Comrie, 1977, 1979), whereas syntactic positions higher up the Accessibility Hierarchy, such as subject and direct object, are said to attract invari-able relative markers (Stark, 2009). By contrast, the evolving tendency in most col-loquial and non-standard Romance varieties, apparently detectible even in Vulgar Latin (Bourciez, 1967:276), involves the use of an invariable relativizer to introduce relative clauses, even in syntactic positions where prescriptive grammars would ordinarily mandate the use of a relative pronoun that agrees with the semantic and/ or morpho-syntactic features of the head NP (Noun Phrase) in which the relative clause is embedded (Fiorentino, 2007:266–7; Stark, 2016:1036). In his seminal analysis of relativization in spoken Brazilian Portuguese, Tarallo (1983:35) observes that invariant *que* has almost completely colonized the relativization system, whereas relative pronouns are conspicuously absent from the everyday spoken lan-guage (op. cit., 88). The same state of affairs is said to obtain in European Portuguese, where *que* is reported to have assumed the status of default relativizer in almost all contexts in the spoken language (Assmann & Rinke, 2017:9, 36).

Turning specifically to locative relativizers, the focus of the present study, the canonical strategies identified in prescriptive accounts involve either the use of a dedicated adverbial relativizer, *onde*, as in (1), or constructions in which the relativ-izer functions as the complement of a preposition, often referred to, following Ross (1967), as pied-piping, illustrated in (2) (examples from Almeida, 2022:50):

(1) Inf: ah **o lugar *onde* eu trabalho**... é um salão tem... três partes... tem a parte da frente né? que cê entra assim é grandão aí tem dois degrau... (AC-024; DE: L. 243–244).[1]
    The place *where* I work

---

[1] The identification of the speaker was produced by Iboruna database (Gonçalves, 2007) represent-ing the number of the speaker (AC0024; AC-050), the identification of textual type (DE—spatial description) and the line where the phrase occurs (L.243–244).

(2) Doc.: (ruído) M. agora eu queria que você... me descrevesse um... um local Inf.: **eu vou descrever a casa *em que* eu estou morando**... (AC-050; DE: L. 193–194)
   I will describe the house *in which* I am living

In addition to the variants listed in (1)–(2), there are two additional options found in colloquial speech. The first involves relativizer *que* employed in conjunction with a resumptive element which is co-referential with the head NP, as shown in (3). Yet another option involves the elimination of a preposition in what is technically referred to as p(repositional) p(hrase)-chopping (hereafter, PP-chopping), as in (4), where [] indicates an omitted preposition[2]:

(3) e um tipo **d'uma salinha pequenininha *que* elas guardava as coisas dela *lá*** e vendia né? (AC-015; DE: L. 639–640)
   like a little room *that* they kept their thing *there*
(4) eu e depois dali nós fomo(s) pra festa que foi na minha... **na casa [] *que* eu morava na Pascoal More(i)ra** ... e fizemos assim uma festa bastante simples (AC-092; NE: L. 38–40)
   in the house [] *that* I used to live in Pascoal Moreira

Of the two variants exemplified in (3)–(4), neither of which is prescriptively endorsed, the resumptive strategy is less frequent, rarely accounting for more than 10% of the variable context (see, e.g., Tarallo, 1983:189; Bispo, 2009:84, 2014:226–227; Assmann & Rinke, 2017:30). It is also more liable to attract prescriptive censure on the grounds of its perceived "redundancy" (see Tarallo, 1983:33; Poletto & Sanfelici, 2017). Indeed, it has a lengthy tradition of being stereotyped by normative grammarians as a mark of illiteracy (see, e.g., Freire, 1842, cited in Tarallo, 1983:33). Despite the negative social meanings that this variant has accrued, some scholars question whether it is relegated to the most informal speech styles and to the most disfavored social groups. Assmann and Rinke (2017:16), for example, claim that both the resumptive and PP-chopping strategies are diffused throughout the general population and exhibit no specific correlation with the level of educational attainment or social status. Other scholars, however, offer more cautious assessments of the social embedding of non-canonical strategies. Tarallo (1983:124) notes that while lower-class speakers of Brazilian Portuguese favor the resumptive strategy, middle- and upper-class speakers occasionally avail themselves of that option too. Drawing on the results of elicited judgment tasks, Tarallo (1983:140) additionally reports that middle-class speakers tend to be more approving of PP-chopping than the resumptive strategy, suggesting that the latter carries more negative social freight. Still, the fact that some speakers recognize pied-piped relative clauses as "better" than the other two variants (Tarallo, 1983:140) would seem to suggest that PP-chopping, although apparently more productive and socially acceptable than its resumptive counterpart, does not enjoy parity with pied-piping. Nevertheless, there are compelling indications that PP-chopping has actually increased over time at the expense of pied-piping, with Tarallo (1983:203) identifying the second half of the nineteenth century as the key period witnessing the emergence and rise of PP-chopping in the spoken language.

---

[2] An analogous construction in other Romance languages (e.g., (Canadian) French) is alternatively referred to as "preposition absorption" (see, e.g., Poplack et al., 2012).

Although marginal in the spoken language, the status of pied-piping in contemporary (Brazilian) Portuguese appears to be sustained by the influence of formal education. In keeping with the norm-enforcing role of the school, higher levels of educational attainment are said to correlate with the use of standard pied-piping (see, e.g., Corrêa, 1998; Duarte, 2011; Alexandre & Hagemijer, 2013), a factor that no doubt enhances the interpretation of this variant as a marker of "careful" speech. But whatever prescriptive influence the school may wield, this is clearly not sufficient to promote the use of normatively sanctioned variants at the expense of non-sanctioned ones, even in written communication, the traditional locus of standardizing processes (Cameron, 2012:43). A recent graphic illustration of this point can be found in Amorim's (2021) study of the written use of oblique relative clauses by 40 undergraduate students with a European Portuguese background. Out of nearly 800 instances of oblique relative clauses generated by the students concerned, 64% comprised a non-canonical relativization strategy, made up overwhelmingly of non-standard PP-chopping, while only 36% of the tokens contained the prescribed pied-piped variant. The fact that pied-piping is said to be "almost non-existent" (Tarallo, 1983:199) in relative clauses in modern vernacular Brazilian Portuguese likely indicates that it does not constitute a natural option in everyday speech (see Corrêa, 1998; Mollica, 2003). Interestingly, Guasti and Cardinaletti (2003:48) arrive at a similar conclusion for French and Italian, equating pied-piping in those languages with the products of explicit teaching.[3] We return to this issue in the results below.

Turning to the linguistic constraints on relativizer choice, there is no general consensus on the conditions governing their use (Assmann & Rinke, 2017:10). Some of this indeterminacy is no doubt traceable to the difficulties in comparing the results of previous studies of relativization, based as they are on divergent data sources and modalities (i.e., speech and writing), not to mention disparate methodological and analytical preferences.

Among the factors commonly cited in connection with variant choice are semantic and morpho-syntactic properties of the head NP in which the relative clause is embedded, as well as processing considerations relating to the length and complexity of the dependency domain. With regard to the resumptive strategy, Tarallo (1985:363) argues that its choice is conditioned by low-level processing constraints on short-term memory, leading it to function as a "last-resort" option that facilitates the processing of complex or long-distance relative clause dependencies. While acknowledging that the resumptive strategy may be sensitive to long-distance dependencies (Mioto & Lobo, 2016:282), some scholars query whether the appeal to processing considerations offers the only explanation for the selection of the resumptive strategy. Alexandre (2000), for example, notes that in colloquial Portuguese, resumptive pronouns are sometimes found in subject and direct object relative clauses (see also Tarallo, 1983:90, Table 4.4; Assmann & Rinke, 2017:30,

---

[3] In English, where pied-piping competes with preposition stranding in oblique relative clauses, McDaniel et al. (1998:309) similarly argue that pied-piping is not a natural option, but is probably picked up during schooling.

Table 4.5) in contexts which are not easily reconciled with processing-based explanations. Subject and direct object are among the most frequently relativized syntactic positions, and both are generally considered to be less complex than oblique or genitive relative clauses, which are reported to be much more favorable to pronoun-retaining strategies (see, e.g., Keenan & Comrie, 1977).

Other factors that are implicated in the choice of the resumptive strategy include the humanness of the head NP (Tarallo, 1983:22, 91) as well as its indefiniteness (Tarallo, 1983:97) although Assmann and Rinke (2017:30) found that the effect of indefinite contexts on the use of the resumptive strategy was negligible in their data.

Turning to PP-chopping, this variant is said to be much more productive in restrictive than non-restrictive relative clauses (Tarallo, 1983:225; Assmann & Rinke, 2017:33). It is also preferentially used to mark relative constructions in lower syntactic positions (i.e., indirect object, oblique and genitive; see Tarallo, 1983:222). Other factors contributing to the use of PP-chopping involve the individual lexical identity of the eliminated preposition, insofar as this information can be reliably identified. Tarallo (1983:226) mentions that *a/para* (to, for), *com* (with), *de* (of), *de/ sobre* (about), *em* (at, in, on), *por* (for, by), and *sobre* (on) are all amenable to PP-chopping, although the relative frequency of elimination appears to be sensitive to idiosyncratic lexical effects. Assmann and Rinke (2017:32) report that *em, com,* and *de* figure among the most frequently eliminated prepositions in locative, temporal, and oblique relative clauses in spoken European Portuguese (see also Bispo, 2007:175).

Summarizing, many previous studies considering possible determinants of relativizer choice, while undoubtedly pertinent to locative relativization, do not have a dedicated focus on that grammatical sub-system. In the following section, we consider how the application of an accountable quantitative methodology to actual usage data can elucidate the social and linguistic partitioning of competing exponents of locative relativization.

Method

Theoretical Framework

Our approach is embedded within the framework of variationist sociolinguistics (Weinreich et al., 1968; Labov, 1972, 1994; Tarallo, 1985; Camacho, 2013b). Of inestimable importance in this framework is the need for copious amounts of community-based vernacular speech, believed to yield "the most systematic data for linguistic analysis" (Labov, 1984:29). The core analytical tool of the variationist approach is the linguistic variable, comprising a number of competing variants that embody the same referential meaning or a generally similar grammatical function (Labov, 1969, 1972). Competition between variants within the same variable context is typically conditioned by multiple social and linguistic factors. It is the patterned organization of competing variants in discourse and their conditioning, as gauged from the extra-linguistic and linguistic environments in which variants occur, which affords a crucial window on the internal structure of variation. We capitalize on this structure for comparative purposes in order to investigate the variable expression of locative relativization in the corpora targeted in the present study.

The Data

The data are drawn from corpora representing two different geographical regions within the state of São Paulo, the most populous state in Brazil, located in the southeast of the country.

The first database is the Iboruna corpus associated with the ALIP project (Gonçalves, 2007), comprising a total of 152 sociolinguistic interviews with speakers residing in the municipality of São José do Rio Preto, located some 270 miles from the city of São Paulo. The interviews are stratified according to speaker sex and age (7–15, 16–25 [aggregated into a single age group, 7–25, in this article],[4] 26–35, 36–55, and 55+) as well as the level of educational attainment, distinguishing elementary school (1st–9th year), high school (10th–12th year), as well as higher education or degree-level studies. The speech recordings that make up the Iboruna corpus straddle a number of different genres, including narratives of personal experience, recounted stories, spatial descriptions, procedural reports, as well as opinion-based texts addressing various topics such as school, family, religion, and politics.

The second corpus is associated with the SP2010 Project (Mendes, 2013), based on 60 sociolinguistic interviews with speakers recorded in the city of São Paulo, the largest Lusophone city in the world, with a population of some 12 million people. The corpus is stratified by speaker sex, age (19–34, 35–49, and 60+), as well as the level of education (high school vs. higher education). The recordings in this corpus are based on personal discussions of neighborhood of residence, childhood, family, work, and leisure, as well as more structured tasks intended to isolate different contextual styles (e.g., reading a news text, a word list, etc.). The principal characteristics of the corpora mined for the purposes of the present investigation are summarized in Table 7.1.

The fact that both corpora contain natural speech data and are constructed according to sociolinguistic principles renders them broadly comparable for scientific purposes. Furthermore, the social parameters (e.g., speaker age, sex, and level of education) associated with the population sample in each corpus can be used to test hypotheses about the contribution of extra-linguistic factors to variant choice. In referring to these two corpora as representations of spoken Brazilian Portuguese, we

---

[4]The amalgamation of the original two age groups into a single broader one in this article is justified on the grounds of the paucity of data generated by the youngest (7–15) age group.

Table 7.1 Characteristics of the corpora

	Amostra Linguística do Interior Paulista (ALIP), Gonçalves (2007)	*Projeto SP2010 Amostra da Fala Paulistana*, Mendes (2013)
No. of words	785,000	Circa one million words
No. of speakers	152	60
Speaker age range	7–89	19–89
Data collection	2003–2005	2009–2013
Speaker geographical origins	Seven cities within the municipality of São José do Rio Preto, São Paulo state	São Paulo city

stress that we are in fact addressing socially stratified and geographically specific varieties of the spoken language, as opposed to colloquial usage in its entirety.

Testing Hypotheses

The extension of the linguistic variable beyond phonology to the study of syntactic variation has been widely discussed in the sociolinguistic literature (e.g., Sankoff, 1973; Labov, 1978; Lavandera, 1978; Romaine, 1982). Many of the long-standing preoccupations with extending the scope of the linguistic variable to syntactic analysis hinge on the contentious problem of meaning. Whereas phonological variants lack a dedicated meaning, syntactic variants are believed to embody meaning-based differences (Romaine, 1982:32), thus problematizing their construal as alternative ways of "saying the same thing," in accordance with classic definitions of the linguistic variable (e.g., Labov, 1969, 1972). Our working hypothesis here, following Sankoff (1988:153), is that even if competing syntactic variants can be associated with different meanings or functions on occasion, these distinctions are not necessarily pertinent every time a variant form is chosen. In other words, differences among competing forms in referential value or grammatical function may be neutralized in discourse.

The variable context in the present study is delimited to locative (restrictive and non-restrictive) relative clauses. These are defined, following Ballarè and Inglese (2022:227), as relative constructions that can encode at least location. Eligible tokens were extracted with the help of the freeware concordancing program *AntConc* (see Tang, 2011), as well as *dmsocio* (Oushiro, 2018), used in the R software environment (Core Team, 2021). In total, over 1000 tokens of locative relative clauses were retained for analysis. These were subsequently coded for a number of factors abstracted from the relevant literature, as well as informal observations of the data, which are hypothesized to motivate variant selection.

Among the independent predictors that we factor into the analysis are those relating to extra-linguistic factors (speaker age, sex, level of education) as well as those associated with features of the linguistic context in which variants occur (e.g., features of the head NP in which the relative clause is embedded, the adjacency of the relative clause to the head NP, as well as semantic properties of the relative clause).

The apparent-time dimension afforded by the age differential in the Iboruna and SP2010 datasets offers a window on possible change in the variable expression of locative relativization. In view of the reported ascendancy of PP-chopping in the spoken language over the last 150 years (Tarallo, 1983:203), we expect that, to the extent that this development represents an ongoing change, PP-chopping should be more frequent in the speech of the younger age cohorts relative to the older ones in each corpus.

Regarding speaker sex, we are aware of no mention in earlier studies that choice of relativizer in Brazilian Portuguese is sensitive to sex differentiation, although in view of women's purportedly greater orientation to prestige norms (Labov, 1990), we speculate that women would be more inclined to favor canonical variants (*onde*, *pied-piping*) and less likely to select non-canonical or vernacular ones (*PP-chopping*, *resumption*).

Previous research (Mollica, 1977, 2003; Corrêa, 1998; Barros, 2000; Burgos, 2003) lends support to our hypothesis that the level of educational attainment should have a measurable effect on relativizer choice, with the most highly educated speakers expected to make greater use of *onde* and pied-piping, although we envisage that the latter variant will be sparsely represented, in line with its documented infrequency in natural speech data. Variants eliciting negative social evaluations, such as the resumptive strategy, are expected to be less frequent in the speech of the highly educated.

Turning to linguistic constraints on variant choice, we speculate that PP-chopping will be sensitive to the syntactic integration of the locative head NP into the verbal argument structure of the relative clause. The locative head NP can function as an obligatory argument of the verb (i.e., as a verbal complement) exhibiting a high degree of syntactic integration, but it can be construed as less integrated into verbal argument structure in the case of quasi-arguments or adverbial adjuncts/modifiers. We hypothesize that the use of PP-chopping strategy will decrease as the syntactic bond between the locative head NP and the verb in the relative clause becomes looser, schematized as follows: verbal complement > quasi-argument > adverbial adjunct. In other words, we would expect PP-chopping to be most highly favored with verbal complements and least favored with adverbial adjuncts or modifiers. In cognitive terms, this would mean that a more explicit coding strategy, such as *onde*, would be favored when the locative head NP is co-referential with an adverbial adjunct or modifier in the relative clause.

Similarly, in terms of possible adjacency effects, we predict that contexts where the head NP and the ensuing relative clause are non-adjacent would be more likely to attract the use of the dedicated locative relativizer, *onde*, to reinforce a locative interpretation. We link this prediction to Rohdenburg's (1996:151) *Complexity Principle*, according to which cognitively complex environments (e.g., non-adjacent contexts) would be expected to favor the use of more explicit coding options.

We also tailored our coding protocol to probe whether the definiteness, specificity, and referential accessibility of the antecedent conjointly influence the choice of locative relativizer. Our hypothesis in this regard centers on processing constraints, specifically the expectation that [+definite/+specific/+accessible] antecedents will correlate with grammatically less explicit relativizers such as PP-chopping because they ostensibly require less cognitive effort to be processed. Conversely when the antecedent is indefinite, non-specific, and less referentially accessible, we anticipate that a more explicit option, such as *onde*, will be preferred (Mollica, 1977, 2003; Tarallo, 1983; Bispo, 2009).

We extend a similar line of reasoning to operationalizing the effect of the semantic properties of the head NP on variant choice. NPs which denote an object are expected to select *onde*, a dedicated locative relativizer, to bolster a locative interpretation, whereas those which explicitly refer to a place (i.e., whose locative meaning is already sufficiently disambiguated) are expected to be more amenable to PP-chopping, a variant that is not confined to relativizing locative NPs.

In terms of the semantic properties of the relative clause, our expectations build on previous reports that restrictive relative clauses (i.e., ones delimiting the denotational reference of the head NP) favor PP-chopping (Tarallo, 1983:225).

Results

A number of key points emerge from the variant distributions depicted in Table 7.2. The first important observation is that the expression of locative relativization in both corpora is essentially a binary variable partitioned between *onde* and the PP-chopping strategy. In the Iboruna database, both variants are used at roughly equivalent rates, whereas in the SP2010, PP-chopping is the dominant variant accounting for over two thirds (67%) of the variable context. With regard to the two remaining variants, the resumptive strategy and pied-piping, the former is marginal accounting for 5% of the aggregated token count, whereas the latter is barely instantiated in the data, in keeping with its reported scarcity in everyday speech. These initial distributional findings reinforce our basic conviction that actual usage norms may differ considerably from those found in prescriptive accounts. The breach between actual and prescribed usage norms is conspicuously illustrated by the fact

Table 7.2 Distributional breakdown of major variants in each corpus

Variant	Iboruna (2003–2005)		SP2010 (2009–2013)		Total	
	N	%	N	%	N	%
Onde	267/554	48	128/453	28	395/1007	39
PP-chopping	249/554	45	300/453	66	549/1007	54.5
Resumptive pronoun	35/554	6.5	15/453	3	50/1007	5
Pied-piping	3/554	0.5	10/453	2	13/1007	1

that PP-chopping, a vernacular option, predominates in the aggregated data, whereas pied-piping, an icon of prescriptivism in the Portuguese grammatical tradition, represents a minuscule proportion of the variable context.

Though neither the resumptive strategy nor pied-piping can be said to play any central role in the variable expression of locative relativization in these data, we can still bring their limited variability to bear on whatever social patterning they exhibit in the data. Table 7.3, based on the aggregated rates of these two variants alone, compares their distribution in each corpus according to speakers' level of educational attainment.

As per earlier reports in the literature (e.g., Tarallo, 1983), pied-piping correlates with the level of educational attainment. Though vanishingly rare in the data overall, the fact that pied-piping is almost exclusively concentrated in the speech of individuals with higher education accords with Tarallo's (1983:175) observation that it is used by those speakers who are most likely to aim consciously at standard norms.

Turning to the resumptive strategy, it is clear that this option is less common in the speech of the most highly educated individuals in both corpora, as we would expect of a stigmatized syntactic variant, but the very fact that highly educated speakers *do* make occasional use of the resumptive strategy is damaging to the trope that this variant is diagnostic of illiterate or uneducated speech.

We are now in a position to return to the two variants that make up the bulk of the variable context in both corpora: *onde* and *PP*-chopping. How are those variants socially embedded? Extrapolating from Tarallo's (1983) earlier observation that PP-chopping is on the rise, we would expect it to be more prevalent in the speech of the younger age groups vis-à-vis the older ones.

Figure 7.1, depicting variant distributions in the discourse of younger and older speakers in the Iboruna corpus, puts the inference of change to the test.

The youngest age group (the 7–25-year-olds) shows the highest overall rate (62%) of PP-chopping and is the only cohort in which its overall rate outstrips that of *onde*. But the absence of any monotonic increase in the use of PP-chopping as the age spectrum is descended militates against change in progress.

Further evidence refuting ongoing change in the use of PP-chopping emerges from the distributional patterns found in the SP2010, shown in Fig. 7.2.

Table 7.3 Comparative distribution of the pied-piping and the resumptive strategy according to the level of speaker education

Variant	Iboruna (2003–2005)				SP2010 (2009–2013)			
	Pied-piping		Resumptive		Pied-piping		Resumptive	
	N	%	N	%	N	%	N	%
Elementary	0/20	0	20/20	100	–	–	–	–
High school	0/9	0	9/9	100	2/12	17	10/12	83
Higher education	3/9	33	6/9	67	8/13	61.5	5/13	38.5

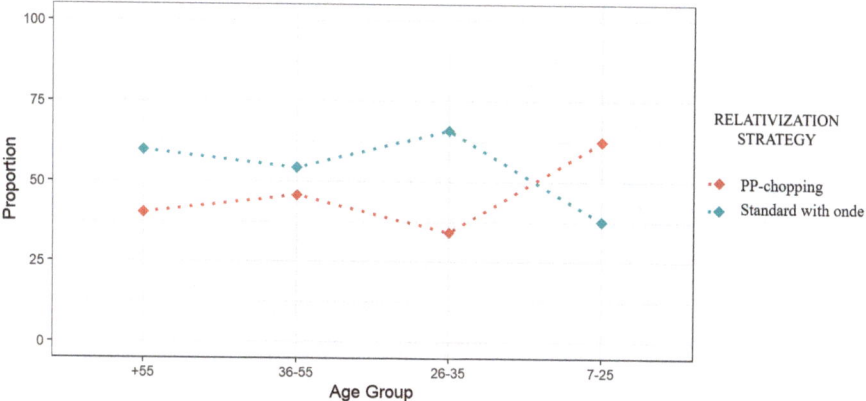

Fig. 7.1 Distribution of *onde* and PP-chopping according to speaker age in the Iboruna corpus

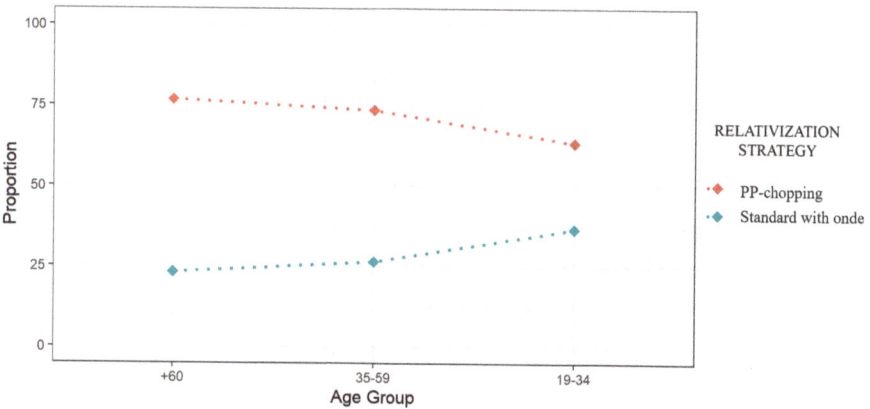

Fig. 7.2 Distribution of *onde* and PP-chopping according to speaker age in the SP2010 corpus

Here we observe that the youngest group in the SP2010 corpus, the 19–34-year-olds, exhibits the lowest overall rate of PP-chopping while also evincing the highest rate of *onde*. Yet again, age distributions do not allow us to pronounce unambiguously in favor of change in progress.

It is well known, however (see, e.g., Poplack, 1997:292), that the apparent impact of certain social factors (e.g., age) on variant choice may mask the effects of other extra-linguistic variables that may make an equal, if not greater, contribution to the choice process. A notable case in point concerns the level of educational attainment. As we observed earlier, the level of education influences rates of the infrequent pied-piping and resumptive options. To explore its potential effect on the majority variants, Fig. 7.3 shows the respective frequencies of *onde* and PP-chopping in both corpora according to the level of educational attainment (elementary vs. high school vs. higher education for Iboruna and high school vs. higher education for SP2010).

Iboruna

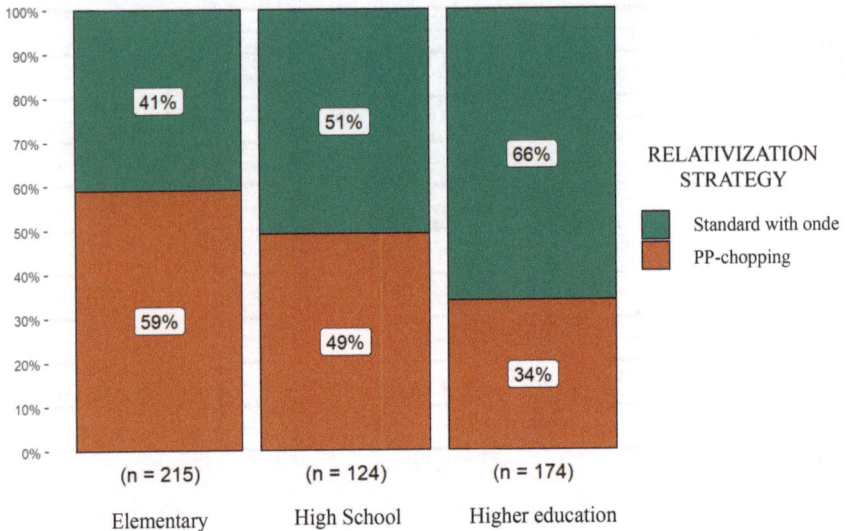

SP2010

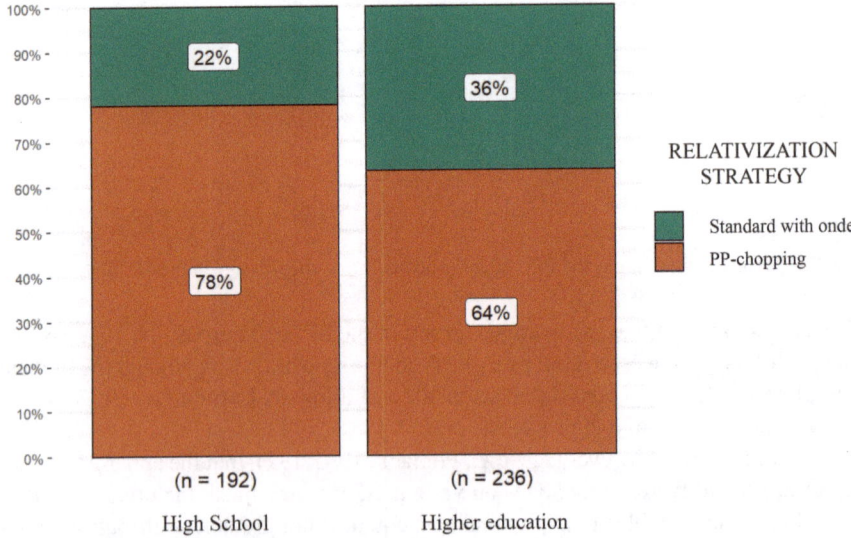

Fig. 7.3 Distribution of standard *onde* and PP-chopping in the Iboruna and SP2010 corpora according to speakers' level of educational attainment

For both corpora, we note that as the level of educational attainment increases, so does the overall rate of *onde*. We nevertheless observe that for the most highly educated speakers, variant distributions in the Iboruna corpus are almost the mirror image of those in the SP2010, with PP-chopping, rather than *onde*, qualifying as the default variant in the latter. Still, in both corpora, the diminution in the use of PP-chopping with increasing education provisionally suggests that the effect of education on linguistic variability is cumulative (Labov, 2001:115), with more highly educated speakers reducing their use of "colloquial" PP-chopping.

It turns out, however, that there is a good reason to believe that age and education are highly correlated with one another, to the point that their combined effect does not allow us to abstract any readily interpretable social pattern from the data. To put the interaction between age and education into sharper relief, we make use of conditional inference trees, a particularly useful tool for scrutinizing "how multiple predictors operate in tandem" (Tagliamonte & Harald Baayen, 2012:135).

Figure 7.4 shows a conditional inference tree exploring the effects of age and education on *onde* and PP-chopping in the Iboruna corpus.

The level of educational attainment (node 1) is at the top of the tree, indicating that it is the most important factor conditioning variant selection. The tree then divides between higher education on the one hand and elementary and high school education on the other. For speakers with lower levels of education (elementary and high school), there is no interaction with age (see node 5). Of particular interest is the split in tree involving speaker age (node 2). For the mostly highly educated speakers, the first (7–25-year-olds) and third (36–55-year-olds) age cohorts show a roughly equal preference in their use of *onde* and PP-chopping (node 4). By contrast, the second (26–35-year-olds) and the fourth (55+) age groups show a greater preference for *onde* (node 3).

Analysis of the corresponding data from SP2010 (Fig. 7.5) reveals a similar interaction between the level of educational attainment and age, although the specific details differ from those associated with the Iboruna dataset.

Once again, for speakers with a lower level of education (high school), there is no interaction with age (see node 5). We observe that those speakers make

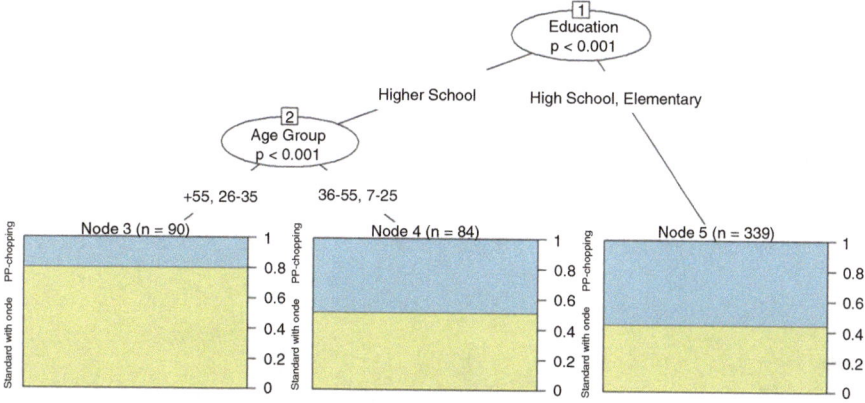

Fig. 7.4 Conditional inference tree exploring the effects of age and education on *onde* and PP-chopping in the Iboruna corpus

comparatively greater use of PP-chopping than *onde*. Turning to speakers with higher education, the youngest age group (node 4), the 19–34-year-olds, partition their usage between *onde* and PP-chopping fairly evenly, whereas the two older age groups, the 35–49-year-olds and the 60+ (node 3) show a greater predilection for PP-chopping.

What can we take from the divergent—and sometimes opposing—patterns observed in the two corpora? Clearly, statistical analysis confirms that age and education interact in influencing variant choice, but not in ways that would allow us to extrapolate an unambiguous trajectory of change in the use of one variant at the expense of the other. Nor would the statistical analysis permit us to correlate the level of education with a clear-cut preference for *onde*. We cannot rule out that the divergent trends in Figs. 7.4 and 7.5 are due to hidden confounds of a structural nature, although judicious cross-tabulation of independent variables incorporated into the analysis reveals no obvious explanation to that effect. Nor does inspection of other extra-linguistic variables reveal additional confounds that could potentially account for the patterns we have uncovered. Speaker sex, for example, a frequently cited concomitant of linguistic change (Labov, 1990), makes no significant contribution to the selection of either *onde* or PP-chopping.

One possibility that bears further consideration is whether any inclination to impose an evaluative categorization of *onde* as "standard" and PP-chopping as "non-standard" results in a distortion of the usage facts (see also Stark, 2009:8–9). These two variants do not appear to exhibit the sharp patterns of social stratification that are routinely associated with other more socially sensitive morpho-syntactic variables in Brazilian Portuguese (e.g., variable nominal and verbal agreement [Scherre & Naro, 2013]; the use of the nominative pronoun *ele* "he" as an accusative pronoun [Mattoso Camara Jr, 2004]). Indeed, the apparent lack of social salience associated with PP-chopping may well have been instrumental in helping it secure a firm foothold in the system of locative relativization.

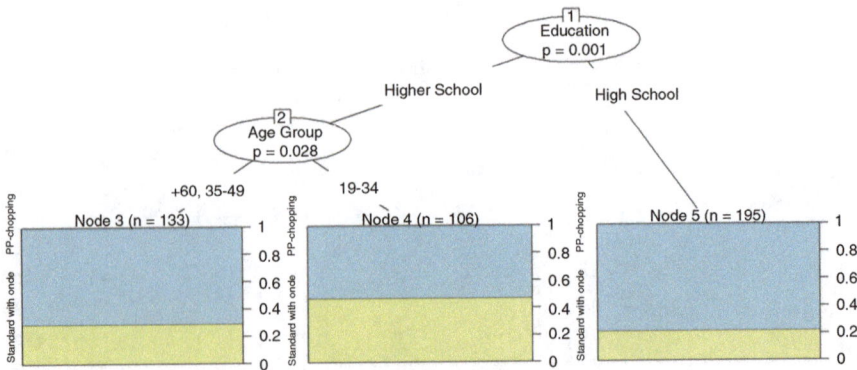

Fig. 7.5 Conditional inference tree exploring the effects of age and education on *onde* and PP-chopping in the SP2010 corpus

Cheshire and Stein (1997:2) observe that the borderlines between standard, non-standard, "colloquial," and "spoken syntax" are often unclear or "fuzzy." In fact, this very indeterminacy foregrounds the ill-defined and abstract nature of a standard language (Milroy & Milroy, 2012:22), a concept which remains notoriously resistant to a linguistically principled definition (Poplack & Dion, 2009:559). Although PP-chopping is clearly prevalent in speech, as opposed to expository prose, it seems not to have attracted the prescriptive opprobrium that the resumptive strategy has accrued. Furthermore, the very fact that the undergraduate students in Amorim's (2021) study, whose usage we would expect to approximate standard Portuguese, actually preferred PP-chopping over other variants, strongly suggests that it would be counter-intuitive to interpret PP-chopping as an icon of non-standard syntax or to construe it as otherwise socially marked.

To achieve a fuller understanding of the factors influencing the selection of *onde* and PP-chopping, we next consider their linguistic conditioning, summarized in Table 7.4.

Contrary to our initial expectations, there is little evidence indicating that these two variants are markedly differentiated in the way they partition the variable expression of locative relativization. Of the multiple linguistic predictors that we factored into the analysis, only two return significant effects (where $p < 0.05$), though not necessarily for both corpora. The results for the semantic identity of the antecedent (i.e., place vs. object) exhibit a significant effect in the Iboruna corpus only and accord with our hypothesis that an antecedent referring to a place is more frequently associated with PP-chopping, while one referring to an object tends to co-occur with *onde*. Definiteness of the head NP also returns a significant effect, but only for the SP2010, where, contrary to our earlier expectation, *onde* is correlated with definite NPs rather than indefinite ones, whereas indefinite heads show a greater propensity to be marked by the PP-strategy.

Discussion

What have we learned from this investigation? One general conclusion we draw from quantitative analysis of over 1000 tokens is that prescriptive accounts fail to capture the details of the variable expression of locative relativization in actual usage. Particularly misleading in the prescriptive enterprise is the inveterate tendency to inflate the importance of normatively sanctioned variants, while side-lining or ignoring other (vernacular) variants which in fact turn out to play a central role in the expression of grammatical functions in spontaneous speech. This was shown to be the case when we compared pied-piping, a prescriptively endorsed but entirely liminal exponent of locative relativization, with its vernacular counterpart, PP-chopping, which accounts for a disproportionate share of the variable context in community-based speech data.

Equally remarkable, if we accept Tarallo's (1983) account of the diachronic evolution of relativization in Brazilian Portuguese, is the rapid ascendancy of

Table 7.4 Comparison of the contribution of linguistic effects to the selection of *onde* and PP-chopping in the Iboruna and SP2010 corpora (shading indicates variables that returned a significant effect)

Variant	Iboruna (2003-2005) Onde		PP-chopping		SP2010 (2009-2010) Onde		PP-chopping		p-Value[a]
Linguistic variable									
Adjacency between the antecedent noun phrase and the relative clause	N	%	N	%	N	%	N	%	>0.05
Adjacent	247/487	51	240/487	49	127/426	30	299/426	70	
Distant	19/26	73	7/26	27	5/8	62	3/8	38	
Semantic classification of the relative	N	%	N	%	N	%	N	%	>0.05
Restrictive	216/409	53	193/409	47	101/369	27	268/369	72	
Non-restrictive	50/104	48	54/104	52	27/59	48	32/59	54	
Morphological class of the locative NP	N	%	N	%	N	%	N	%	>0.05
Pronoun	-	0	1/1	100	-	0	2/2	100	
Common noun	245/478	51	233/478	49	89/359	25	270/359	75	
Proper noun	11/19	56	8/19	42	25/52	48	27/52	52	
Adverb	10/15	67	5/15	33	14/15	93	1/15	7	
Syntactic function of the relative marker	N	%	N	%	N	%	N	%	>0.05
Verb complement	138/264	52	126/264	48	67/201	33	134/201	67	
Quasi-argument	72/147	49.7	74/147	50.3	29/136	21	109/136	79	
Adverbial adjunct	55/102	54	47/102	46	32/90	36	58/90	64	
Semantic identity of the antecedent	N	%	N	%	N	%	N	%	<0.05
Place	213/440	48	227/440	52	132/424	30	298/424	70	
Object	53/73	73	20/73	27	-	0	4/4	100	
Definiteness of the head NP	N	%	N	%	N	%	N	%	<0.05
Indefinite NP	177/330	54	153/330	51	34/169	20	135/169	80	
Definite NP	89/183	49	94/183	51	94/259	36	165/259	64	

[a]The statistical tests of significance are generated in two steps. First, *p-value* was obtained by applying the Pearson's Chi-squared test in the programming language R. For a second validation, we apply a generalized linear mixed model of regression that only selected as p < 0.05 the semantic identity of the antecedent and definiteness of the head NP

PP-chopping in the spoken language at the apparent expense of pied-piping. This development is all the more striking because it overlaps with cumulative efforts to promote mandatory education in Brazil in the twentieth century, a turn of events that we would ordinarily associate with the propagation of prescriptively ratified variants, given the pivotal role of the school in diffusing codified forms. That prescriptive ideologies have had no appreciable effect, as far as we can tell, on the rise of PP-chopping in spoken Portuguese is borne out by our quantitative analyses of locative relativization, demonstrating that this variant, along with *onde*, constitutes the norms of everyday usage in community-based grammars.

Why PP-chopping has not attracted the same degree of prescriptive stigma ascribed to other vernacular options such as the resumptive strategy merits further investigation. To the best of our knowledge, subjective reaction tests have never been used to probe speakers' sensitivity to potential differences in the social evaluation of *onde* or PP-chopping in locative relative clauses. Statistical analysis of the data at our disposal, while illuminating the effects of age and education on variant choice, failed to reveal any convincing evidence that these variants are sharply differentiated in terms of social meaning. We cannot rule out the possibility that our analytical tools have failed to detect such differences, if they exist. A more fined-grained analysis of the combined effects of age and education on variant selection may turn up motivations for variant choice that our current analysis missed. Nor do we rule out the prospect that other varieties of spoken Portuguese may harbor social differences in the use of *onde* and PP-chopping that were not revealed in the present study. One remaining possibility is that the contemporary system of locative relativization in spoken Brazilian Portuguese, essentially comprising just two variants, is a relatively covert, unobtrusive variable that has not been conscripted for the purposes of marking social differences (see also Tottie & Rey, 1997:245).

Situated in a broader cross-linguistic perspective, we reiterate that there is nothing typologically exceptional or "dysfunctional" about the use of *onde* and PP-chopping to express locative relativization. The relative absence of pied-piping in the system of locative relativization in spoken Brazilian Portuguese is entirely consistent with typological generalizations that account for relative constructions in other vernacular varieties of Romance, where relative particles are commonly used to mark the syntactic function of the relativized element, even in oblique relative clauses (see, e.g., Poplack et al., 2012 for French). In fact, from a typological perspective, Stark (2009:9) goes so far as to argue that it is the respective *standard* varieties of Romance that are marked and perhaps even "artificial" in deviating from regular morpho-syntactic processes of encoding relativization.

The issue of linguistic change, which preoccupied earlier studies of relativization in Brazilian Portuguese (e.g., Tarallo, 1983), is one which we have not been able to fully address here. Contrary to what we had initially hypothesized building on Tarallo (1983), our expectation that corpus analysis would reveal apparent-time increments in the use of PP-chopping was not borne out. The possibility of change is one that would clearly benefit in future research from the availability of appropriate *real-time* data reflecting antecedent stages of locative relativization in colloquial Brazilian Portuguese. In the interim, we note that while our current results do not militate in favor of an increase in PP-chopping over time, they do provide grounds for suspecting possible change in the use of *onde*. One such development concerns the use of *onde* to relativize non-locative antecedents, as in (5):

(5) **é um jogo de baralho... éh *onde*... cada carta tem um valor diferente...** (AC-049; RP: L. 153–155)

it's a card game... yeah *where*... each card has a different value...

Yet again, once we situate examples such as (5) in a cross-linguistic perspective, we observe that in numerous languages, relativizers that have a locative origin may undergo functional expansion, enabling them to relativize other syntactic positions higher up the Accessibility Hierarchy (Keenan & Comrie, 1977, 1979). The extended functional range of locative relativize markers has been noted in the colloquial varieties of diverse languages such as Italian (Ballarè & Inglese, 2022); English (Radford, 2019); and German (Brandner & Bräuning, 2013), to name but a few. And it is well known that in Modern Greek, what was originally a locative relativizer subsequently evolved to become a generalized relative marker capable of marking the full range of syntactic positions in the Accessibility Hierarchy (see Nicholas, 1998). Only more accountable analyses of speech-based data representing Brazilian Portuguese will allow us to determine whether *onde* is developing into a more general marker of clause linkage along the lines proposed for other languages (Ballarè & Inglese, 2022).

We conclude by briefly considering some of the broader societal ramifications of our investigation. Among the practical implications of this research is the need to develop socially realistic frameworks of Brazilian Portuguese based on accountable analysis of actual usage data. If educators and allied professionals are to develop effective strategies for understanding and nurturing children's syntactic development, it is imperative that they should have a scientifically grounded knowledge of the systematic and structured nature of the community-based grammars that children bring to school with them (Milroy, 1987:200). Without such knowledge, language professionals run the risk of mistakenly equating structured variability in everyday speech with ungrammaticality or, worse still, linguistic deficiency (Cheshire & Edwards, 1993:35). Such negative appreciations, as we noted as the outset of this article, can fuel the perpetuation of exclusionary ideologies and discriminatory practices that have real-world impacts on equity and social mobility.

Acknowledgments The authors would like to thank the São Paulo Research Foundation FAPESP (Grant 2020/00593-5 – Milena Aparecida de Almeida) and the National Council for Scientific and Technological Development CNPq (Grant 306464/2019-5—Rosane Andrade Berlinck).

References

Alexandre, N. M. P. A. (2000). *A estratégia resumptiva em relativas restritivas do Português Europeu*. Dissertation, FLUL.

Alexandre, N., & Hagemijer, T. (2013). Estratégias de relativização de PPs no mundo luso-atlântico: crioulos de base lexical portuguesa e variedades do português. In M. Moura & M. A. Sibaldo

(Eds.), *Para a história do português brasileiro. Volume III- Sintaxe comparative entre o português brasileiro e linguas crioulas de base lexical portuguesa* (pp. 49–71). EDUFAL.

Almeida, M. A. (2022). *A sociolinguística das estratégias de relativização em contextos locativos na fala paulista*. 2022. Dissertation, Faculdade de Ciências e Letras, Universidade Estadual Paulista (UNESP).

Amorim, C. (2021). O domínio das frases relativas preposicionadas por estudantes do ensino superior. *Linguística: Revista de Estudos Linguísticos da Universidade do Porto – N.° Especial, 2021*, 215–233.

Assmann, E., & Rinke, E. (2017). Relative clauses in a corpus of spoken European Portuguese. *Revista de Estudos Linguísticos da Universidade do Porto, 12*, 9–39.

Bagno, M. (2000). *Dramática da língua portuguesa: tradição gramatical, mídia & exclusão social*. Edições Loyola.

Bagno, M. (2001). *Português ou Brasileiro? Um convite à pesquisa*. Parábola Editorial.

Bagno, M. (Ed.). (2002). *Lingüística da Norma*. Edições Loyola.

Ballarè, S., & Inglese, G. (2022). The development of locative relative markers. From typology to sociolinguistics (and back). *Studies in Language*, 1–38. https://doi.org/10.1075/sl.20013.bal

Baronas, R. L., & Cox, M. I. P. (2013). Por uma vida melhor na mídia: discurso, aforição e polêmica. *Linguagem em (Dis)curso, 13*(1), 65–93.

Barros, A. L. (2000). *O uso da relativa cortadora na fala pessoense*. Dissertation, Universidade Federal da Paraíba.

Bispo, E. B. (2007). Oração adjetiva cortadora: análise de ocorrências e implicações para o ensino de português. *Linguagem & Ensino, 10*, 163–186.

Bispo, E. B. (2009). *Estratégias de relativização no português brasileiro e implicações para o ensino: o caso das cortadoras*. Thesis, UFRN.

Bispo, E. B. (2014). Orações relativas em perspectiva histórica: interface uso e cognição. *Veredas, 18*(1), 222–235.

Bourciez, É. (1967). *Éléments de linguistique romane*. Klincksieck.

Braga, M. L., & Manfili, K. (2004). Essa é a preocupação onde eu quero chegar: "onde" em referências anafóricas no português do Brasil. *Veredas, 8*, 233–243.

Brandner, E., & Bräuning, I. (2013). Relative *wo* in Alemannic: Only a complementizer? *Linguistische Berichte, 234*, 131–170.

Britto, L. P. L. (2002). Língua e ideologia: a reprodução do preconceito. In M. Bagno (Ed.), *Linguística da norma* (pp. 135–154). Edições Loyola.

Burgos, L. E. S. (2003). *Estratégias de uso das relativas em uma comunidade de fala afro-brasileira*. Dissertation, Universidade Federal da Bahia.

Callou, D., & Lopes, C. R. S. (2004). Contribuições da Sociolinguística para o ensino e a pesquisa: a questão da variação e mudança linguística. *Revista do GELNE (UFC), 5*, 63–74.

Camacho, R. G. (2013a). Construções relativas nas variedades do português: uma interpretação discursivo-funcional. *Filologia linguística, 15*(1), 179–214.

Camacho, R. G. (2013b). *Da linguística forma à linguística social*. Parábola Editorial.

Camara, J. M., Jr. (2004). Ele como um acusativo no português do Brasil. In C. E. F. Uchôa (Ed.), *Dispersos de J. Mattoso Câmara Jr* (pp. 47–53). Editora Lucerna.

Cameron, D. (2012). *Verbal hygiene*. Routledge.

Castilho, A. T. (2006). Apresentação. In C. S. Jubran (Ed.), *Gramática do Português Culto Falado no Brasil*. Vol. I: Construção do texto falado. Campinas (pp. 7–25). Editora da Unicamp.

Cheshire, J., & Edwards, V. (1993). Sociolinguistics in the classroom; exploring linguistic diversity. In J. Milroy & L. Milroy (Eds.), *Real English: The grammar of English dialects in the British Isles* (pp. 34–52). Longman.

Cheshire, J., & Fox, S. (2016). From sociolinguistic research to English language teaching. In K. P. Corrigan & A. Mearns (Eds.), *Creating and digitizing language corpora* (pp. 265–310). Palgrave Macmillan.

Cheshire, J., & Stein, D. (1997). The syntax of the spoken language. In J. Cheshire & D. Stein (Eds.), *Taming the vernacular: From dialect to written standard language* (pp. 1–12). Routledge.

Chomsky, N. (1956). Three models for the description of language. *IRE Transactions on Information Theory, 2*, 113–124.

Core Team. (2021). *R: A language and environment for statistical computing.* R Foundation for Statistical Computing, 2018. Disponível em: https://www.R-project.org/.

Corrêa, V. R. (1998). *Oração relativa: o que se fala e o que se aprende no português do Brasil.* Thesis, Universidade Estadual de Campinas.

Cyranka, L. F. M. (2014). Avaliação das variantes: atitudes e crenças em sala de aula. In M. A. Martins, S. R. Vieira, & M. A. Tavares (Eds.), *Ensino de português e Sociolinguística* (pp. 133–155). Editora Contexto.

De Villiers, J. G., Tager Flusberg, H. B., Hakuta, K., & Chen, M. (1979). Children's comprehension of relative clauses. *Journal of Psycholinguistic Research, 8*, 499–518.

De Vries, M. (2002). *The syntax of Relativization.* Netherland Graduate School of Linguistics, lot, Universiteit Utrecht.

Diessel, H., & Tomasello, M. (2005). A new look at the acquisition of relative clauses. *Language, 81*(4), 882–906.

Duarte, I. (2011). Modo oral e modo escrito, estructuras sintácticas de desenvolvimento tardio e escolarização. In A. Valente & M. T. Pereira (Eds.), *Lingua portuguesa: descrição e ensino* (pp. 15–30). Parábola.

Figueiredo-Silva, M. C. (2019). Uma história das relativas do português brasileiro. In C. Galves, M. A. Kato, & I. Roberts (Eds.), *Português brasileiro: uma segunda viagem diacrônica* (pp. 283–312). Editora da Unicamp.

Fiorentino, G. (2007). European relative clauses and the uniqueness of the relative pronoun type. *Rivista di Linguistica, 19*(2), 263–291.

Flynn, S., Foley, C., & Vinnitskaya, I. (2004). The cumulative-enhancement model for language acquisition: Comparing adults' and children's patterns of development in first, second and third language acquisition of relative clauses. *International Journal of Multilingualism, 1*(1), 3–16.

Freire, F. J. (1842). *Reflexões sobre a língua portugueza.* Typografia da Sociedade Propagadora dos Conhecimentos Úteis.

Gonçalves, S. C. L. (2007). Banco de dados Iboruna: amostras eletrônicas do português falado no interior paulista. Available at: http://www.iboruna.ibilce.unesp.br.

Görski, E. M., & Coelho, I. L. (Eds.). (2006). *Sociolinguística e Ensino: contribuições para a formação do professor de língua.* Editora da UFSC.

Guasti, M. T., & Cardinaletti, A. (2003). Relative clause formation in romance child's production. *Probus, 15*, 47–89.

Keenan, E. L., & Comrie, B. (1977). Noun phrase accessibility and universal grammar. *Linguistic Inquiry, 8*, 63–99.

Keenan, E. L., & Comrie, B. (1979). Data on the noun phrase accessibility hierarchy. *Language, 55*, 332–352.

Kersch, D. F. (1996). *A palavra ONDE no português do Brasil.* Dissertation, Universidade Federal do Rio Grande do Sul.

Labov, W. (1969). Contraction, deletion and inherent variability of the English copula. *Language, 45*(4), 715–762.

Labov, W. (1972). *Language in the inner city.* University of Pennsylvania Press.

Labov, W. (1978). Where does the linguistic variable stop? A response to Beatriz Lavandera. *Working papers in sociolinguistics*, 44. Southwest Educational Development Laboratory.

Labov, W. (1982). Objectivity and commitment in linguistic science: The case of the black English trial in Ann Arbor. *Language in Society, 11*, 165–201.

Labov, W. (1984). Field methods of the project on linguistic change and variation. In J. Baugh & J. Sherzer (Eds.), *Language in use* (pp. 28–54). Prentice Hall.

Labov, W. (1990). The intersection of sex and social class in the course of linguistic change. *Language Variation and Change, 2*, 205–254.

Labov, W. (1994). *Principles of linguistic change: Internal factors.* Blackwell.

Labov, W. (2001). *Principles of linguistic change: Social factors.* Blackwell.

Lavandera, B. (1978). Where does the sociolinguistic variable stop? *Language in Society, 7,* 171–182.

Lippi-Green, R. (2012). *English with an accent: Language, ideology and discrimination in the United States* (2nd ed.). Routledge.

Martins, M. A., & Abraçado, J. (Eds.). (2015). *Mapeamento sociolinguístico do português brasileiro.* Contexto.

Mattos e Silva, R. V. (2004). *'O português são dois...': Novas fronteiras, velhos problemas.* Parábola Editorial.

McDaniel, D., Mckee, C., & Bernstein, J. B. (1998). How children's relatives solve a problem for minimalism. *Language, 74,* 308–334.

Mendes, R. B. (2013). Projeto SP2010: Amostra da fala paulistana. Available at http://projetosp2010.fflch.usp.br

Milroy, L. (1987). *Observing and analysing natural language: A critical account of sociolinguistic method.* Basil Blackwell.

Milroy, J., & Milroy, L. (2012). *Authority in language* (4th ed.). Routledge.

Mioto, C., & Lobo, M. (2016). Wh-movement: Interrogatives, relatives and clefts. In W. Leo Wetzels, S. Menuzzi, & J. Costa (Eds.), *The handbook of Portuguese linguistics* (pp. 275–293). Wiley-Blackwell.

Mollica, M. C. (1977). *Estudo da cópia em relativas em português.* Dissertation, Pontifícia Universidade Católica.

Mollica, M. C. (2003). Relativas em tempo real no português brasileiro contemporâneo. In M. C. de Paiva & M. E. L. Duarte (Eds.), *Mudança lingüística em tempo real* (pp. 129–138). Contra Capa.

Murelli, A. (2011). Relative constructions in European languages: A look at non-standard. *JournaLIPP, 1,* 1–21.

Nicholas, N. (1998). *The story of pu. The grammaticalisation in space and time of a modern Greek complementiser.* Unpusblished PhD dissertation, University of Melbourne.

O'Neill, P., & Massini-Cagliari, G. (2019). Linguistic prejudice and discrimination in Brazilian Portuguese and beyond. *Journal of Language and Discrimination, 3,* 32–62.

Oushiro, L. (2018). *dmsocio.* v0.2.0. Available at oushiro.shinyapps.io/dmsocio

Paiva, M. C., & Duarte, M. E. L. (2003). *Mudança lingüística em tempo real.* Contra Capa.

Paiva, M. C., & Gomes, C. A. (2014). *Dinâmica da variação e da mudança na fala e na escrita.* Contra Capa.

Poletto, C., & Sanfelici, E. (2017). Relative clauses. In A. Dufter & E. Stark (Eds.), *Manual of romance morphosyntax and syntax* (pp. 804–838). Walter de Gruyter.

Poplack, S. (1997). The sociolinguistic dynamics of apparent convergence. In G. Guy, C. Feagin, J. Baugh, & D. Schiffrin (Eds.), *Towards a social science of language: Papers in honor of William Labov* (pp. 285–309). Benjamins.

Poplack, S., & Cacoullos, R. T. (2015). Linguistic emergence on the ground: A variationist paradigm. In B. MacWhinney & W. O'Grady (Eds.), *The handbook of language emergence* (pp. 267–291). Wiley Blackwell.

Poplack, S., & Dion, N. (2009). Prescription vs. praxis: The evolution of future temporal reference in French. *Language, 85,* 557–587.

Poplack, S., Zentz, L., & Dion, N. (2012). Phrase-final prepositions in Quebec French: An empirical study of contact, code-switching and resistance to convergence. *Bilingualism: Language and Cognition, 15,* 203–225.

Radford, A. (2019). *Relative clauses: Structure and variation in everyday English.* Cambridge University Press.

Ramos, H. (2011). *Por uma vida melhor.* Ação Educativa Global.

Ribeiro, I. (2009). As sentenças relativas. In D. Lucchesi, A. N. Baxter, & I. Ribeiro (Eds.), *O Português Afro-Brasileiro* (pp. 1985–1208). EDUFBA.

Rickford, J. R. (1997). Unequal partnership: Sociolinguistics and the African American speech community. *Language in Society, 26,* 161–197.

Rohdenburg, G. (1996). Cognitive complexity and increased grammatical explicitness in English. *Cognitive Linguistics, 7*(2), 149–182.

Roland, D., Dick, F., & Elman, J. (2007). Frequency of basic English grammatical structures: A corpus analysis. *Journal of Memory and Language, 57*, 348–379.

Romaine, S. (1982). *Socio-historical linguistics: Its status and methodology.* Cambridge University Press.

Ross, J. R. (1967). *Constraints on variables in syntax.* Unpublished Ph.D. dissertation, MIT.

Sankoff, G. (1973). Above and beyond phonology in variable rules. In C. J. Bailey & R. Shuy (Eds.), *New ways of analyzing variation in English* (pp. 44–62). Georgetown University Press.

Sankoff, D. (1988). Sociolinguistics and syntactic variation. In F. J. Newmeyer (Ed.), *Linguistics: The Cambridge survey* (Vol. III, pp. 140–161). Cambridge University Press.

Scherre, M. M. P. (2005). *Doa-se lindos filhotes de poodle: variação lingüística, mídia e preconceito.* Parábola Editorial.

Scherre, M. M. P., & Naro, A. J. (2013). Sociolinguistic correlates of negative evaluation: Variable concord in Rio de Janeiro. *University of Pennsylvania Working Papers in Linguistics, 19*(2), 181–190.

Silva, R. V. O. (2011). *Análise da estrutura das orações relativas no português falado de Belo Horizonte: uma abordagem variacionista.* Dissertation, Pontifícia Universidade Católica de Minas Gerais – PUC/MG.

Silva, G. M. O., & Scherre, M. M. P. (Eds.). (1996). *Padrões Sociolinguísticos: análise de fenômenos variáveis do português falado na cidade do Rio de Janeiro.* Tempo Brasileiro.

Silva, J. C. (2018). *As orações relativas no português falado em Feira de Santana – BA.* Dissertation, Universidade Estadual de Feira de Santana.

Stark, E. (2009). Romance restrictive relative clauses between macrovariation and universal structures. *Philologie im Netz, 47*, 1–15. Available at http://web.fu-berlin.de/phin/phin47/p47i.htm.

Stark, E. (2016). Relative clauses. In A. Ledgeway & M. Maiden (Eds.), *The Oxford guide to the romance languages* (pp. 1029–1040). Oxford University Press.

Tagliamonte, S. A., & Harald Baayen, R. (2012). Models, forests, and trees of York English: Was/were variation as a case study for statistical practice. *Language Variation and Change, 24*, 135–178.

Tang, W. (2011). *A Simple Guide to Using Antconc.* Available at: http://www.laurenceanthony.net/software/antconc/resources/help_AntConc321_english.pdf

Tarallo, F. (1983). *Relativization strategies in Brazilian Portuguese.* PhD Dissertation. University of Pennsylvania, Philadelphia.

Tarallo, F. (1985). *A pesquisa sociolinguística.* Editora Ática.

Tottie, G., & Rey, M. (1997). Relativization strategies in earlier African American vernacular English. *Language Variation and Change, 9*, 219–247.

Vandresen, P. (Ed.). (2002). *Variação e mudança no português falado da Região Sul.* EDUCAT.

Vieira, S. R., & Brandão, S. F. (Eds.). (2007). *Ensino de gramática: descrição e uso.* Contexto.

Weinreich, U., Labov, W., & Herzog, M. I. (1968). Empirical foundations for a theory of language change. In W. P. Lehmann & Y. Malkiel (Eds.), *Directions for historical linguistics: A symposium* (pp. 95–188). University of Texas Press.

Zilles, A. M. S., & Faraco, C. A. (Eds.). (2015). *Pedagogia da Variação Linguística: língua diversidade e ensino.* Parábola Editorial.

Chapter 8
Pronominal Variation in Spoken Portuguese in "Rurban" Communities: Reflections on Evaluation, Prestige, and Stigma

Letícia Gaspar Pinto ⓘ and Rosane Andrade Berlinck ⓘ

Introduction

In establishing the foundations for a theory of linguistic change (and variation), Weinreich et al. (1968) highlight evaluation as one of the central problems to be faced by the researcher. If it is essential to investigate and describe the place of variable phenomena within the linguistic structure, we cannot lose sight of the fact that the existence of variation does not take place outside a social space, historically conditioned. The *status* of the variants, their possibilities of expansion leading to a process of change, crucially depends on how the community perceives and evaluates these forms, positively or negatively. Or, still, without being aware of the different uses that circulate in the group. In this sense, the problem of evaluation is closely related to what the authors defined as the problem of social embedding, and it is also fundamental to determine the extralinguistic factors that condition the processes. As Paiva and Duarte (2006) point out, when considering the role of evaluation on the path of variation and change, the Weinreich, Labov, Herzog (WLH) proposal attributes an agentive role to the speaker: they are able to accelerate or restrict the pace of change, depending on how they position themselves in relation to the variation, even if it happens unconsciously.

Since all these aspects are so strongly interconnected, we will find the issue of evaluation explored, to a lesser or greater extent, less or more explicitly, since the first studies that developed from the proposal launched in WLH and the initial works of William Labov. Labov's iconic study on Martha's Vineyard reveals precisely that the social meaning that the community attributes to a local linguistic mark is what makes it possible to understand the ongoing process of change, through the defense or rejection of the identity bond with the island (Labov, 1972).

L. G. Pinto · R. A. Berlinck (✉)
Unesp – São Paulo State University, Araraquara, São Paulo, Brazil
e-mail: leticia.gaspar@unesp.br; rosane.berlinck@unesp.br

© The Author(s), under exclusive license to Springer Nature Switzerland AG 2023
G. Massini-Cagliari et al. (eds.), *Understanding Linguistic Prejudice*,
https://doi.org/10.1007/978-3-031-25806-0_8

It is worth mentioning, however, that the concept of evaluation was often linked to the notion of *prestige* (or its absence) defined by the speaker's position in a hierarchy of social classes. Although being an important and inescapable aspect of the analyses, it is not always sufficient, as other values in force in the group can be linked to linguistic forms, attributing prestige or stigma to them. In addition, considering the Brazilian scenario (but not only it), an important factor in the evaluation of forms is their relationship with the standard norm; the language model thus established is correlated with social classes, but is not limited to this link, and has a strong coercive action on uses (Milroy, 2001; Faraco & Zilles, 2017).

It is also worth remembering that the set of explanatory principles of variation and change, inferred from the robust empirical base built up by decades of studies, mainly portrays the universe of urban communities. Looking at the urban space would have been a way of, on the one hand, establishing a counterpoint to dialectologically oriented research and, on the other hand, investigating linguistic processes in dense and heterogeneous communities that became the main focuses of population concentration from the second half of the twentieth century, in much of the world (Labov, 1965). Bearing this in mind, we should ask ourselves whether the conclusions obtained in such studies, often elevated to the status of more general principles, would apply in the same way to communities with a less urbanized profile.

These questions guide us to investigate how the assessment of linguistic uses influences the picture of variation and/or change in communities that have been left off the radar of sociolinguists. We selected as *locus* of study two neighboring cities, located in the southwest of Minas Gerais, close to the interior of the state of São Paulo – Cabo Verde-MG and Muzambinho-MG. The location of these municipalities can be seen in Fig. 8.1:

Cabo Verde-MG and Muzambinho-MG, in addition to having a low population concentration, 13,823 inhabitants and 20,430 inhabitants (IBGE, 2010), respectively, have some rural features. Such traits are present in this region because the main economic activity developed there is coffee cultivation. Therefore, these communities are still very much focused on the countryside, being formed, above all, by people who have or have had a certain type of bond with the countryside and who preserve some of their cultural background. Thus, it appears that these cities can be considered rurban areas (Bortoni-Ricardo, 2004).

Although these municipalities are neighbors, there are some structural and functional differences (Veiga, 2004) between them that can be reflected in the linguistic variety spoken by the residents. In relation to the number of inhabitants in rural areas, a census carried out by the IBGE in 2010 showed that 45% of Cabo Verde people still lived in the countryside, while only 23% of Muzambinhenses lived in rural places. Another difference is the educational structure of these cities: in Muzambinho-MG, there are private elementary schools and a public higher education institution, while in Cabo Verde-MG, there are no such educational centers. Therefore, from the analysis of these aspects, it is observed that, even if these communities are close to each other, they differ in terms of their degree of urbanization, Cabo Verde-MG can be considered a less urbanized city than Muzambinho-MG.

Fig. 8.1 The location of Cabo Verde-MG and Muzambinho-MG (The purple-dashed line on this map marks the boundary between the states of Minas Gerais and São Paulo). (*In:* Diretorioderuas (Available at: https://www.diretorioderuas.com/BR/Minas-Gerais/Mesorregiao-Sul-Sudoeste-De-Minas/Microrregiao-Sao-Sebastiao-Do-Paraiso/Mapa-Da-Cidade/. Accessed on September 08, 2021))

In order to verify possible differences in the framework of linguistic variation in these communities related to their social organization, we chose for the study a phenomenon that is demonstrably variable in Brazilian Portuguese – the alternation between the pronominal forms of the first-person plural. The choice of this phenomenon was based on a specificity found in the speech of this region: in addition to the variation between *nós* and *a gente*, a very common variation in Brazilian Portuguese, there is also a phonological variation, since the inhabitants make use of the variants *nóis* and *nói*. When analyzing these forms, it is noted that *nós* underwent a diphthongization process, resulting in *nóis*. The use of the form *nói* is also very frequent, probably generated from the deletion of the sibilant /S/ in the coda position of the form *nóis*.

In this research, these phonological variants were included in our analysis, not only because this look at morphophonology is still little explored by Brazilian sociolinguistics but also because their presence, possibly, causes other values to be attributed to the forms in variation. Thus, one of the main objectives of this chapter, as already explained, is to identify and discuss the social meanings of the variants analyzed in these communities, in order to reflect, more specifically, on the concepts of evaluation, prestige, and stigma.

To this end, we will initially expose the theoretical assumptions that guide this study (sections "The Social Meanings of Linguistic Variation" and "The Phenomenon Under Study") and our theoretical-methodological decisions (section "Theoretical-Methodological Decisions"). Subsequently, we will present the results of the subjective reactions questionnaire (section "Subjective Reactions Questionnaire"), in which we seek to identify the local meanings of the analyzed variants. Through them, we will discuss the results of linguistic production (section "Linguistic Production: Analysis of Social Variables"), focusing on some social variables (*place of birth*, *sex/gender*, and *education*), which can help us understand issues related to the prestige and stigma of forms. Finally, we will approach, in a more specific way, such concepts, reflecting on the social values of the variants in the investigated communities (section "Final Considerations: The Role of Social Meanings in Linguistic Variation Processes").

The Social Meanings of Linguistic Variation

According to Ochs (1992), linguistic structures indirectly point to social categories, through a chain of semiotic associations, which is configured in the phenomenon of *indexicality*. It is important to highlight that these categories are not inherent to the linguistic form, but due to co-occurrence in a group, this form can indicate a certain idea. Assuming that language is a heterogeneous system (Weinreich et al., 1968), it is considered that linguistic variation can point to different social meanings and, through them, speakers can construct their identities by using a variant instead of another.

Also based on this notion of indexicality, Silverstein (2003) creates the model of "indexical order," which classifies linguistic features into two groups: *first-order indices* and *second-order indices*. The former refers to geographic or diastratic variants that indicate the participation of individuals in a given speech community and do not differ in degrees of formality. Such an index can become second-order if the social evaluation of speakers who use these variants is associated with the index, internalizing itself in the subjects' dialects in order to index other specific elements. Thus, *second-order indices* index both macrosocial categories and speakers' social evaluation and ideology in relation to variant forms.

This model proposed by Silverstein (2003) dialogues with the Labovian concepts of *indicators*, *markers*, and *stereotypes*. Labov (1972) proposed this classification based on the level of awareness of individuals about the forms in linguistic variation and change. For him, the indicators are linguistic traits that present social stratification but that appear to have little evaluative force and do not have a pattern of stylistic variation,[1] similar to Silverstein's (2003) *first-order indices*. In contrast, *markers* exhibit not only social stratification but stylistic stratification as well. In tests of subjective reactions, although the phenomena are often below the level of consciousness, speakers almost always produce cohesive responses. *Stereotypes*, in turn, differ from the latter because they are socially marked forms, being targets of evaluative metacomments. From this perspective, it is possible to perceive that the linguistic traits considered *markers* and *stereotypes* are similar to the *second-order indices* of Silverstein (2003).

However, when comparing the proposals of these two authors, we observe that they differ insofar as Silverstein's (2003) indices admit reinterpretations, allowing new meanings and social judgments to be indexed as they are used by speakers in different social practices. Thus, it is noted that the indices are in a constant process of reconstruction, not being fixed, contrary to what appears from the classifications of Labov (1972). Due to this fact, the idea of Silverstein (2003) is taken as a basis in the conception of *indexical fields* proposed by Eckert (2008).

As this author defends that the study of variation should be centered on social meaning, she proposes the concept of *indexical fields*, which allows describing correlations between certain meanings and the use of certain linguistic traits. According to her views:

> [...] the meanings of variables are not precise or fixed but rather constitute a field of potential meanings – an indexical field, or constellation of ideologically related meanings, any one of which can be activated in the situated use of the variable. The field is fluid, and each new activation has the potential to change the field by building on ideological connections. Thus variation constitutes an indexical system that embeds ideology in language and that is in turn part and parcel of the construction of ideology. (Eckert, 2008:454)

In opposition to the first sociolinguistic studies, Eckert (2008) shows that the variables do not have static social meanings; these are dynamic and subject to constant reinterpretation. This happens because speakers do not use certain linguistic traits only to reaffirm their place in society but also to make ideological moves. To exemplify this fact, the author cites some studies, such as the one by Labov (1963) on the island of Martha's Vineyard, in which the social meaning of variation is based on ideologies about what the locality is and what are the practices, the beliefs, and the customs present in it. From this perspective, she points out that "local identity claims are about what it means to be from 'here' as opposed to some identified 'there'" (Eckert, 2008:462).

To access these social meanings, it is necessary that, in addition to studies of linguistic production, evaluation, attitude, and perception studies are also carried out (Oushiro, 2015, 2021; Sene, 2019). Although these three concepts are often treated as synonyms in current research, in this study they will be approached as distinct concepts, since here it is understood that they differ in terms of the speakers' degree of awareness.

---

[1] For Labov (1972), stylistic variation is associated with the degrees of formality of a social interaction, that is, how much the individual monitors his speech in a given communicative situation.

Therefore, we consider that *evaluation*, one of the five empirical problems for the study of linguistic variation and change (Weinreich et al., 1968), is the way in which speakers/listeners, through their beliefs, relate certain values to linguistic production of themselves or of other speakers, being, therefore, a metalinguistic activity. When speakers/listeners express this assessment explicitly, we call it a *linguistic attitude*, that is, it is a form of reaction to what is thought about a particular variant or variety (Garcia, 2018). According to Lambert and Lambert (1972:78), attitude can be defined as:

> [...] an organized and coherent way of thinking, feeling, and reacting in relation to people, groups, social issues or, more generally, to any event that occurs in our surroundings. Its essential components are thoughts and beliefs, feelings (or emotions) and tendencies to react.[2]

On the other hand, we consider that *sociolinguistic perception* is associated with subjective reactions and inferences made by speakers/listeners when listening to another individual (Oushiro, 2021). This perception can be conscious or unconscious and happens based on what has already been learned and recognized by the subjects (Jekosch, 2005, apud Sene, 2019). Therefore, from these definitions, it is clear that *evaluation*, *attitude*, and *perception* are complementary concepts that must be studied together so that we can understand how the linguistic forms point to social meanings in the investigated communities.

The Phenomenon Under Study

According to Lopes (2003), the pronominalization of the noun *gente*[3] in Brazilian Portuguese was slow and gradual, involving a "covariation of associated changes over a long period of time" (Lopes, 2003:73). As a result of this process, there was a restructuring of the verbal paradigm, as it loses its inflectional richness, going from six basic forms to three (e.g., *eu canto, tu/você/ele/a gente canta, vocês/eles cantam*). Therefore, as a way of avoiding ambiguity, Brazilian Portuguese is ceasing to be a language with a null subject and becoming a language with an explicit subject (Duarte, 1995), which "gives the new pronouns the status of only indicators of the category of person, hence their presence has become increasingly mandatory"[4] (Lopes, 2007:104).

---

[2] Translated from the Portuguese version: "[...] uma maneira organizada e coerente de pensar, sentir e reagir em relação a pessoas, grupos, questões sociais ou, mais genericamente, a qualquer acontecimento ocorrido em nosso meio circundante. Seus componentes essenciais são os pensamentos e as crenças, os sentimentos (ou emoções) e as tendências para reagir" (Lambert & Lambert, 1972:78).

[3] This noun, according to Lopes (2003:9), "originates from the Latin noun gĕns, gĕntis: 'race,' 'family,' 'tribe,' 'the people of a country, region or city'."

[4] "[...] dá aos novos pronomes o status de únicos indicadores da categoria de pessoa, daí sua presença ter se tornado cada vez mais obrigatória" (Lopes, 2007:103).

After the consolidation of this grammaticalization process, *a gente* starts to exist in the Brazilian Portuguese pronominal system together with the variant *nós*, being used as one of the strategies to refer to the first-person plural. This alternation between *nós* and *a gente* has been the object of study of many sociolinguistic works in different regions of the country (Vianna & Lopes, 2015). The work of Omena (1986) was the first to address this phenomenon in Brazilian Portuguese. Using a sample from the Projeto Censo database, the author analyzed the speech of non-educated informants in Rio de Janeiro, noting a preference for the use of *a gente* (73%) in the subject position. With regard to the social factors investigated, she pointed out that the age group is important for the use of the forms in variation, with a favoring of *a gente* by the young and a disadvantage by the older ones, which indicated that a change in progress could be occurring. Regarding the gender of the speakers, the researcher showed that this group of factors did not influence the choice of forms so much. Finally, she analyzed education and social class, noting that individuals who had a higher level of education and who were from higher social classes preferred to use *nós*.

Based on this study, Lopes (1993) investigated such variation in the speech of educated people in three Brazilian capitals: Salvador-BA, Porto Alegre-RS, and Rio de Janeiro-RJ. To do so, she used the NURC Project *corpus*, made up of interviews collected in the 1970s. Regarding extralinguistic factors, age, sex/gender, and city were the most strongly correlated with variation. The results showed that *a gente* was favored not only by young people but also by women, which differs from the results of Omena (1986) on the role of the sex/gender variable. With regard to cities, it was found that, in Rio de Janeiro, there was a greater use of *a gente* than in the other analyzed capitals.

In the state of Minas Gerais, the phenomenon in question has also been investigated, having its first description in Maia (2003). In this study, the researcher analyzed two *corpora* made up of interviews carried out in Pombal, a rural area of Mariana-MG, and in Belo Horizonte-MG. Discussing the results obtained, she pointed out that there are evident differences linked to the geographic distribution of the variants, since, in Belo Horizonte, the capital of Minas Gerais, *a gente* was more used (70%), while in the countryside, *nós* (64%) was more frequent, which indicates that the implementation of *a gente* is happening more slowly in rural areas. This fact was also observed by Foeger (2014), who analyzed the speech of individuals who live in the rural area of Santa Leopoldina-ES, comparing the linguistic behavior of these residents with the behavior of those who live in Vitória-ES – the capital of Espírito Santo state (Mendonça, 2010; Benfica, 2013).

In São Paulo capital, the variation in the use of first-person plural pronouns has already been analyzed both in the capital and in the interior of the state. In São Paulo, there is the work of Coelho (2006), who investigated this variation and verbal agreement in the speech of individuals who live in Brasilândia, a peripheral community in the North Zone of São Paulo. For this, the sociolinguist built a sample with 24 interviews with speakers who represent the different social groups of the community in question. Supported by this investigation, he found that there is not a strong presence of *a gente* in the speech of this locality (53%).

Through a careful ethnographic observation of the neighborhood under study, the author reported that there is a social hierarchy of the residents, and this seems to influence the use of forms in variation. In this context, it was noticed that the construction *Nóis* + V-zero is more used by the "manos," young people of lower social class, to differentiate themselves from the "good guys," children of the members of the community association. These boys, in turn, belong to the group with the highest expectation of social ascension, identifying with values of higher social classes. In the speech of these young people, it was possible to notice another type of construction: the use of *a gente* with the verbal agreement foreseen for this pronoun.

In addition to these linguistic behaviors, it was observed that male employees and daycare teachers, residents who have more contact with the middle class, tend to distance themselves from the local vernacular. Therefore, they use the variant *a gente* together with the verb with the morpheme *–mos* (as in *a gente vamos*), a construction that could be interpreted as a case of *hypercorrection*. Other social groups, such as single mothers who work outside the neighborhood, participants in the community project, and the upper working class, show an oscillating behavior between the pronouns *nóis* and *a gente*, accompanied by the verbal ending zero. Thus, these results indicate that the social ascension of the residents is more linked to the replacement of *nóis* by *a gente* than to the use of the ending *–mos*.

Rubio (2012) investigated the alternation between *nós* and *a gente* in Brazilian Portuguese and European Portuguese. To carry out this research, speech samples from the Iboruna Database and samples from different regions of Portugal, belonging to the Reference Corpus of Contemporary Portuguese, were used as *corpora*. Concerning the pronominal alternation in the São Paulo variety of Brazilian Portuguese, the researcher observed that there is a preference for the use of *a gente* (73.8%) to the detriment of *nós* (26.2%).

Analyzing the social variables that motivate such preference, Rubio (2012) found that, as young people are the ones who use *a gente* the most, a process of linguistic change seems to be taking place. Another aspect observed was that the behavior of speakers with a lower level of education is similar to that of those with a higher level, and sex/gender was not a relevant factor in pronominal variation. Such results may indicate that the use of *a gente* is not stigmatized in the community in question, since, according to Rubio (2012, p. 226), "schooling and gender tend to function as a 'thermometer' to indicate the degree of acceptance of a linguistic variant in a process of variation."[5]

In the Brazilian northeast region, the variation between *nós* and *a gente* has also been extensively researched. As an example, there is the work of Mendes (2007), who investigated this phenomenon in popular Portuguese in the city of Santo Antônio de Jesus-BA, located in the Recôncavo Baiano. The results of this research showed that the speakers of this municipality prefer to use the innovative form (93%) – *a gente* –, mainly those who live in the urban perimeter; in rural areas,

---

[5] "a escolarização e o gênero tendem a funcionar como 'termômetro' para indicar o grau de aceitação de uma variante linguística em um processo de variação" (Rubio, 2012:226)

however, there is a greater use of *nós* than in the municipality's urban territory. In addition, individuals who have lived their entire lives in Santo Antônio de Jesus-BA use the variant *nós* more than those who have lived in other cities. In this way, the author concluded that *a gente* is more present in the speech of those individuals who have greater contact with large urban centers and those who have more access to the media.

This observation was also pointed out by Mattos (2013), in a study on the speech of several municipalities in Goiás. She found that there is a predominance of *a gente* (77%) in the speech of Goiás. Among the groups of social factors analyzed, the age group indicates that there is a change in progress, since young people are the ones who use *a gente* the most and the older people are the ones who most disfavor the use of the form in question. In order to better understand the implementation process of this variant, the researcher analyzed, from 1970 onward, the urban development of Goiás, hypothesizing that, as a result of this process, *a gente* was incorporated into the Goiás speech, which could be related to the urban nucleus and to the idea of modernization (Mattos, 2013).

In the southern region of the country, there are also different studies on the alternation between these pronominal forms. Among them, we can mention Zilles (2005), who, using the NURC and VARSUL databases, carried out studies in *apparent time* and in *real time*, comparing the 1970s and 1990s. When data from 1990 were analyzed, there was a preference for *a gente* (69%) to the detriment of *nós* (31%). Regarding the extralinguistic factors investigated, the sociolinguist stated that there is a change in progress, led by young people and women. With regard to schooling, it was found that there is little difference in the linguistic behavior of less and more educated speakers. Therefore, a cross-tabulation between the variables sex and education was carried out, in which it was possible to observe that men and women with an intermediate or higher level of education had a very similar behavior regarding the use of *a gente*. On the other hand, men with elementary education used *a gente* less than women with the same level of education.

In summary, considering the various studies mentioned, it is observed that the pronoun *a gente* is widely used in Brazilian Portuguese as one of the strategies to represent the first-person plural in the subject position. In general, it can be said that the process of implementing *a gente* is advanced in the different Brazilian regions; however, there are some differences in relation to the location (Vianna & Lopes, 2015), since, in rural areas, this process is happening more slowly than in more urbanized communities.

Theoretical-Methodological Decisions

Based on the theory of linguistic variation and change (Weinreich et al., 1968; Labov, 1972, 1994, 2001), we initially investigated what are the linguistic and social variables that motivate the alternation between the first-person pronominal forms of the plural in the subject position. Therefore, in a first analysis, our variation envelope was composed of the variants *nós* and *a gente*, and the phonological variants (*nóis* and *nói*) were all classified as *nós*.

However, in order to better understand the social meanings of the forms in variation, it was necessary to verify how these factors are associated with the phonological variants that are behind the *nós* data. In this sense, we investigated, in a second moment, the four pronominal forms: *nós*, *nóis*, *nói*, and *a gente*.[6] Although the variants *nóis* and *nói* are of a different nature from the variants *nós* and *a gente*, they were included in the same analysis because they can alternate in the same context. Such forms can be seen in the following excerpts:

(a) Acolhedor/ respeitador/ como eu disse/ e o que eu acho difícil/ não que eu não goste/ mas que eu acho que precisa melhorá/ **nós estamos trabalhando** muito pra isso/ é a questão de trabalho/ aqui falta bastante trabalho (CV, F, F3, ES).[7,8]

(b) É/ aqui/ só entrava em casa pa comê, né?! / Ia na escola/ chegava da escola e ficava o dia intero pa rua/ brincano/ andano de bicicleta /jogano futebol na rua/ nos campinho de terra/ hoje/ nem isso existe mais/ então/ nesse sentido/ **nóis aproveitamo** muito como criança (CV, M, F2, ES).[9]

(c) aí **nói vortamo** pa cidade/ eu fiquei cuidano do L. e do Z. na casa deles/ mas depois eles precisaro da casa/ queria vim embora/ morá lá/ eu vim embora traveiz cum o E./ aí puis o E. no pré pra ele podê vim embora porque ele num queria vim/ aí puis o E. no pré/ e viemo pra cá traveiz/ mas aí eu ia daqui panhá café na roça todo dia (MZ, F, F3, SES),[10]

(d) Quando **a gente tava voltano** tipo daqui da cidade e aí um/meio que um cara apontô a arma pra gente/ só que tipo assim eu tava dormino no banco/ só que aí tipo eu acordei/ assustada/ chorano/ aí eu levantei e aquela foi a imagem que eu

---

[6] It is important to emphasize that, unlike Zilles (2002, 2005), in this work, there were no occurrences of phonetic reductions of *a gente* (*ahente*, *a'ente*, and *'ente*). As a result, these were not included in our variation envelope.

[7] After each example presented, there is a caption with the speaker's characteristics: place of birth, Cabo Verde-MG (CV) or Muzambinho-MG (MZ); sex/gender, female (F) or male (M); the age group, age group 1 – 18–25 years old (F1), age group 2 – 35–50 years old (F2), or age group 3 – over 60 years old (F3); and the level of education, without higher education (SES) or with higher education (ES).

[8] Welcoming / respectful / as I said / and what I find difficult / not that I don't like it / but that I think it needs improvement / we are working hard for it / it's a matter of work / we lack a lot of work here (CV, F, F3, ES)

[9] It's/here/ I only used to go into the house to eat, right?! / I went to school / I came home from school and stayed all day on the street / playing / riding a bicycle / playing football in the street / in the dirty fields / today / not even that exists anymore / so / in that sense / we enjoyed it a lot as a child (CV, M, F2, ES)

[10] then we went back to the city/ I took care of L. and Z. at their house/ but then they needed the house/ I wanted to leave/ live there/ I came back again with E./ then I put E. in preschool so he could come back because he didn't want to come / then I put E. in the pre-school / and we came here again / but then I used to go from here to get coffee in the countryside every day (MZ, F, F3, SES)

tive, entendeu? / Aí eu num parava de chorá/ num parava de chorá/ mas eu tinha tipo/ sei lá/ uns dez/ onze anos (CV, F, F1, ES).[11]

In the first analysis, based on Rubio's (2012) thesis, the following linguistic variables were investigated: *degree of subject determination*, *phonic salience*, *verb tense*, and *verbal agreement*; and the extralinguistic variables were *place of birth*, *sex/gender*, *education*, *age group*, and *the informant's relationship with the field*. In the second stage of investigation, the extralinguistic variables remained the same, and the only linguistic variable analyzed was the *verbal agreement*, since we consider that, unlike the others, this one can point out certain trends that will help us understand more what are the values of the forms in this region.

To carry out this study, 24 informants were selected, 12 from Cabo Verde-MG and 12 from Muzambinho-MG. In each of these municipalities, informants are divided into three distinct and non-continuous age groups: age group 1 (18–25 years old), age group 2 (35–50 years old), and age group 3 (over 60 years old). This division was made so that it is possible to investigate the different phases of life of the inhabitants of these cities – the young phase, the adult phase, and the elderly phase – and how these can be linguistically marked through the use of the studied variants. These informants are also divided between men and women: there are six men and six women from each municipality, so that we can analyze sex/gender issues. In addition to this age group and sex/gender division, they are divided between those who have higher education and those who do not.

The speech of these communities was analyzed through sociolinguistic interviews that followed a script of questions that induced the informant to talk about him and someone else or about him and another group of people to make him use the variants of the linguistic phenomenon studied more spontaneously. In addition, these questions addressed issues associated with the informant's city of origin and his or her relationship with the countryside, in order to observe how these aspects are reflected in the variety spoken by these individuals.

At the end of this interview script, the social meanings of the forms in variation were investigated. According to Oushiro (2019), one of the methods used in variationist sociolinguistics to access such meanings is the formulation of *explicit questions* in the interview. Based on this idea, we applied a questionnaire of subjective reactions, in order to investigate the attitudes and perceptions of the informants in relation to the variants. In the first moment, we asked the participants what they think about the way of speaking in their city and why, in order to verify how they evaluate their linguistic variety.

Then, we started the second moment of the questionnaire, in which we tried to capture the residents' perception without them knowing what our object of study was. To this end, we prepared three audios for them to listen to: audio 1 (*nói*), audio

---

[11] When we were coming back, like from here from the city and then a / kind of a guy pointed the gun at us / just like I was sleeping on the bench / then like I woke up / scared / crying / then I got up and that was the picture I had, see? / Then I couldn't stop crying / I couldn't stop crying / but I was like / I don't know / about ten / eleven years old (CV, F, F1, ES)

2 (*a gente*), and audio 3 (*nóis*). The variant *nós*, although produced by the inhabitants of this region, was not included in this questionnaire, since, as it was prepared before we carried out the sociolinguistic interviews, we had to rely only on the results obtained by Pinto (2019), in which there was no considerable amount of *nós* data (only three occurrences). Thus, we consider that it would be more coherent to include in this questionnaire only the pronominal forms that were more frequent in the speech of the individuals who participated in the previous study.

Furthermore, the duration of the audios listened to varied between 11 and 15 seconds, and, in each of them, the analyzed variant was produced only twice by the speaker, in order to prevent the number of repetitions of these forms from affecting the perception of the informants. It is also necessary to mention that all the individuals listened to the stimuli in the same order, which may have, in some way, interfered with the results, since it is possible that the participants had a more neutral position in relation to the first recording and used it as a basis for evaluating others.

In order to mitigate the effects of external factors, such as the voice and content of these audios, in the participants' perception, we made some methodological decisions: the three audios were staged by the same speaker – a young man from Muzambinho-MG who always lived in the city, and, before the subjects listened to them, they were warned that they would hear the voices of young people, in order to avoid this being a point mentioned throughout the questionnaire. In addition, in all recordings, the subject addressed was, in general, the climate.

In addition to controlling voice and content, we also controlled verb agreement, to reduce the possibility of participants judging this question instead of the pronominal form. In this sense, the verbs that accompany the pronouns *nói* and *nóis* are all with the ending *–mos*, with only the deletion of the *-s*, and the verbs that accompany the pronoun *a gente* are conjugated in the third-person singular. Through these audios, we then started the first moment of the questionnaire.

At first, we played audio 1 and asked the participants some questions. After they answered these questions, we played audio 2, repeating the same questions and so on. The questions asked in this second moment were the following:

1. From this person's way of speaking, do you think she is from Muzambinho or Cabo Verde? Why?
2. Is there anything in particular that caught your attention in this audio?
3. If you had to describe this person to someone, how would you describe it?

After the participants answered all these questions about the three audios listened to, we started the third moment of the questionnaire. At that moment, individuals become aware of the variable being studied, so that their beliefs in relation to the variants could be investigated. For this, we repeated the recordings and asked the following questions:

4. In this audio, the person used the *nói/a gente/nóis* to refer to her and another group of people. Do you use this form? In what situations?
5. Do you think that people from Cabo Verde/Muzambinho use this form?

After these interviews were carried out, they were transcribed, and the data collected and analyzed using the R statistical program (R Core Team, 2021). The linguistic production results obtained in these investigations were interpreted according to the hypotheses underlying the controlled (structural) linguistic variables and according to the social meanings of the variants in each of the communities, which were identified through the questionnaire of subjective reactions.

Bearing in mind that the main objective of this work is to reflect on the concepts of evaluation, stigma, and prestige, we will first report the main results of the subjective reactions questionnaire. From them, we will establish the local meanings of the variants and interpret the production results of the four variants in relation to social variables, more specifically *place of birth*, *sex/gender*, and *education* of the speakers, since we consider that such variables can help us better understand the notions of stigma and prestige. Therefore, in this study, we will not approach the results of linguistic variables as much as the results of some social variables, such as the informant's *relationship with the field* and *age group*.

Results of the Study in Cabo Verde-MG and Muzambinho-MG

Subjective Reactions Questionnaire

In the second moment of the questionnaire, in which our objective was to capture the perception of the informants without them being aware of the analyzed variable, we played the three stimuli with the pronominal forms: *nói*, *a gente*, and *nóis*. As mentioned in section "The Phenomenon Under Study", the first question asked in relation to these audios was the following: From the way this person speaks, do you think he is from Muzambinho-MG or from Cabo Verde-MG? Why?

This question was designed to verify whether participants think that the use of the studied variants differs from one city to another, given that these communities, despite being neighbors, have differences, as we explained in the introduction to this chapter. The answers to this question can be seen in Fig. 8.2:

Based on this figure, it can be seen that 58% (7) of the participants from both municipalities, when listening to the stimulus with the *nói* variant, associated the form in question when talking about their own speech. This result indicates that the informants seem to recognize, even if unconsciously, that the residents of their cities use this pronominal form, which suggests that this is a variant that indicates regionality in the investigated speech communities.

On the other hand, it is noted that, when we play the stimulus with the *a gente* variant, 50% (6) of Cabo Verde participants and 58% (7) of Muzambinho participants said that the speaker is from Muzambinho-MG. This result caught our attention, since we expected that most residents of Cabo Verde-MG would also relate the

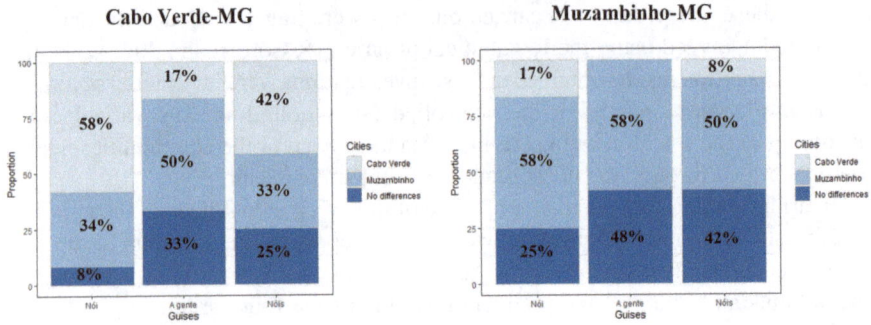

Fig. 8.2 Audio analysis by city. (Author's elaboration)

use of this form to their own linguistic variety. So, to try to understand this issue, we analyzed what the participants' justifications were.

An informant from Muzambinho-MG stated that this speaker is from her own city because he appears to be "less rural" than the speaker in the previous audio, possibly due to living in a larger municipality and less dependent on the countryside. In addition, this statement may indicate that the informants associate the use of *a gente* with the feature [− rural] and the use of *nói* with the feature [+ rural], since the speaker in audio 1 was characterized as "more rural." Another informant, a resident of Cabo Verde-MG, stated that this speaker is from Muzambinho-MG, given that, in relation to the speaker of the first audio, she considers him "more chic." This perception points out that Cabo Verde people have the image that Muzambinho-MG is a more developed city and, therefore, its inhabitants are "more chic." In the same way as the one from Muzambinho, this participant also seems to attribute opposite social meanings to the use of the variants *nói* and *a gente*: while *nói* appears to be linked to the speech of the less refined, *a gente* seems to be linked to talking about more refined people.

Considering these justifications, it is clear that the variant *a gente* can be related to positive social values in these communities. In this sense, Cabo Verde people, when stating that the speaker of this audio is from Muzambinho-MG, showed a certain linguistic insecurity (Calvet, 2004). It should be noted that we cannot categorically state that it was the use of this pronominal form that led to such assessments or whether other linguistic aspects present in the audio also contributed to this assessment, so we must consider these correlations with caution.

When the participants listened to the audio with the variant *nóis*, they gave more diverse answers than in the previous audios, but the result that stood out the most was that 42% (5) of the participants from Cabo Verde-MG and 50% (6) of the participants from Muzambinho-MG related the use of this pronominal form to their own way of speaking. This shows that, in a way, they also recognize each other when they listen to the *nóis* variant, as happened in the audio with *nói*.

Finally, it is also observed that, in all recordings, there were participants who said that there are no differences between the ways of speaking in these municipalities. These stated that the speakers could be from both Cabo Verde-MG and

Muzambinho-MG, since these cities are neighbors and have very similar characteristics, including their linguistic repertoire. After asking the municipality of the speaker of each audio, we asked the informants the following question: Is there anything in particular that caught your attention in this audio?

Regarding the first stimulus, in which the speaker used the *nói* variant, some participants from Cabo Verde-MG and Muzambinho-MG pointed out that something that caught their attention was the fact that this voice is similar to the way they speak, which may signal that they feel familiar when they hear the variant in question. Another point mentioned was the absence of first-person plural verb agreement. Although this was controlled in the audios, it was an aspect often mentioned by the participants. This may have happened for two reasons: (i) because individuals already associate the use of *nói* with verbs in the third-person singular, since they mention that this individual said *nói vai*, and (ii) because the first-person plural verb agreement is an overrated feature in Brazilian Portuguese, being the target of metacommentary. In this way, we can think that the social meanings attributed by the informants may be linked not only to the use of the pronoun but also to the verbal agreement.

Furthermore, the participants mentioned that the speaker of this first stimulus speaks very fast, cutting out some words and syllables. To exemplify this fact, they mentioned some linguistic aspects, such as the verbal form "chuveno," in which the consonant [d] is deleted, and the word "memo," which, like the variant *nói*, undergoes the process of erasing the sibilant /S/ in coda position. Taking into account the points mentioned by the informants, it can be seen that, even though they mentioned the *nói* variant to demonstrate the absence of verb agreement, they did not specifically talk about the use of this pronominal form, which indicates that it is not a target of metacomments in these speech communities, and its use seems to be below the level of consciousness.

In the same way that occurred with the variant *nói*, the individuals, when answering about the second audio, did not mention, in a specific way, the presence of the variant *a gente*; they only mentioned this form, claiming that, in comparison with the previous audio, the person was speaking more "right," since he used verb agreement properly. Other informants said that nothing in particular caught their attention in this audio, thus showing that the variant *a gente* is not the target of metacomments either.

Thus, it is noted that, although there are similarities with the first audio, there are differences between the answers given. One of them is that, in this case, no speaker tried to approximate the way of speaking in question to his own way of speaking, possibly due to linguistic insecurity (Calvet, 2004), given that this variant seems to have some social prestige in relation to the phonological variants *nóis* and *nói*. However, it is important to emphasize that, in this second stimulus, other linguistic phenomena were not performed, such as the deletion of the consonant [d] in verbs in the gerund and the suppression of /S/ in coda in lexemes.

On the other hand, when answering about the third audio, in which the speaker used the variant *nóis*, the participants pointed out that there is an approximation between this speaker's way of speaking and their own way of speaking, which indicates that they also feel familiar when listening to this form. In addition to this issue of familiarity, the participants also mentioned that the speaker in question is very similar to the speaker of the first audio, arguing that both have a more "slurred" accent. This approximation between the first and the third audios was not something expected in this work, since our hypothesis was that these variants were different in social terms. In this sense, it is possible to think that this happened because (i) these variants have similar social meanings, (ii) the informants identify themselves with the use of the two pronominal forms, and/or (iii) because, in this audio, there is also the deletion of the consonant [d] in the verb that is in the gerund.

To finish this second moment of the questionnaire, we asked the following question: If you had to describe this person to someone, how would you describe it? To describe the speaker in audio 1, who used the *nói* variant, the participants used several adjectives that were organized into word clouds, as can be seen in Fig. 8.3:

It is noted that the informants from each municipality shared traits in common when they answered about this first stimulus. One of the adjectives most used by them was "familiar": they believe that, by the way of speaking, this person resembles someone they know or with themselves, since, according to these participants, the individual who speaks in this way can be from the countryside or not.

Another aspect shared by the residents of these cities were the [+ rural] and [− urban] traits of this variant. Such traits were evidenced through the use of different expressions: those that are more general and refer to the relationship with the countryside ["rural" and "caipira" (redneck)], those that refer to the level of education ["pouco estudado" (little studied) and "informal"], others that refer to personality ["simples" (simple), "humilde" (humble), "relaxado" (relaxed), and "deselegante" (inelegant)], and those that refer to places where there are these traits ["interior de São Paulo" (São Paulo countryside), "Gomes," and "São Bartolomeu de Minas," the latter two being names of rural neighborhoods in the municipalities]. Thus, it is noted that all these expressions make up the image of the stereotyped redneck as one who is socially backward and who, therefore, has a low level of education.

Fig. 8.3 Adjectives used to describe the speaker of the first audio (*nói*). (*In:* Author's elaboration)

In addition to these traits, in Muzambinho-MG, informants characterized this person as "apavorado" (terrified), "descontraído" (relaxed), "ansioso" (anxious), and "comunicativo" (communicative), justifying that he speaks very fast, seeming to "want to say everything at once." This perception may have occurred, in part, due to the process of erasing the sibilant in coda that takes place in the variant in question. Another aspect that draws attention in these adjectives is that "relaxado" (relaxado) and "ansioso" (anxious) are opposite terms, which show us that the same recording can generate different perceptions.

Still, the people of Muzambinho also described this individual as a "molecão" (immature man) and "malandro" (rascal), arguing that he appears to be immature and without responsibilities. The informants may have had this perception for two reasons: (i) because one of the topics addressed in this first stimulus was "party" and (ii) because they associated the use of *nói* with the way of speaking from younger people, considering that, in Pinto (2019), it was found, in both communities, that this age group tends to use this pronominal form frequently.

To describe the speaker of audio 2, who used the form *a gente*, the participants used expressions that seem to oppose those presented for audio 1, as can be seen in Fig. 8.4:

As in the previous audio, it is noted that the responses of informants from both cities are, to a certain extent, cohesive, indicating that they share the same traits in relation to the variant *a gente*. These features contrast with those used to describe the previous variant: while the form *nói* was characterized as [+ rural] and [− urban], the variant *a gente* was characterized as [− rural] and [+ urban], as can be seen if we analyze the adjectives used. Such adjectives refer to the individual's level of education ["escolarizado" (schooled), "formal," "culto" (cultured), "preparado" (prepared)], to his social class ["classe social alta" (upper social class), "condomínio fechado" (gated community)], and to his personality ["fino" (fine), "playboy," "sofisticado" (sophisticated)], building the image of a person who has a high level of education and who lives in a bigger city. Thus, the informants seem to associate

Fig. 8.4 Adjectives used to describe the speaker of the second audio (*a gente*). (*In:* Author's elaboration)

positive social values with this variant, insofar as the same man, previously evaluated as poorly educated, rustic, and resident of rural neighborhoods, is now considered educated, of high social class, and resident of gated communities.

Also, there are two other traits that contrast with those mentioned in the previous audio: calmness and maturity. At the same time that the speaker of the first audio was characterized as "apavorado" (terrified), in the second one, he was described as "calmo" (calm), "sereno" (serene), "atento" (attentive), and "claro" (clear). According to informants, this person can be described in this way because he speaks more slowly compared to the previous one, facilitating the understanding of what was said. It is possible that this perception has to do with the fact that, in this audio, there was no erasure of the final sibilant. Another trait associated with the use of this variant was the maturity of this individual, as the informants claimed that, even if this individual is also young, he seems to be someone more "maduro" (mature), "sério" (serious), and "responsável" (responsible).

Finally, when answering about the third audio, in which the speaker used the variant *nóis*, the participants used different adjectives to characterize it, as can be seen in Fig. 8.5:

In a similar way to what was observed in the first audio, participants from Cabo Verde-MG and Muzambinho-MG characterized the speaker in question as "familiar," justifying that his way of speaking is similar to the way in which the people with whom they live together speak. In addition to this similarity, it can be seen that this pronominal form was also associated with features of [+ rural] and [− urban], given that this speaker is described as "rural," "caipira" (redneck), "informal," and "simples" (simple).

Although the variant *nóis* seems to have a well-established use in Brazilian Portuguese (Hora & Aquino, 2012), it was associated with traits of rurality in these communities, probably because the participants identify with the use of this form and, also, identify themselves with such traits, as could be seen in the most general

Fig. 8.5 Adjectives used to describe the speaker of the third audio (*nóis*). (*In:* Author's elaboration)

moment of this questionnaire. Therefore, it seems that everything that these informants believe is close to their way of speaking is linked to traits that signal rurality, since that is how they recognize themselves.

Comparing the results of both cities, the participants differed when talking about the degree of maturity of this speaker, as the Cabo Verde informants described him as "maduro" (mature) and "responsável" (responsible), while the people from Muzambinho described him as "molecão" (immature man). In this way, it is noted that, unlike the previous audios, the answers are not so cohesive, with some divergences between the municipalities. This variation in the answers may be related to the fact that this form, despite not being in accordance with the standard norm, is present in the speech of most people, regardless of whether they live in the countryside or in the city, thus being able to point to diverse social meanings.

In the third moment of the questionnaire, in which the participants become aware of the variable being studied, we repeated the three audios heard in the first moment and asked them some questions. The first question is as follows: In this audio, the person used the form *nói/a gente/nóis* to refer to himself and another group of people. Do you use this form? In what situations?

When answering about the *nói* variant, 58% (seven) of the participants from Cabo Verde-MG and 67% (eight) of the participants from Muzambinho-MG said they use this pronominal form. However, some individuals emphasized that this use is often unconscious, and others pointed out that it depends on the communicative situation, since, according to the informants, this variant is more used in informal contexts and with people with whom they are more intimate. Another aspect that caught our attention was the speech of a participant in age group 1 (18–25 years old) who always lived in the rural area of Muzambinho-MG. He stated that he uses this variant a lot, justifying that, in his city, people have a certain tendency to cut out words. This perception may indicate that the deletion of the sibilant in coda does not occur only in the *nói* variant but also in other words, being something recurrent in the linguistic variety of this community.

On the other hand, 42% (five) of Cabo Verde informants and 33% (four) of Muzambinho informants said they did not use this pronominal form. In general, all these participants are in the age group 2 (35–50 years old) and age group 3 (over 60 years old), including people with and without higher education. Analyzing the production data of these individuals, it is clear that this variant was used by the majority, except for three people who have a degree. Those people who did not use the variant in question said that they do not speak that way because of the work environment, which requires them to use the forms prescribed by normative grammars. This shows that, in certain contexts, this variant is stigmatized.

In addition, there were graduated participants who mentioned that they do not use the *nói* variant, because it is more used by young people, and, according to them, this age group speaks more "wrongly" and with more slang. On the other hand, participants who do not have a degree claimed that the form *nói*, in particular, is not used by them, but they use other expressions present in this first audio, such as the form "memo," in which the process of erasing the sibilant /S/ in coda also occurs.

Regarding the variant *a gente*, 67% (eight) of the participants from both Cabo Verde-MG and Muzambinho-MG stated that they use this form. In both cities, they mentioned that this use also depends on the communicative situation, since, unlike *nói*, this variant is more used in formal contexts, which allows us to notice a certain social prestige of this form in the investigated speech communities. In addition, another speech that caught our attention was that of a graduated informant from Muzambinho in age group 3 (over 60 years old). She said that she prefers to use the variant *a gente* to the detriment of other pronominal forms to avoid deviations in verb agreement, since, in this case, the verb is usually conjugated in the third-person singular.

On the other hand, 33% (four) of Cabo Verde informants and 33% (four) of Muzambinho informants said they did not use the *a gente* variant, these being of different age groups and all without higher education. However, analyzing the production data of these participants, it is noted that only one Muzambinho participant, in fact, did not use the variant in question. This participant, who is young and has lived in the countryside all his life, emphasized that he only uses *nói* and *nóis*. Like this participant, other individuals also said that they only use the phonological variants of *nós* because they are "more rustic," which indicates that these are more associated with country life than *a gente*.

Finally, when the informants answered about the *nóis* variant, 83% (10) of Cabo Verde informants and 92% (11) of Muzambinho informants said they used this form. Analyzing these percentages, it is noted that they were higher than the percentages referring to the previous variants, indicating that, in general, the participants seem not to be so afraid when speaking that they use this form, probably because it is present in the speech of most Brazilians. From this perspective, some informants even mentioned that this is the pronominal form most used by them, arguing that it seems to be in the middle of a kind of scale, between *a gente* and *nói*.

In the same way that happened with the variant *nói*, these informants also mentioned that the use of this variant depends on the communicative situation, being more used in informal situations, since, in other situations, there is a preference for the use of the variants *nós* and *a gente*. This fact is highlighted in the speech of the participants who said that they do not use the *nóis* variant, due to the environment in which they work – women in age groups 2 and 3 who have higher education.

After this question, to end the third moment of the questionnaire, we asked the participants if they think that people from Cabo Verde/Muzambinho use each of the forms. In both speech communities, all questionnaire participants stated that individuals from their cities use the three pronominal forms: *nói*, *a gente*, and *nóis*. However, they made some reservations similar to those stated in the previous question. From these results, it is clear how individuals evaluate and perceive the forms in variation. Despite the limitations of the methodology used here,[12] we were able to

---

[12] The formulation of explicit questions in the interview script does not allow us to capture the hidden reactions of individuals in relation to the analyzed variants, being, therefore, one of the limitations of this methodology. To solve it, we intend, in future studies, to apply an experiment based on the matched-guise technique (Lambert et al., 1960).

access the different social meanings of the variants in the investigated speech communities. This will allow us to better understand not only the functioning of such communities but also the linguistic behavior of their residents.

Linguistic Production: Analysis of Social Variables

First, it is important to highlight that, in total, we obtained 697 tokens from the variable analyzed in this study, 314 tokens in Cabo Verde-MG and 383 tokens in Muzambinho-MG. The distribution of the four variants according to the place of birth of the informants can be seen in Fig. 8.6:[13]

The figure indicates that *a gente* is the variant most used by residents of both communities; however, Cabo Verde informants use this form less (49%) than Muzambinho informants (58%). When we go back to the results of the subjective reactions questionnaire, we observe that the variant *a gente* indicate [− rural] and [+ urban] traits in these communities. Based on this, it is possible to think that the residents of Muzambinho-MG, considering that their hometown is less rural than Cabo Verde-MG, identify themselves more with [+ urban] traits, tending to use *a gente* more frequently.

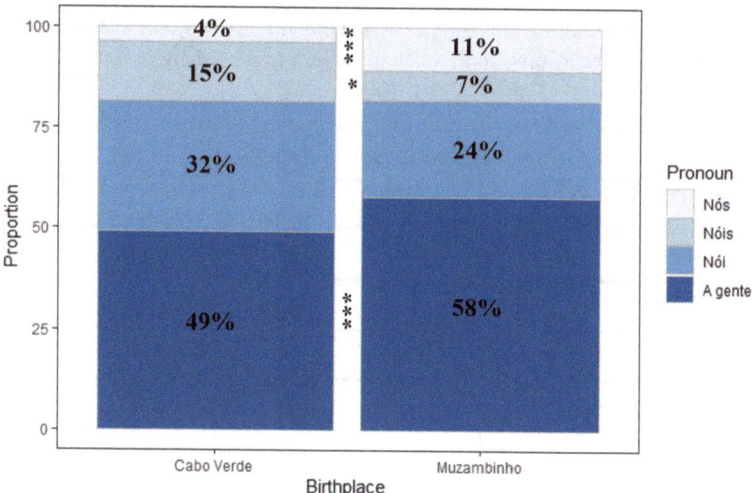

Fig. 8.6 Proportion of the use of pronouns according to place of birth. (*In*: Author's elaboration)

---

[13] To verify if the variables are statistically significant, we performed a chi-square test between the rows of the table. The results of this test will be between the bars of the graph, next to each one of the analyzed variants. To understand them, it is necessary to keep in mind that: (i) without statistical significance – p-value greater than 0.05: without asterisks $p > 0.05$; (ii) with statistical significance – p-value less than 0.05: $*p < 0.05$; $**p < 0.01$; and $***p < 0.001$.

Furthermore, it is observed that the phonological variant most used by individuals from Cabo Verde-MG and Muzambinho-MG is *nói*, 32% and 24%, respectively. Considering that, in this region, this form indirectly points to [+ rural] and [− urban] traits, it can be thought that it is used more frequently by individuals because they identify with these aspects. Even the residents of Muzambinho-MG, who believe they live in a less rural area than Cabo Verde-MG, use adjectives that refer to such traits to describe their way of speaking. Therefore, the use of the *nói* variant can be considered a mark of regionality in these communities, even if this happens unconsciously.

Despite these similarities, there are differences between these municipalities in relation to the second most used phonological variant. While, in Cabo Verde-MG, residents use more *nóis* (15%), in Muzambinho-MG, they use more *nós* (11%). We think it is possible to associate this result with the differences observed in the profile of the cities: as they have a greater link with the rural area, Cabo Verde people would use more of the variants linked to the countryside, such as the variant *nóis*, which points to [+ rural] and [− urban] traits. On the other hand, the people of Muzambinho would try to use forms that distance themselves from these traits, like *nós*, which is present in the speech of people with a greater knowledge of the standard norm.

Regarding the sex/gender variable, it is important to mention that, with the changes that have taken place in society, especially from the twentieth century onward, the role of women has changed. Therefore, the explanations for understanding the relationship between this variable and the phenomena in variation are, little by little, also changing (Freitag, 2015). They are no longer restricted to circular or essentialist interpretations, such as "women are more sensitive to the social prestige of linguistic forms" (Labov, 1990, 2001).

In this work, in order to avoid such types of explanations, we seek to understand the role of women in the investigated speech communities. Through sociolinguistic interviews, we observed that all the women who participated in this study work or have worked outside the home, which indicates that this role has indeed changed over the years. However, as these cities have some rural traits, patriarchal patterns are still very present, sexism being something recurrent.

To exemplify this fact, we can cite some situations described in the episode *Elas* of the radio special produced by Ribeiro (2021). In this context, the journalist portrayed, among other aspects, the lives of Cabo Verde women who work in the countryside. Many of them talked about their double working hours: they work exhaustively in the countryside and then at home, since, in most cases, there is no division of domestic tasks. In addition to this overload, they also face sexist attitudes in the work environment. Among the reports presented, a Cabo Verde woman mentioned that, because she works in the countryside, she was sometimes called a "machona" (macho woman). This is because, possibly, this activity is associated with man, which illustrates a prejudice on the part of the population.

These situations, although they have portrayed the lives of women from Cabo Verde-MG who work in the countryside, are also recurrent in the lives of Muzambinho women and others who have other occupations; that is, regardless of city and profession, women in this region still suffer from patriarchal patterns rooted in society both at home and at work. We believe that, in order to reaffirm their role and be more heard by the community in general, they are more subject to normative pressures than men. Therefore, they would make greater use of locally more prestigious linguistic forms. To verify whether this hypothesis is confirmed, we analyzed this variable and the results are shown in Fig. 8.7:

Analyzing these figures, it is possible to observe that, in Cabo Verde-MG, women use the *a gente* variant more (64%) than men (39%). We have already seen that *a gente* in this region is associated with positive values, being linked to talking about people with a higher level of education and belonging to a high social class. Thus, one interpretation of these results is that women, even if unconsciously, use this variant more as a way of being more socially heard.

As for the phonological variants, Cabo Verde men and women more often use the same form: *nói*. However, there is a difference between the proportions of the use of this form, since men (39%) tend to use it more than women (23%). As we have seen, the analysis of the social values that are linked to this variant revealed that it is the least prestigious pronoun in this community, as it points to negative values, such as the notion of little schooling. Thus, one might think that women avoid the use of *nói* more than men, possibly because they tend to police themselves more linguistically, even if this is done unconsciously.

Furthermore, it is observed that *nóis* is the second most used phonological variant by men (19%) and women (8%) in Cabo Verde-MG, being even more frequent among males. Reviewing the results of the questionnaire, it appears that *nóis* was not specifically related to either positive or negative values, but it indicates a series of meanings associated with country life. Taking this into account, it is possible to say that men use more *nóis* than women due to the fact that they have a greater relationship with the rural area, since most interviewees work or have worked in the countryside, while women have other occupations, with only one working in the countryside during the coffee harvest season. Another aspect that can be noticed in this figure is that the form least used by Cabo Verde people of both sexes is *nós*, with no statistically significant difference between the use they make.

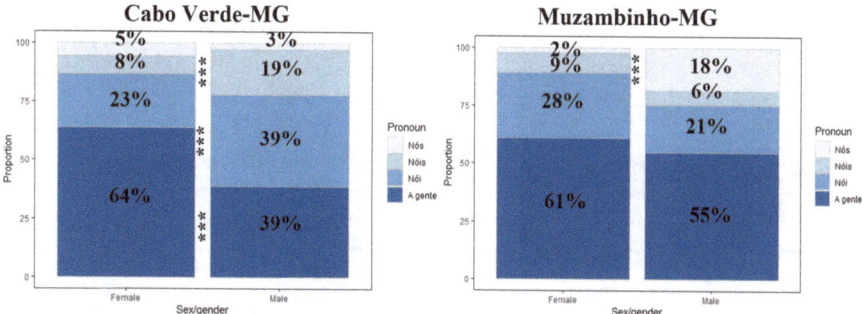

Fig. 8.7 Proportion of the use of pronouns according to sex/gender. (*In*: Author's elaboration)

132 L. G. Pinto and R. A. Berlinck

In Muzambinho-MG, the variant *a gente* is the most used among the variants by both women (61%) and men (55%); although, in percentage terms, women use this pronoun more frequently than men, the difference is not as wide as what was seen in the data from Cabo Verde and is not statistically significant. The *nói* variant is the second most used form, 28% and 21%, respectively, a difference that is also not statistically significant. Such results surprised us, as we expected that there would be a statistical difference between female and male informants in the use of these variants, as they seem to be associated with opposite values in this community. The only statistically relevant difference was in the use of *nós* – men use this form more (18%) than women (2%).

Investigating what are the local meanings of this last variant, it seems to be linked to the speech of educated people, being more socially prestigious. Considering that, this production result goes in the opposite direction to what was initially hypothesized, since we believed that women from Muzambinho would tend to use this form more than men. When analyzing these tokens of *nós* to try to better understand this fact, we observed that they are mostly concentrated on the speech of a man with higher education who was quite conservative regarding the use of the Portuguese language during the interview. Thus, it would not be, in fact, a representative use of a social segment, but an idiosyncratic trait of a speaker.

With regard to the *level of education* of speakers, it is expected that, as the school is one of the main places where the individual has contact with the standard norm (Bortoni-Ricardo, 2004), individuals who have a higher level of education use comparatively more variants endorsed by the grammatical norm, transmitted and reinforced by the school, while those who have a lower level of education more often use forms with less prestige associated with the standard norm, even though they can make use of variants that have a certain local prestige. To verify if and how such correlations are manifested in these communities, we analyzed this variable, with results shown in Fig. 8.8:

From these figures, it can be seen that, in Cabo Verde-MG, there were no statistically significant differences in the use of the *a gente* variant between those with and without higher education. On the other hand, in Muzambinho-MG, speakers who

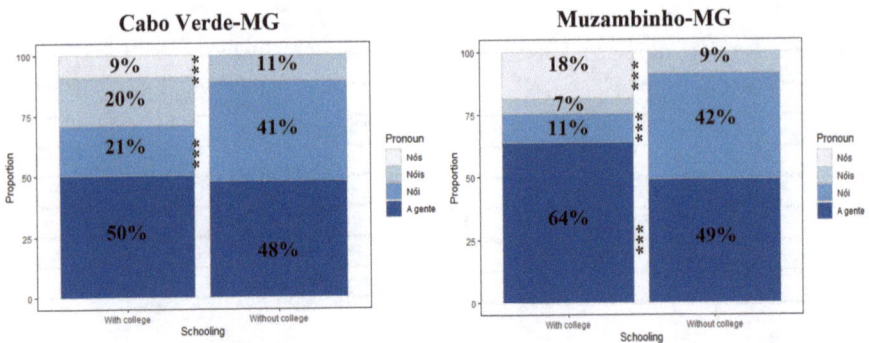

Fig. 8.8 Proportion of the use of pronouns according to schooling. (*In*: Author's elaboration)

have a degree use the variant *a gente* (64%) more than those who do not (49%). In view of the way in which individuals evaluate and perceive forms, it appears that *a gente* has a greater social prestige, because it was linked to the speech of people with higher social classes and with a higher level of education. Possibly, as a result of this, people from Muzambinho with higher education tend to use it more frequently, or, conversely, one might think that this variant has this prestige precisely because it tends to be used more by speakers who have a higher level of education.

As for the *nói* variant, it is the most used by Cabo Verde people and Muzambinho informants without a degree, 41% and 42%, respectively. This result may be related to the fact that it is the least prestigious form in these communities, as it is linked to the speech of people who are little studied and simpler. However, it is important to highlight that, in both municipalities, this variant is also present in the speech of people with higher education, albeit in smaller proportions, 21% in Cabo Verde-MG and 11% in Muzambinho-MG. Another aspect that can be observed through these results is that there were no statistically significant differences in the use of *nóis* between those with and without higher education in the two cities analyzed.

Finally, in relation to the *nós* variant, both in Cabo Verde-MG and in Muzambinho-MG, it is present only in the speech of individuals who have a degree, 9% and 18%, respectively, and these indices are statistically significant ($p < 0.001$). Comparing these results to the questionnaire (cf. section "Subjective Reactions Questionnaire"), it is possible to observe that *nós* is the form that has the most prestige, because, according to the informants, it is "more correct," being present only in the speech of people who they believe have greater knowledge of the standard norm, such as teachers. Therefore, it can be thought that, due to this prestige, this form is restricted to the use of certain social groups with a high socioeconomic level and a high degree of literacy.

Thus, the positive and negative values locally attributed to the forms investigated during the questionnaire of subjective reactions helped us better understand the differences between those residents with and without higher education, confirming our initial hypothesis that the years of schooling may interfere with the use of less or more prestigious variants.

Final Considerations: The Role of Social Meanings in Linguistic Variation Processes

Our main objective in this study was to investigate to what extent we could identify correlations between variants of a very recurrent phenomenon studied in Brazilian Portuguese (the pronominal realization of the first-person plural) and social meanings that emerge in a context little explored in sociolinguistic research – the less urbanized or *rurban* communities (Bortoni-Ricardo, 2004). We understand that the perception and evaluation that speakers have in relation to different forms of expression of the same idea can influence the "life" of these variants, in the sense that there may be a tendency to maintain and even expand the use of certain forms associated with positive values in the community and rejecting the employment of others. This rejection can be general, a reaction of the whole community, but it can, on the contrary, be linked to specific social segments.

The first important observation was to verify that the variants are all present in the speech of the two communities studied. And even speakers who do not use (or think not to use) any of them have a clear perception of the values that are associated with each of them. It is this sharing of usage norms that underlies the concept of a *speech community*. Naturally, it is necessary to investigate a set of linguistic phenomena to establish whether, in fact, we are facing a *speech community*[14] that encompasses both cities, but we have here an important indication in this sense.

From the analysis of the evaluations, perceptions, and productions of the speakers who composed the sample, we identified the social meanings of each one of them. We saw that the *a gente* form is associated in the community with positive values: high social class, high level of education, formality, sophistication, and maturity. In contrast to this set of values, we have the *nói* form, which is associated with poorly educated, simple, rustic, humble, and immature people and with informal contexts of interaction. The form *nóis* shares many of the meanings of *nói* but presents itself with a comparatively more positive evaluation than this. Finally, the form *nós*, which is infrequent, is clearly linked to quite formal contexts and to the domain of the standard norm, via schooling.

A central aspect that underlies these meanings is the rural/urban contrast and the perception evidenced in the interviewees' speech that the communities are characterized by a less urban and more rural way of life. Gradual differences between the two cities are also perceived and correspond to the proportion of the use of the variants: *a gente* being relatively more used in Muzambinho-MG, a city evaluated as comparatively more developed, that is, more urbanized; *nói* being relatively more used in Cabo Verde-MG, a community to which it is attributed a more rural profile.

The role we identified for the variant *a gente* shows that there is no necessary correspondence between standard norm and prestige. The pronoun *a gente* is rarely mentioned in normatively oriented works, and if it is, it appears marginally even classified as a form of address and not as a true pronoun (Almeida, 1973:150). However, it is this form that has the most prestige discovered in the communities, being associated with more formal communicative situations, a higher level of education, and a higher socioeconomic level.

Another facet of how prestige is manifested in these communities has to do with the accentuated use of *nói*. Traits such as [+ rural], caipira (redneck), poorly educated, molecão (immature man) were associated with this variant. However, the usually negative evaluation applied to these characteristics, which are often a source of stereotypes, does not prevent speakers from using the variant and, at times,

---

[14] According to Guy (2001:33), "the speech community is a group of speakers who: share linguistic traits that distinguish this group from others; communicate relatively more with each other than with people outside their community; share norms and attitudes towards the use of language" (Translated from the Portuguese original paper).

expressing explicitly that it is something inherent to their identity. We consider, then, that it would be possible to speak of a situation of *covert prestige* (Trudgill, 1972; Labov, 1972). Studies by Pinto (2019, 2022) have identified a correlation between the *nói* form and younger speakers in the communities. Contrary to the expectation of an increase in the use of *a gente*, the historically innovative form, this group reveals a predominant use of *nói*. The author notes that this form is even more frequent among young males and among those who have not been away from cities to work or study in other locations for a period. These characteristics reinforce our interpretation that the form *nói*, which indicates regionality, would have acquired/ would be acquiring a strongly positive value for the community.

We see, then, that social forces acting on processes of variation (and change), in general, are also essential to understand the specific picture of these two rurban communities – such as schooling, sex/gender, and age. However, precisely the specificities that define the sociodemographic space studied establish particular values for each form in variation, configuring norms of use and practices of interaction between the members of the communities.

Acknowledgments The authors would like to thank the Brazilian Federal Agency for Support and Evaluation of Graduate Education [Coordenação de Aperfeiçoamento de Pessoal de Nível Superior – CAPES – Letícia Gaspar Pinto) and The National Council for Scientific and Technological Development - CNPq (Grant 306464/2019-5 – Rosane Andrade Berlinck).

References

Almeida, N. M. d. (1973). *Gramática metódica da língua portuguesa* (24th ed.). São Paulo: Edição Saraiva.

Benfica, S. d. A. (2013). *Os "nós" da concordância verbal na fala capixaba*. Artigo apresentado como requisito parcial de nota para conclusão de disciplina de Mestrado do Programa de Pós-Graduação em Estudos Linguísticos da Universidade Federal do Espírito Santo.

Bortoni-Ricardo, S. M. (2004). *Educação em língua materna: A Sociolinguística na sala de aula*. São Paulo: Parábola Editorial.

Calvet, L.-J. (2004). *Sociolinguística: uma introdução crítica* (Tradução Marcos Marcionilo). São Paulo: Parábola Editorial.

Coelho, R. F. (2006). *É nóis na fita! Duas variáveis linguísticas na periferia de São Paulo*. (O pronome de primeira pessoa do plural e a marcação do plural no verbo). Dissertação de mestrado. USP.

Duarte, M. E. L. (1995). *A perda do princípio 'Evite pronome' no português brasileiro*. 161 f. Tese (Doutorado em Linguística) – Universidade Estadual de Campinas, Campinas, SP.

Eckert, P. (2008). Variation and the indexical field. *Journal of Sociolinguistics, 12*(4), 453–476.

Faraco, C. A., & Zilles, A. M. S. (2017). *Para conhecer norma linguística*. São Paulo: Contexto.

Foeger, C. C. (2014). *A primeira pessoa do plural no português falado em Santa Leopoldina*. 158 f. Dissertação (Mestrado em Linguística) – Universidade Federal do Espírito Santo, Vitória.

Freitag, R. M. K. (2015). (Re)discutindo sexo/gênero na sociolinguística. In *Mulheres, linguagem e poder*. Estudos de gênero na sociolinguística brasileira, Freitag, Raquel Meister Ko, and Cristine Gorski Severo (orgs.). 17–73. São Paulo: Blucher.

Garcia, B. L. (2018). *Identidade social e atitude linguística*: um estudo da fala de Bonfim Paulista. Dissertação (Mestrado em Linguística e Língua Portuguesa) – Universidade Estadual Paulista "Júlio de Mesquita Filho", Araraquara.

Guy, G. (2001). As comunidades de fala: fronteiras internas e externas. In ABRALIN. Disponível em: https://www.abralin.org/site/wp-content/uploads/2020/03/ABRALIN_26.pdf. Accessed 25 May 2022.

Hora, D. d., & Aquino, M. d. F. d. S. (2012). Da fala para a leitura: análise variacionista. *ALFA: Revista de Linguística, 56*(3).

Instituto Brasileiro de Geografia e Estatística. (2010). Cidades. Disponível em: http://mapasinterativos.ibge.gov.br/sigibge/. Accessed 13 July 2017.

Jekosch, U. (2005). *Voice and speech quality perception. Assessment and Evaluation.* New York: Spring.

Labov, W. (1963). The social motivation of a sound change. *Word, 19, 1–42.*

Labov, W. (1965). Stages in the Acquisition of Standard English. In R. W. Shuy (Ed.), *Social dialects and language learning: Proceedings of the Bloomington, Indiana, conference, 1964* (pp. 77–103). National Council of Teachers of English.

Labov, W. (1972). *Sociolinguistic patterns.* Philadelphia: University of Pennsylvania Press.

Labov, W. (1990). The intersection of sex and social class in the course of linguistic change. *Language Variation and Change, 2*, 205–254.

Labov, W. (1994). *Principles of linguistic change. Vol. 1: Internal factors.* Blackwell Publishers.

Labov, W. (2001). *Principles of linguistic change. Vol. 2: Social factors.* Blackwell Publishers.

Lambert, W. W., & Lambert, W. E. (1972). *Psicologia social* (Vol. 3). Zahar Editores.

Lambert, W. E., et al. (1960). Evaluational reactions to spoken languages. *The Journal of Abnormal and Social Psychology.*, American Psychological Association, 60(1).

Lopes, C. R. d. S.. (1993). *Nós e a gente no português falado culto do Brasil.* Rio de Janeiro. 189 f. Dissertação (Mestrado em Letras Vernáculas) – Faculdade de Letras, Universidade Federal do Rio de Janeiro.

Lopes, C. R. d. S. (2003). *A inserção de "a gente" no quadro pronominal do português.* Frankfurt am Main/Madrid: Vervuert/Iberoamericana.

Lopes, C. R. S. (2007). Pronomes pessoais. In: Vieira, Sílvia Rodrigues, and Brandão, Sílvia Figueiredo (orgs) *Ensino de gramática: descrição e uso. São Paulo: Contexto, p. 103–114.*

Maia, F. P. S. (2003). *A variação "nós" / "a gente" no dialeto mineiro: investigando a transição.* 166 f. Dissertação (Mestrado em Estudos Linguísticos) – Universidade Federal de Minas Gerais, Belo Horizonte.

Mattos, S. E. R. (2013). *Goiás na primeira pessoa do plural.* 137 f. Tese (Doutorado em Linguística) – Universidade de Brasília, Brasília.

Mendes, R. P. S. (2007). *O perfil da alternância do sujeito nós e a gente em Santo Antônio de Jesus:* um recorte no português popular do interior da Bahia. 141 f. Dissertação (Mestrado em Letras e Linguística) – Instituto de Letras, Universidade Federal da Bahia, Salvador.

Mendonça, A. K. d. (2010). *Nós e a gente em Vitória:* uma análise sociolinguística da fala capixaba. Vitória. 100 f. Dissertação (Mestrado em Linguística) – Centro de Ciências Humanas e Naturais, Universidade Federal do Espírito Santo.

Milroy, J. (2001). Language ideologies and the consequences of standardization. *Journal of Sociolinguistics, 5*(4), 530–555.

Ochs, E. (1992). Indexing gender. In A. Duranti & C. Goodwin (Eds.), *Rethinking context: Language as an interactive phenomenon* (pp. 335–358). Cambridge: Cambridge University Press.

Omena, N. P. d. (1986). A referência variável da primeira pessoa do discurso no plural. In A. J. Naro et al. (Eds.), *Relatório final de pesquisa: Projeto Subsídios do Projeto Censo à Educação* (pp. 286–319). UFRJ.

Oushiro, L. (2015). *Identidade na Pluralidade*: Avaliação, produção e percepção linguística na cidade de São Paulo. Tese (Doutorado) – Curso de Letras, Linguística, Universidade de São Paulo, São Paulo.

Oushiro, L. (2019). Conceitos de identidade e métodos para seu estudo na sociolinguística. *In Estudos linguísticos e literários*, 304-325. Salvador, n. 62. Disponível em: https://doi.org/10.9771/ell.v0i63.33777. Accessed 20 July 2020.

Oushiro, L. (2021). Avaliações e percepções sociolinguísticas. In Estudos Linguísticos (São Paulo. 1978), v. 50, n. 1, 318–336. https://doi.org/10.21165/el.v50i1.3100. Disponível em: https://revistas.gel.org.br/estudos-linguisticos/article/view/3100. Accessed 20 September 2021.

Paiva, M. d. C. A. d., & Duarte, M. E. L. (2006). Quarenta anos depois: a herança de um programa na Sociolinguística brasileira. In *Fundamentos empíricos para uma teoria da mudança linguística* (posfácio à edição brasileira), Uriel Weinreich, William Labov, and Marvin I. Herzog, 131–151. São Paulo: Parábola Editorial.

Pinto, L. G. (2019). *A gente vai, nóis vamo, nói vai*: Variação Pronominal e Identidade na região de Muzambinho-MG. Monografia (Trabalho de Conclusão de Curso) – Curso de Letras, Universidade Estadual Paulista Júlio de Mesquita Filho, Araraquara.

Pinto, L. G. (2022). *O que que nói vai fazê cuisso?* Um estudo sobre alternância pronominal e significados sociais em Muzambinho-MG e em Cabo Verde-MG. 160 f. Dissertação (Mestrado em Linguística e Língua Portuguesa) – Faculdade de Ciências e Letras, Universidade Estadual Paulista Júlio de Mesquita Filho, Araraquara.

R Core Team. (2021). 2018. R: A language and environment for statistical computing. In *R Foundation for Statistical Computing*, Vienna, Austria. Disponível em: https://www.R-project.org/

Ribeiro, M. d. P. (2021). lugar. Youtube. Disponível em: https://www.youtube.com/watch?v=rQUnXT066Kc. Accessed 01 December 2021.

Rubio, C. F.. (2012). *Padrões de concordância verbal e de alternância pronominal no português brasileiro e europeu*: estudo sociolinguístico comparativo. Tese (Doutorado em Estudos Linguísticos) – Instituto de Biociências, Letras e Ciências Exatas, Universidade Estadual Paulista "Júlio de Mesquita Filho", São José do Rio Preto.

Sene, M. G. (2019). Percepções sociolinguísticas, avaliações subjetivas e atitudes linguísticas: três domínios complementares. In *Revista todas as letras* (MACKENZIE. Online), v. 21, 304–323.

Silverstein, M. (2003). Indexical order and dialectics of sociolinguistic life. In *Language & communication*, 193–229, University of Chicago, n. 23.

Trudgill, P. (1972). Sex, covert prestige and linguistic change in the urban British English of Norwich. *Language in Society, 1*(2), 179–195.

Veiga, J. E. d. (2004). A relação rural-urbano no desenvolvimento regional. In *Anais do II Seminário Internacional sobre Desenvolvimento Regional*. Santa Cruz do Sul, RS.

Vianna, J. S., & Lopes, C. R. d. S. (2015). Variação dos Pronomes "NÓS" e "A GENTE". In: Martins, Marco Antônio; Abraçado, Jussara. *Mapeamento sociolinguístico do português brasileiro*. São Paulo: Contexto, p. 109–132.

Weinreich, U., Labov, W., & Herzog, M. I. (1968). Empirical foundations for a theory of language change. In W. P. Lehmann & Y. Malkiel (Eds.), *Directions for historical linguistics* (pp. 95–195). University of Texas Press.

Zilles, A. M. S. (2002). Grammaticalization of 'a gente' in Brazilian Portuguese. *University of Pennsylvania Working Papers in Linguistics, 8*(3), 297–310.

Zilles, A. M. S. (2005). The development of a new pronoun: The linguistic and social embedding of a gente in Brazilian Portuguese. *Language Variation and Change, 17*(1), 19–53.

Chapter 9
Approaching Gender and Sexuality Issues from a Sociolinguist Corpus-Based Analysis: A Methodologic Challenge

Angélica Rodrigues ⓘ, Camila Bordonal Clempi ⓘ, and Rafael de Almeida Arruda Felix ⓘ

Introduction

Sociolinguistics has been developing as a theoretical model of linguistic analysis that, from the founding works of Weinreich et al. (1968) and Labov (1972), in the 1960s, changed how we understand the relationship between language and society and designed a methodology that allowed us to analyze language as a heterogeneous entity. This theoretical and methodological model is based on the idea that the heterogeneity of the language is ordered, that is, it is not random but regulated by a set of factors that lead to the process of variation and/or linguistic change inherent in the linguistic system (Weinreich et al., 1968).

The verification and interpretation of variable phenomena, in this perspective, assume the apprehension not only of linguistic aspects (at the phonetic-phonological, morphosyntactic, semantic-discursive levels) but also of extralinguistic aspects (macro- and microsociological categories), to the extent that they can jointly condition the favoring or restraining of a change. In other words, Weinreich et al. (1968) postulate that the analysis of linguistic heterogeneity should consider that "linguistic and social factors are closely interrelated in the development of language change" (Weinreich et al., 1968:188).

A method that allows us to verify how different groups of speakers use the language is the analysis of independent variables, or groups of factors, which are the linguistic or extralinguistic contextual aspects that shape, influence, and motivate the occurrence of one variant instead of others, which are semantically and functionally equivalent. Among the linguistic factors, Tagliamonte (2006) states that each group of factors should be discussed based on the hypothesis that it would, in fact, influence the way people speak. Concerning the groups of extralinguistic factors, since the initial research carried out by Labov (1972), it is possible to observe

A. Rodrigues (✉) · C. B. Clempi · Rafael de Almeida Arruda Felix
Unesp Sao Paulo State University, Araraquara, Sao Paulo, Brazil
e-mail: angelica.rodrigues@unesp.br; camila.clempi@unesp.br; rafael.felix@unesp.br

© The Author(s), under exclusive license to Springer Nature Switzerland AG 2023
G. Massini-Cagliari et al. (eds.), *Understanding Linguistic Prejudice*,
https://doi.org/10.1007/978-3-031-25806-0_9

a refinement of the social variables, with macrosocial factors such as age, education level, and sex/gender being traditionally analyzed (Eckert, 2012).

The variable "sex/gender," however, is treated as a synonym for biological sex. Eckert and MacConnell-Ginet (1992) discuss this essentialist view on sex and gender within sociolinguistics, stating that notions such as "women" and "men" are frequently taken for granted in sociolinguistics, as a result of frequent abstraction from stereotypical views on what it is like to be a "man" and a "woman" and the social practices associated with them and, consequently, from the little theorization regarding this social category in the analysis of variable phenomena. For the authors:

> Abstracting gender and language from the social practices that produce their particular forms in given communities often obscures and sometimes distorts the ways they connect and how those connections are implicated in power relations, in social conflict, in the production and reproduction of values and plans. (Eckert & MacConnell-Ginet, 1992:1–2)

According to Bucholtz (2002), in order to understand gender identities in their entirety, it is not enough to consider only "gender" or only the relationship between "gender" and "sex," because gender theories are often underlain by sexuality theories. According to Bucholtz (2002, p. 35), "like gender, sexuality underlies a great deal of what has been labeled 'sex' in variationist sociolinguistics."

Based on the results of analyses concerning the role of the female gender in the implementation of the periphrastic future in Brazilian Portuguese, and the use of superlatives by gay men, this chapter aims to discuss methodological aspects related to the sex/gender and sexuality factors. We emphasize that the adoption of a social perspective of gender leads to the inclusion of not only other groups of social factors, but it also, and mainly, requires a socially sensitive choice of the research corpus. We also reinforce that the stratification of speakers based on their sexualities makes it possible to perform an analysis that goes beyond the stereotypes of identities that are, in fact, so diverse.

The chapter is organized as follows: in section "Social Variables Related to Gender and Sexuality", we briefly review the history of sociolinguistics and discuss how "gender" and sexuality are understood in variationist research; in section "Including Gender and Sexuality in Methodological Alignment", we consider and detail research on the implementation of the periphrastic future in BP (Clempi, 2019) and on the use of the superlative adjectives as a possible index of *gay* identity (Felix, 2016), highlighting their proposals to address notions of gender and sexuality; in section "Gender and Sexuality Issues in Sociolinguistics", we present a reflection on how existing spoken linguistic databases in Brazil consider only the biological sex of speakers disregarding their sexualities; and we also offer contributions so that research which focuses on gender and sexuality can obtain broader and more reliable data and results, addressing linguistic heterogeneity with greater care.

Social Variables Related to Gender and Sexuality

One of the social variables traditionally considered in sociolinguistic studies as underpinning variation/change is gender, also referred to as sex, sex/gender, and gender/sex. Unlike other categories of analysis, the operationalization and analysis of gender have mostly been done without entailing the accommodation of social theories. This lack of theorization has resulted in excessive abstraction and consequently led to interpreting gender through an essentialist perspective (Eckert & MacConnell-Ginet, 1992; Bucholtz, 2002; Wodak & Bank, 2017).

On the one hand, second- and third-wave sociolinguistic studies[1] have changed the entire view of the relation between language and society; have proposed a model of analysis focused, respectively, on locally defined speech communities and on relations between structure and practice, as stated by Eckert (2012); and, thus, have verified gender either as a category [+abstract], within a specific social context, or as a result of social engagements in interaction practices. On the other hand, Brazilian sociolinguistics has developed, as pointed out by Freitag, Martins, and Tavares (2012, p. 926), mostly from the first-wave approach.

We emphasize that, according to Eckert (2012), the first-wave studies are responsible for defining the methodological basis for the study of variation, showing the correlations between linguistic variables and social categories, such as socioeconomic class, gender, age, etc., in which the speech style is analyzed according to the prestige/stigma traits. According to Eckert (2012:90):

> [...] Studies in the first wave interpreted the social significance of variation on the basis of a general understanding of the categories that served to select and classify speakers rather than through direct knowledge of the speakers themselves and their communities.

First-wave sociolinguistic studies developed in Brazil often make use of databases based on broad sociodemographic categories (age, education, and sex/gender), aiming at verifying general trends of speech communities (Freitag et al., 2012). In our understanding, the constitution of databases of Brazilian Portuguese speech is one of the aspects that collaborate so that the control of the variable sex/gender is, generally, done without a theoretical discussion of gender being taken into account. The question that arises in face of the first-wave sociolinguistic research supported by databases is that the stratification of the informants, besides being based on biological sex (given category), does not consider the intersection with other social variables, which are so important for the understanding of gender, such as ethnicity and sexuality.

In this matter, Freitag (2015:46, our translation) argues that:

> Because it is the default stratification of sociolinguistic databases, controlling the variable sex/gender is a formality; having or not a hypothesis of its effect on the phenomenon, there

---

[1] Sociolinguistic waves represent, as proposed by Eckert (2012), distinct (and coexisting) trends in the analysis of the social context of linguistic variation.

is no operational effort in adding it in the analysis, since its characterization is ready-made and doesn't require analytical thinking by the researcher.[2]

We can cite as examples the studies on the variable future (synthetic future and periphrastic future) in Brazilian Portuguese, from databases that control the sex of informants in female/male, namely, Projeto Varsul (Variação Linguística na Região Sul do Brasil), with the study of Gibbon (2000), and Projeto NURC (Norma Urbana Culta), with the study of Oliveira (2006). Gibbon (2000) and Oliveira (2006) reach similar conclusions regarding the conditioning of the female gender in the implementation of the innovative variant of future (periphrastic future). The authors' results point to female leadership in linguistic change, and their interpretations are grounded in Labov's (1990, 2001) gender paradox:

(i) "For stable sociolinguistic variables, women show a lower rate of stigmatized variants and a higher rate of prestige variants than men" (Labov, 2001:266).
(ii) "In linguistic change from above, women adopt prestige forms at a higher rate than men" (Labov, 2001:274).
(iii) "In linguistic change from below, women use higher frequencies of innovative forms than men do" (Labov, 2001:292).

The conclusions of Gibbon (2000) and Oliveira (2006) fit into principle (iii). Regarding the social role played by women in the conditioning of the innovative variant (periphrastic future), interpretations may often fall into a stereotypical view, based on common-sense, without taking into account the specific social context of the speech communities investigated and of a hypothesis about the general social context. The authors explain in similar terms that linguistic innovation, in general, may be related to the new social position women have achieved in society. Within a specific social theory, this issue can be addressed and analyzed, since this interpretation is valid only for a class of women, which means that understanding the role of women as workforce is complex, as hooks (2000, p. 49) points out: "work would not necessarily liberate us" [women], because "this fact does not change the reality that economic self-sufficiency is needed if women are to be liberated."

These aspects, therefore, contribute to the fact that hypotheses are not formed a priori and that the results are analyzed through decontextualized interpretations of the linguistic behavior of men and women, for example. In this perspective, we agree with Wodak and Bank (2017, n. p.) in the sense that "studies of gender-specific variation are often contradictory, depending on the author's implicit assumptions about sex and gender, the methodology, the samples used, etc."

This issue reveals that, although the theoretical and methodological assumptions of sociolinguistics consider linguistic heterogeneity, when it comes to the factor sex/gender, the diversity of women and men (black men and women, indigenous

---

[2] "Por ser estratificação default nos bancos de dados sociolinguísticos, controlar a variável sexo/gênero é uma praxe; tendo ou não uma hipótese do seu efeito sobre o fenômeno, não há custo operacional em incluí-la na análise, na medida que a categorização já vem pronta, sem requerer reflexões analíticas do pesquisador" (Freitag, 2015:46).

people, LGBTQIA+, people with disability, etc.) is not part of the agenda of the first researches of Labovian sociolinguistics. Eckert and MacConnell-Ginet (1992) point to the fact that many research studies, by using some women and some men, mostly white, present the data analysis in such a way that the linguistic usages seem to represent everyone. Generalizing the results, in cases like these, can be controversial. The discussion and problematization of gender and sexuality as complex social variables in the conditioning of language change, therefore, remain far from being addressed based on a critical approach.

Bucholtz (2002) states that for us to understand gender identities in all their full complexity, it is not only necessary to take into account gender or its relation with sex but also a third factor which is directly implicated in the various gender performances: sexuality. The author uses a text by Milroy (1992) that carries important ideological information about gender and sexuality:

> Burchfield (1981) reports difficulties experienced by the BBC in persuading regional radio stations in the UK to adopt the high-status accent known as RP; he quotes a Radio Carlisle spokesman as replying, "If we pronounced everything in the way suggested-here our northern listeners would feel we're a bunch of poofters." (Burchfield 1981:7) (Milroy, 1992 *apud* Bucholtz, 2002, p. 36)

Bucholtz (2002) asserts that comments of this nature indicate that sexuality, very strongly linked to gender, deserves further investigation as a sociolinguistic variable, since social meanings based on different ideologies of sexuality are attributed to the linguistic use of each gender. Furthermore, the author states that sexuality includes, in addition to sexual orientation, defined by the gender to which a person feels sexually attracted to, an orientation to sexuality, which would be a compilation of sexual and sexualized practices and ideologies that shape the interactions of everyday life. Such discussion is inscribed in sociolinguistic studies of the third wave, which focus on this stylistic practice and shift the place the speaker, who is no longer seen as a stable and passive carrier of the language that adapts her/his speech according to the formality of the situation, but as a stylistic agent, which continuously combines styles to create her/his identity (Eckert, 2012).

It is important to remember that Bucholtz (2002) does not deny the importance and use of concepts of sex, gender, and sexuality. What she proposes, however, is a renewal of the existing conflicting theories of definition for sex and gender and the implementation of the concept of sexuality in the variationist research. The author further explains that these connections and differentiations between the terms sex, gender, and sexuality show that all these dimensions must be carefully considered in any sociolinguistic study involving any of them.

However, including these dimensions in sociolinguistic research implies taking on the challenges faced by the operationalization and analysis of gender and sexuality along the lines of sociolinguistic research, such as collecting speech data with stratification of informants according to social categories that intersect with gender and sexuality or the recovery of the informant's social profile in past written data. The researcher who sets out to consider these variables, therefore, needs to make methodological decisions, especially with regard to the corpus of analysis, since, as we have pointed out, Brazilian databases only control broad sociodemographic categories. Thus, research by Clempi (2019) and Felix (2016) presents methodological alternatives (Sections "Approaching Gender Issues: The Woman's Role in the Implementation of Periphrastic Future in Brazilian Portuguese" and "Approaching Sexuality Issues: The Superlative of Adjectives in the Speech of Gay Men in Brazilian Portuguese") to show how taking gender and sexuality theories into account can enable data analysis from a [+social] and [−biological] perspective.

Including Gender and Sexuality in Methodological Alignment

Approaching Gender Issues: The Woman's Role in the Implementation of Periphrastic Future in Brazilian Portuguese

From the discussions in (2), we infer that the analysis of the sex/gender variable as a conditioning factor of linguistic variation and change is mostly carried out in Brazilian sociolinguistics far from a social theory, without raising the crossing of social, cultural, and historical issues in the constitution of gender (being a woman/ being a man as a performance).

In diachronic studies, which focus on the language's past, the challenge can be even greater, as the available written texts do not provide reliable information about authorship and, consequently, about the information of the informants' social profiles. As stated by Auer et al. (2015), the produced written texts of past synchronies are usually attributed to literate white men from the upper classes of society. Clempi (2019) and Clempi and Rodrigues (2020) address this issue by showing that the gender category, focusing on the role of the female gender in linguistic change, needs to be considered in view of the role of women in society even in historical analysis. In this sense, the authors propose to analyze how we can attest, as foreseen in the gender paradox, the role of women in the implementation of the periphrastic future in Brazilian Portuguese from a diachronic study, based on written data. The great challenge, according to the authors, is to determine a control method for the analysis of this extralinguistic variable in writing, since the main sources of historical data (newspapers and official documents) are written by male authors.

Referring to the bases of sociolinguistic research and the hypothesis about the role of women in the implementation of an innovative variant, Clempi (2019) starts from an investigation of the conditioning of the female gender variable in the process of linguistic change of the future (synthetic future > periphrastic future) in written Brazilian Portuguese in two time periods (1920s and early 1970s). The following examples, transcribed as shown in the samples, illustrate the dependent variable and the *corpora* used:

(a) Synthetic futures (conservative variant):

(01) *Se porventura conheces alguem capaz de affirmar ter eu amado sinceramente,*
If you happen to know someone capable of claiming to have loved me sincerely,

   *escreva-me e eu te **responderei**,*
                  [ANSWER-FUT-1SING]
   write to me and I **will answer** you,

   provando que as settas de Cupido ainda não feriram o coração desta tua amiguinha
   proving that Cupid's arrows have not yet wounded the heart of this little friend of yours.

   (*A Cigarra*, June, 1920).

(02) [...] *alludindo o assumpto que ora occupa a imprensa do Rio,*
   [...] alluding to the issue that now occupies the press in Rio,

   inseriu "A Gazeta", ha dias, o seguinte topico:
   inserted "A Gazeta", a few days ago, the following topic:

   *"Trata-se de saber quaes **serão** os resultados da "medida aventada*
                       [TO-BE-FUT-3PL]
   "It is about knowing what   **will be** the results of the "measure proposed

   no Congresso Nacional de Educação" sobre o celibato compulsorio das professoras"
   in the National Congress of Education" on the compulsory celibacy of teachers"

   (*A Gazeta*, February, 1928).

(b)Periphrastic future (innovative variant):

(03) *[...] você nunca mais   **vai**   **conseguir** uma hora vaga*
                  [GO-PRES-2SING   GET-INF.]
   [...] you **will** never **find** spare time

   para fazer a música que você tanto ama.
   to make the music you love so much.

   (*A Cigarra*, July 1970).

(04) *A letra do Hino do Congresso foi escolhida mediante concurso [...] e foi ganho por uma*
   The lyrics of the Congress Anthem was chosen through a contest [...] and was won by a

   *senhora residente em Minas Gerais que **vai receber** um prêmio de mil cruzeiros novos*
                       [GO-PRES-3SING   RECEIVE-INF.]
   lady residing in Minas Gerais who   **will receive**   a prize of one thousand new cruzeiros.

   (*Correio da Manhã*, March, 1970).

The author collected her data from letters which were published in the magazine *A Cigarra* (female audience). The results are interpreted based on the comparison and data confrontation with data extracted from readers' letters from the newspapers *A Gazeta* and *Correio da Manhã*, which was assigned as the "control group," as they represent a broader set of readers, not genderly specified.[3]

Although it is a common practice to stratify the sex/gender of each informant in sociolinguistics, one of the major questions in the research carried out by Clempi (2019) is, therefore, dealing with texts in which the authorship is not attested. Clempi (2019) adopts, in this sense, gender as a performance, that is, as a representation of a socially diffused image (Butler, 1999), and assumes that working with texts written in women's magazines can be favorable to this type of (socio)linguistic analysis.

Women's magazines, at different time periods, accommodate practices and roles considered feminine, in a model that creates and standardizes identifications of femininities. We have not lost sight of the fact that the press which targets women builds the image of its readership based on a hegemonic pattern and represents the image of women based on stereotypes of an era. In this perspective, Buitoni (1981, p. 142) states that "[t]he white, smiling woman is the label and brand of a product called the female press" (Buitoni, 1981:142, our translation) and points out that "[f]rom paper to paper, the Brazilian female press collaborates for the mystification of the female being, helping to maintain standards" (Buitoni, 1981:144, our translation).

Therefore, we can assume that the publications are not necessarily written by women, but represent and reproduce society's interpretations of what it is like to be a woman and womanhood in general. Authorship, in these cases, does not need to be attested, since the letters reveal writing related to a gender (female). In addition, even though it represents a particular woman (white, from higher socioeconomic classes), working with the written text, more specifically with the written text chosen for the constitution of the research *corpora*, can be favorable to the treatment of the gender variable, in view of the more marked elaboration and conception of this social category in the written modality of the language than the work with sociolinguistic speech databases. The discussions made by Clempi (2019), in this way, were only made possible due to the constitution of *corpora*, since they consider a sample which is sensitive to social gender matters.

Following this methodological proposal, the results of the study, based on 1105 tokens – *A Cigarra* (621 occurrences: 490 tokens from the synthetic future and 131 tokens from the periphrastic future) versus control group (484 occurrences: 426 tokens from the synthetic future and 58 tokens from the periphrastic future) – are presented in Fig. 9.1, generated from non-parametric regression calculations with the help of R (R Core Team, 2021):

---

[3] Clempi (2019) maintains that the newspaper has men as target readers in the sense that they published alleged manly oriented content, like economy and politics.

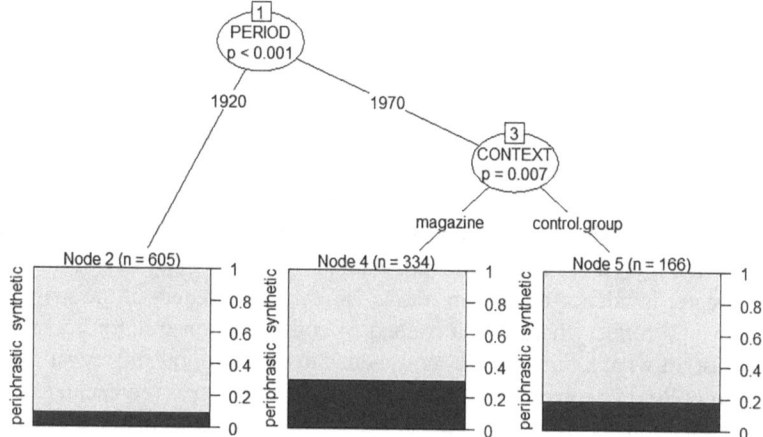

Fig. 9.1 Significance of the variables "period" and "context" in the use of the periphrastic future

From the diagram, we can see the statistical significance and the way in which the independent variables (period and context) act simultaneously with the dependent variable (synthetic and periphrastic future). The branches represent lower p-value numbers (p below 0.05) obtained by the set of variables. The first segmentation node refers to the period of 1920, with 605 occurrences (58 data from the innovative variant in *corpora*, corresponding to 9.6% of the general data of this time period). The second node refers to the 1970s period, which segments the context ($p = 0.007$): magazine (node = 334, with 32% of PF data) and control group (newspaper) (node = 166, with 18% of PF usage).

The results, therefore, point to a greater significance of the use of the periphrastic future variant in the 1970s in the *corpus* of *A Cigarra*. The study by Clempi (2019) corroborates the Labovian hypothesis (Labov, 2001) that in changes without social awareness (*changes from below*), women use innovative ways more often than men, showing innovative behavior, and are less conformist (*nonconforming*) with norms that are not openly prescribed.

Furthermore, the analysis based on gender (female) performance allows new discussions regarding the role of this variable in linguistic change. Clempi (2019), thus, mobilizes other aspects that may be involved and intertwined with the greater use of the innovative variant (periphrastic future) in the data from the *A Cigarra* sample (female audience). The stylistic dimension of the letters, for example, is taken into account in the explanation and interpretation of the results, considering that the set of factors that combine in the configuration of the magazine's texts can act in the choice of the innovative variant.

Clempi (2019) verifies that the linguistic and social approach established by the magazine, whose proposal is to establish a relationship of friendship with the target audience, supports the formation of the readers' identity and corroborates a certain performance of the female gender. The opposite is observed in the control group (letters from the newspapers *A Gazeta* and *Correio da Manhã*), in which there is a greater social distance between newspaper readers and a greater degree of formality in writing. The author, in this sense, verifies that readers' letters, which reveal greater intimacy and less formality, as is the case of themes related to personal drama, frequent in the *A Cigarra corpus*, can promote linguistic innovation.

In general, Clempi (2019) analyzes that the meaning that the readers' letters in *A Cigarra* manifest in the historical context, through the magazine-readers interaction, is an important mechanism of social practice. This includes, then, a more frequent and relevant use of the periphrastic future when compared to the letters of the control group, more resistant to ongoing change.

The greater incidence of the innovative variant in the letters of the magazine *A Cigarra* would reflect, therefore, a context of collective construction (consciously made or not) of what feminine identity is, added to the temporal and stylistic dimensions. This collective construction, however, cannot be taken as representative of the female gender, since the profile of women's magazine readers, in general, points to the identification of white and middle-class women, whose interests are understood to be restricted to themes related to personal care and romantic-love relationships. Clempi (2019) contrasts this profile of the magazine, including the possible readers and authors of the letters and the illustrated female identity itself with the profile of the newspaper, in which the possible readers and authors of the letters are identified in the absence of an orientation to gender, that could mark a certain neutrality, if that would not constitute anything but a patriarchal falsehood. The author, thus, offers new discussions regarding the effects of the gender variable on linguistic change in written texts in Brazilian Portuguese, showing how the adoption of a social gender perspective can allow an interpretation of the results beyond the scope of the gender paradox.

Approaching Sexuality Issues: The Superlative of Adjectives in the Speech of Gay Men in Brazilian Portuguese

Felix (2016) developed his research based on the observation that the usage of the superlative in the Brazilian Portuguese could be associated with the speech of gay men. In Portuguese, superlatives can be analytical and synthetic. Analytical superlatives are formed with the use of other intensification words (such as an adverb) as in "o mais bonito" (the most beautiful). Synthetic superlatives are formed with the addition of a superlative suffix, which can be "-íssimo" as in "belíssimo" (very beautiful), "-érrimo" as in "chiquérrimo" (very fancy), and the most colloquial one "-ésimo" as in "elegantésimo" (very elegant). Felix (2016) focused mainly on the ones formed by the suffixes -érrimo(a) and -ésimo(a). Such observation was made possible after searching the terms "superlative gay" on *Google*. The first two entries presented a list with ten tips to discover if a man is gay and the first item of the list was the use of synthetic superlatives:

(5) "Usa superlativo sintético. Homem de verdade não fala
    He uses synthetic superlatives. A real man doesn't say:

    "isso está **chiquérrimo**",   "estou **atrasadíssimo**"
    "this is a way sophisticated",   "I'm unbelievable late"

    "que **caríssimo**",   "você está **lindérrima**"
    "that's super expensive",   "you're very beautiful".

    Se o cara que você quer usa essas expressões, caia fora amiga! Esse pitbull é Lessie!"
    If the guy you are into uses these expressions, run away. This Pitbull is Lassie.

    (Felix, 2016:4)

Even though this allegedly funny text is filled with prejudice and homophobia, it is evident that, at that time, the use of adjectives in the synthetic superlative was not socially associated with the speech of "real men," that is, heterosexual men, and therefore being a characteristic of the speech of gay men. A more academic evidence of the association of the use of superlative with gay man can be found in the study conducted by Gonçalves (2003) which also signals that the use of synthetic superlatives might be linked with a flamboyant speech generally used by gay men and avoided by heterosexual ones. The author describes a conversation he eavesdropped in a bar. He describes that there were only men sitting at the table and that they were talking about a gay man they knew. In a certain point of the conversation, the author transcribes what one of them said about the gay man stressing his gayness and queerness:

(6) "O cara né, gozadão... Nem um pouco discreto... O cara vive soltando a franga.
    The guy, right, funny guy... Not at all discreet... The guy is always letting loose.

    Lá na faculdade, ele vai todo afetado dizendo pras meninas: (mudança de voz com trejeitos)
    At college, he goes all affected saying to the girls: (voice change with grimaces)

    —aí eu cheguei ar-ra-san-do, de salto,
    " —then I arrived ar-ra- san-do (killing it), in heels,

    chiquésima, elegantérrima, ma-ra-vi-lho-sa! (risos)"
    very chic, very elegant, gor-geous!! (laughs)"

    (Gonçalves, 2003:54).

It is clear by this quote that when describing the gay man's speech, the straight man used the intensifying suffixes "-ésimo" and "-érrimo," two ways to form the synthetic superlative in Portuguese, reinforcing the idea that these constructions might be used more frequently by gay men. Based on this stereotypical assumption that gay men tend to use synthetic superlatives very frequently, Felix (2016) aimed at systematically analyzing this phenomenon by the use of corpora based on sociolinguistic interviews.

Considering, therefore, this alleged use of superlatives by men, Felix (2016), when proposing to analyze these uses from speech samples, reports a difficulty in selecting a speech database, because despite the existence of several databases of Brazilian Portuguese speech data that enabled numerous sociolinguistic research in the country, none of them has controlled gender and all its possibilities or the sexuality of the speakers as a methodology. In the databases of the NURC project (Norma Linguística Urbana Culta), PEUL (Programa de Estudos sobre o Uso da Língua), and ALIP (Amostra Linguística do Interior Paulista), for example, informants are divided into "man" and "woman," disregarding all the intersectionalities which are intrinsic to the term "gender" and the sexuality of the speakers. Because of this, the author organized and collected a sample which would meet the needs of the research, which aimed to analyze the speech of openly gay men.

For the elaboration of the research database, Felix (2016) followed the basic methodological precepts of Labovian sociolinguistics. However, as it is a set of interviews that document the speech of gay men, "sex" was not a variable. Felix (2016) aimed at analyzing speech samples from 24 sociolinguistic interviews carried out with gay men in the city of Ribeirão Preto, in the countryside of the State of São Paulo, in order to check the frequency of the use of adjectives with superlative derivation and the possible linguistics and extralinguistics factors that could be associated with the use of these forms. Considering the examples mentioned above and the preliminary results, Felix (2016) hypothesized that, as it is a highly stigmatized and stereotyped linguistic form, the use of the superlative would also be related to questions of identity and style. Since, as previously exemplified, heterosexual men avoid the use of this derivation because they associate it with the speech of gay men and that, in the words of Thorne and Henley (1975:115 *apud* Gonçalves, 2003:52), this gay way of talking is characterized by an exaggerated approach to what is socially perceived as being feminine, the author sought to compare the data from the sample of gay speakers with speech data from men and women, resorting to Brazilian Portuguese speech databases previously compiled by other researchers, in this case, the database developed by the Iboruna/ALIP Project (Gonçalves, 2007).

Felix (2016) states that the negative methodological effect of this procedure is that this database selected its informants considering only sex; therefore, it is not possible to access information about gender, gender identity, and sexuality of these informants. Despite recognizing that the effect of comparing the data of the sample of speech of gay men, which was organized by Felix (2016), and those of the Iboruna Project is not completely reliable with regard to the contrast between the speech of homosexuals and heterosexuals, the author chose to carry out this procedure, mainly because it would be very difficult to draw conclusions about the frequency of use and linguistic and extralinguistic factors without considering a "control" group. Thus, Felix (2016) also analyzed 24 interviews with men and 24 interviews with women, taken from the Iboruna database, in order to verify whether the results obtained from the speech sample of men who self-identified as gay contrasted in some aspect with the speech sample of men and women who were not selected considering their sexual orientation and/or gender identity.

Felix (2016) analyzed 5972 adjectives that appeared in both databases, the ones recorded by the author and the ones originating from the Iboruna database, using the Goldvarb program. Adjectives with neutral degree; superlatives in "-issimo," "-érrimo," and "-ésimo"; and also adjectives with diminutive and augmentative suffixes were considered, since they also intensify the idea expressed by the adjective either for less or for more. The results are shown in Fig. 9.2:

Felix (2016) infers from the data that when we look only at those referring to the speech of gay men, it doesn't seem to express a frequency of use so high as to characterize the speech of this group. However, when compared with data from the control group, the results may indeed indicate the existence of a trend toward greater use of the synthetic absolute superlative by gay men. On the other hand, Felix (2016) affirms that we cannot state that the use of adjectives in this derivation is in fact an indexing feature of gay speech just from these results, even with such high amount of data. There are many factors which may have motivated the low frequency of the use of superlatives, such as their frequent association with the speech of effeminate gay men and the strong homophobia still present in the country. It should also be noted that the performance of effeminate gay is also very strongly repressed within the gay community itself, as pointed out by Nogueira (2011), who, when analyzing 50 profiles of men looking for sex with other men on the website *disponivel.com*, states that most of the profiles explicitly stated their lack of interest in effeminate gays.

To complete his analysis, while collecting data for his database, Felix (2016) also conducted a semi-structured interview with the informants based on the following question: "What is your opinion about the gay characters that appear in soap operas, magazines, the media in general?", intending to verify the degree of empathy of the speakers toward the stereotypical image of gay men and, consequently, to verify if the speaker intended to approach this image in order to affirm his identity as gay or to move away from it in order to deny or, at least, conceal it. The answers obtained were varied, but in general all the informants agreed on the same point: the

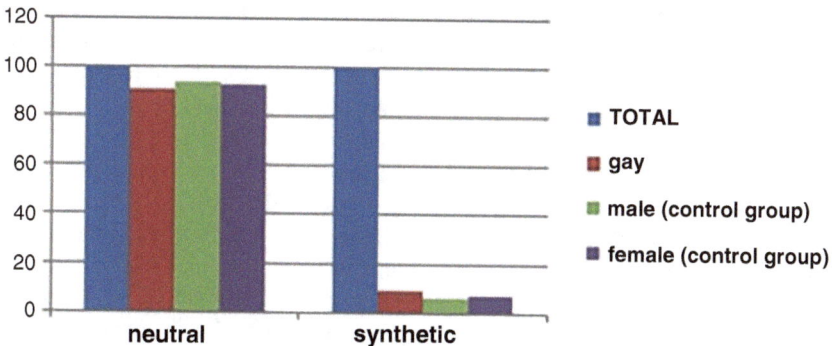

Fig. 9.2 Frequency of neutral and superlative adjectives in interviews with gay men versus control group. (*In*: (Felix, 2016, p. 61))

characters are too effeminate. The judgment made by each speaker interviewed, however, of this effeminacy was also quite varied. Informant G1, for example, states that:

(7) whenever they bring the homosexual he is very effeminate, right? In these programs. He is very effeminate, he has some jargon.. as if it were like that... in general, right for everyone and I don't find it interesting because... [...] I believe that making the homosexual issue a funny thing or is it... that you can make a joke is a way of reducing the situation of the homosexual person to a joke, right? So it's not credible, right? (G1) (Felix, 2016:64, own translation)

This informant, therefore, fears that this "effeminate" view of gays will discredit their voices and reduce them to a joke. Therefore, for him, this representation of gay men is perceived to be negative, which could motivate him to want to escape this stereotype. Felix (2016) highlights that in the speech of this informant, no adjective with a synthetic absolute superlative degree was used.

Informant G2, on the other hand, states that:

(8) A lot of people must think it's stereotyped, I think it's real [...] I don't really give a fuck to this cisgender gays who are like "oh but I'm not a fag like that" it's your loss, babe you... you got fucked you could have been born cooler you know. (G2) (Felix, 2016:64, own translation)

Unlike G1, this informant negatively evaluates the "cisgender queers" who criticize the representations of effeminate gay men. Felix (2016) reinforces that throughout the interview, G2 reinforces his sexuality quite frequently. It was also in this interview in which the informant used a greater number of adjectives with synthetic absolute superlative degree derivation in "-íssimo," "-érrimo," and "-ésimo," which are the intensification suffixes more associated with the speech of gay men; he did it 19 times from a total of 84 total uses by all the 24 openly gay men who were interviewed. It means that this speaker alone was responsible for more than 22% of the total uses of the superlatives derived in "-íssimo," "-érrimo," and "-ésimo," way above the average of uses of the other speakers. Felix (2016) believes that if the speaker intends to make his sexual orientation explicit, it seems natural that he will use the so-called marked or stigmatized forms linked to this group more often than the one who prefers not to make this characteristic explicit.

In other words, it is clear that the interpretation of these results depends on a wide range of factors. Nevertheless, it is evident that Felix's (2016) research shows that all these results were only found and could only be analyzed because the speakers were stratified taking the variable "sexuality" into account. It is important to emphasize that the objective of Felix's (2016) research was not to describe a single gay speech, since within the "gay man" subgroup of the LGBTQIA+ community there are several identities and ways of speaking. According to Campbell-Kibler et al. (2001:177), "the assumption that there is a singular gay way of speaking homogenizes the diversity within the gay community, erasing or at least deeming unimportant to sociolinguistic inquiry the many subcultures comprising the community."

Finally, a more complete description of Brazilian Portuguese and the nuances which are intrinsic to the variables gender and sexuality will only be possible when these variables are actually included in the methodological processes of stratification of speakers in sociolinguistic research.

Gender and Sexuality Issues in Sociolinguistics

Disregarding social theories about gender and sexuality contributes to the fact that stereotypes and generalizing explanations permeate sociolinguistic analysis. In this chapter, therefore, we bring to light the analyses of different texts, written and spoken, in a diachronic and synchronic perspective, based on Clempi (2019) and Felix (2016), which show us that the constitution of data samples focused on social aspects of the variables gender and sexuality can help in the operationalization and analysis of social factors conditioning the variation and linguistic change.

Clempi (2019) demonstrates how it is possible to work with written texts of past synchronicities, with the absence of information from the social profiles of each writer, and, even so, test the influence of the gender role, through a critical and social and *corpora* approach which is sensitive to gender issues. The author, in addition, draws attention to the fact that a social perspective of gender allows us to have a broader view of linguistic change.

Sex/gender analysis based on traditional principles and explanations, based, for example, on trends pointed out by first-wave sociolinguistic studies, results in the reduction of women into a single profile. The analysis that takes a social perspective into account, on the other hand, highlights that the results point to only a portion of women, mainly white and cisgender, a representation that does not cover the broader concept of womanhood. Clempi (2019) shows, from her results, that although there is a tendency for women to lead the implementation of the periphrastic future, this is a specific group of women, given that the women's magazine is made for a specific profile – white, from higher social status, with reading and writing power – in addition to limiting that audience to specific themes, allegedly described as "feminine" themes. To this extent, the sociolinguistic verification of gender as a category based on social theories helps the analyses perceive women as a diverse group of speakers and also avoids stereotypes, not considering them as an explanation of change by themselves.

In Felix (2016), on the other hand, the author problematizes that no database until the time of publication had stratified speakers based on their sexuality and that, therefore, we did not have a representative analysis of the diversity of speeches of different types of speakers. Felix (2016) also demonstrates, through the work of Gonçalves (2003), that a stratification based solely on the essentialist notion of "sex" as "biological sex" is not enough for a more complete analysis, since within a single group, for example, of "masculine," speakers demonstrate differences in linguistic usages and choices based on performativity and social practices arising from what they believe to be masculine. Gay men are still men, belonging to the masculine gender, but it is clear from Gonçalves (2003) and from Felix's own work (2016) that straight and gay men can and do use language in different ways. In line with the works of the third wave of linguistic studies, Felix (2016) cites Queen (2014) who affirms that:

> the theoretical position of identity has been replaced by the more fluid concepts of stance, style, and personae. These concepts are meant to capture the inherent instability in any presentation of a social self and to capture more robustly the nature of intraspeaker variability rather than focusing centrally on interspeaker variability. (Queen, 2014:207)

Felix (2016) defends, therefore, the need to consider "sexuality" and "gender identity" as a group of factors when defining speech data collection, since there is not only one gay speech model but as many "gay speeches" as there are speakers.

According to Bucholtz (2002):

> as we shift our focus from sex differences to the whole range of phenomena captured by the term gender variation, we engage with issues of style and ideology, social practice and performance, that contributed distinctively linguistic perspective to the analysis of the diversity and complexity of the social world, thereby setting the entire field of sociolinguistics in its wider context. (Bucholtz, 2002:42, 43)

Throughout this chapter, we have shown, by correlating the results found in Clempi (2019) and Felix (2016), that the analyzes of variation and change in Brazilian Portuguese can be enriched if our analyzes are not limited to gender and sexuality stereotypes, demonstrating, at the light of socially inclusive extralinguistic factors, a more faithful portrayal of the linguistic diversity of our speakers.

References

Auer, A., et al. (2015). Historical sociolinguistics: The field and its future. *Journal of Historical Sociolinguistics, 1*(1), 1–12.

Bucholtz, M. (2002). From 'sex differences to gender variation in sociolinguistics. *University of Pennsylvania Working Papers in Linguistics, 8*, 33–45.

Buitoni, D. H. S. (1981). *Mulher de papel: A representação da mulher na imprensa feminina brasileira*. Edições Loyola.

Burchfield, R. W. (1981). The spoken word: a BBC guide. London: British Broadcasting Corporation.

Butler, J. (1999). *Gender trouble. Tenth Anniversary Edition* (2nd ed.). Routledge. https://doi.org/10.4324/9780203902752

Campbell-Kibler, K., Podesva, R. J., & Roberts, S. J. (2001). Sharing resources and indexing meanings in the production of gay styles. http://web.stanford.edu/~eckert/Courses/ParisPapers/PodesvaEtAl2001.pdf. Accessed 07 April 2022.

Clempi, C. B. (2019). *Variação entre futuro sintético e perifrástico em textos escritos*: um estudo diacrônico sobre o papel do gênero feminino na mudança linguística. Dissertation, São Paulo State University.

Clempi, C., & Rodrigues, A. (2020). O papel do gênero social nos estudos sociolinguísticos: desafios metodológicos na análise do futuro variável. *Revista Estudos Linguísticos, 49*, 452–470. https://doi.org/10.21165/el.v49i1.2481

Eckert, P. (2012). Three waves of variation study: The emergence of meaning in the study of sociolinguistic variation. *Annual Review of Anthropology, 41*, 87–100.

Eckert, P., & MacConnell-Ginet, S. (1992). Think practically and look locally: Language and gender as community-based practice. *Annual Review of Anthropology, 21*(1), 461–488.

Felix, R. d. A. A. (2016). *Adjetivo superlativo na fala de homens gays:* uma discussão sociolinguística. Dissertation, São Paulo State University.

Freitag, R. M. K. (2015). (Re)discutindo sexo/gênero na sociolinguística. In R. M. Ko & C. G. Severo (Eds.), *Mulheres, Linguagem e Poder – Estudos de Gênero na Sociolinguística Brasileira* (pp. 14–74). Blucher.

Freitag, R. M. K., Martins, M. A., & Tavares, M. A. (2012). Bancos de dados sociolinguísticos do português brasileiro e os estudos de terceira onda: potencialidades e limitações. *Alfa: Revista de Linguística, 56*(3), 917–944.

Gibbon, A. d. O. (2000). *A expressão do tempo futuro na língua falada de Florianópolis:* Gramaticalização e Variação. Dissertation, Federal University of Santa Catarina.

Gonçalves, C. A. (2003). A função indexical das formações X-íssimo, X-ésimo e X-érrimo no português do Brasil. *Veredas, 5*(2), 47–59.

Gonçalves, S. C. L. (2007). Banco de dados Iboruna: amostras eletrônicas do português falado no interior paulista. Available in: http://www.alip.ibilce.unesp.br. Acess in [01/12/2016].

Hooks, B. (2000). *Feminism is for everybody: Passionate politics.* Pluto Press.

Labov, W. (1972). *Sociolinguistic patterns.* University of Pennsylvania Press.

Labov, W. (1990). The intersection of sex and social class in the course of linguistic change. *Language Variation and Change, 2*(2), 205–254.

Labov, W. (2001). *Principles of linguistic change. Social factors.* Blackwell.

Milroy, L. (1992). New perspectives in the analysis of sex differentiation in language. In K. Bolton & H. Kwok (Eds.), *Sociolinguistics today: International perspectives* (pp. 163–179). Routledge.

Nogueira, G. (2011). Ânus rebeldes – gêneros normativos. Paper presented at the VII Encontro de Estudos Multidisciplinares em Cultura, Federal University of Bahia, Salvador, 3–5 August 2011.

Oliveira, J. M. d. (2006). *O futuro da língua portuguesa ontem e hoje:* variação e mudança. Thesis, Federal University of Rio de Janeiro.

Queen, R. (2014). Language and sexual identities. In S. Ehrlich, M. Meyerhoff, & J. Holmes (Eds.), *The handbook of language, gender and sexuality* (pp. 203–219). Wiley.

R Core Team. (2021). *R: A language and environment for statistical computing.* R Foundation for Statistical Computing. https://www.R-project.org/

Tagliamonte, S. A. (2006). *Analysing sociolinguistic variation.* Cambridge University Press.

Thorne, B., & Henley, N. (1975). *Language and sex.* Newbury House.

Weinreich, U., Labov, W., & Herzog, M. (1968). *Empirical foundations for a theory of language change.* University of Texas Press.

Wodak, R., & Bank, G. (2017). Gender as a sociolinguistic variable: New perspectives on variation studies. In F. Coulmas (Ed.), *The handbook of sociolinguistics* (pp. 127–150). Blackwell.

Chapter 10
Language Prejudice and Language Structure: On Missing and Emerging Conjunctions in Libras and Other Sign Languages

Angélica Rodrigues ⓘ **and Roland Pfau** ⓘ

Introduction: Language Prejudice

Language prejudice can be analyzed either from a community-internal perspective, where nonstandard variants are commonly contrasted with standard ones, or be based on the contrast between different linguistic communities. In the latter case, languages spoken by socioeconomic groups with higher prestige tend to be assigned a higher linguistic status in global perspective and are often taken to be more consistent and efficient, especially when used in international interactions. On the other hand, languages without a written tradition, spoken by, for instance, traditional and indigenous communities, have commonly been considered as less complex, or even primitive, or have been described as "dialects." Behind this alleged distinction between primitive and developed languages are often biased ideas about civilization, culture, and language – as entertained, for instance, by French scholars during the nineteenth century, who considered languages with a literary tradition, such as European languages, as *langue de culture* ("language of culture"), opposing them to languages without a writing system. However, as Lyons (1981: 301–302) points out, the term *culture*, as defined under such a label, presumes that there would be culturally more advanced and culturally less advanced languages, an idea that evidently is in conflict with an anthropological perspective on culture as socially acquired knowledge that an individual learns as a member of a given society.

Moreover, the use of the terms "language" and "dialect" also implies a hierarchical perspective on language varieties. Haugen (1966: 922) points out that these

A. Rodrigues (✉)
Unesp – Sao Paulo State University, Araraquara, Sao Paulo, Brazil
e-mail: angelica.rodrigues@unesp.br

R. Pfau
University of Amsterdam, Amsterdam, Netherlands
e-mail: r.pfau@uva.nl

© The Author(s), under exclusive license to Springer Nature Switzerland AG 2023
G. Massini-Cagliari et al. (eds.), *Understanding Linguistic Prejudice*,
https://doi.org/10.1007/978-3-031-25806-0_10

terms are loaded with "ambiguities and obscurities" that may allow an interpretation according to which language is superordinate to dialect or that may reduce dialect to a form of language that is excluded from polite society. In fact, typological, sociolinguistic, and ecolinguistic studies provide evidence that language diversity should not be understood in such terms, as there is plenty of evidence that every language ever studied – including what might be considered a dialect – represents a complex and highly developed system of communication (Lyons, 1981: 27).

Crucially, language diversity and linguistic variation are not the exception, but rather central hallmarks of actual language use. Members of any linguistic community are used to deal with linguistic heterogeneity, i.e., multilingual and multidialect environments, on a daily basis without compromising communication. Still, language evaluation (Labov, 1972) within the linguistic community may lead speakers to negatively evaluate certain variants, e.g., variants associated with illiterate members of the community, while variants used by higher educated speakers, usually associated with standard grammar usage, may be more positively evaluated. For instance, in Brazil, even though there are significant discrepancies between the rules described in scholarly grammars as standard Portuguese and the Portuguese actually spoken by the majority of speakers, we can observe – especially in the media – that a vast number of nonstandard variants suffer language prejudice. Take agreement as an example. Studies conducted by Scherre and Naro (1998) revealed that both verb agreement and noun phrase-internal agreement are used in Brazilian Portuguese under variable rules, with social variables (in particular, age, sex/gender, and years of schooling) influencing the frequency of the use of overt agreement markers. Nevertheless, the lack of agreement marking, characteristic of the nonstandard variant, is considered highly marked and is the target of linguistic prejudice.

Within an approach to language prejudice that takes the contrast between linguistic communities as point of departure, it appears natural to extend the scope of inquiry to deaf communities and their sign languages. After all, sign languages are unwritten – and for the longest time undocumented[1] – languages, and they, as well as their communities of users, are often marginalized within the hearing mainstream communities. In the past, sign languages – just like indigenous languages – have commonly been considered primitive communication systems, which may fulfill basic communicative purposes but do not allow for conveying complex messages and abstract ideas. Such prejudices against sign languages and their users are rooted in no small part in the concepts of able-bodiedness and of disability. As Padden and Humphries (1988) point out, deaf people are usually defined by what they lack, i.e., their inability to perceive sounds. This medical view underlies the concept of disability as "a problematic characteristic inherent in particular bodies and minds" (Kafer, 2013: 5). As a consequence, a disability is seen as something that should be "cured" or "fixed." For members of the deaf community, this often implies being

---

[1] While sign languages are still unwritten languages, they are, since the advent of analogue and digital recording techniques, no longer undocumented (e.g., Supalla, 2001; Legg, 2016; Geraci et al., 2019).

denied access to sign language and being pushed to acquiesce in technologies of normalization, such as cochlear implant surgery (Lane, 2002).

Thanks to more than 60 years of linguistic research (e.g., Stokoe, 1960; Klima & Bellugi, 1979), it is now clear that sign languages are full-fledged natural languages, which – despite the use of different articulators – display striking similarities with spoken languages at all levels of linguistic description (see, e.g., chapters in Quer et al., 2021) and, at the same time, differ from each other typologically in significant ways (Pfau & Zeshan, 2016; Zeshan & Palfreyman, 2017, 2020). Still, prejudices persist, and, as mentioned above, these extend to the communities of users, who are commonly marginalized and stigmatized rather than recognized as what they are: minority groups with their own languages and culture, which is characterized by distinct traditions, customs, networks, and cultural expressions (e.g., Senghas & Monaghan, 2002; Ladd, 2003; Friedner & Kusters, 2020). Taken together, combating prejudices against sign languages requires a broader understanding of the history of deaf communities and their fight against repeated (and ongoing) efforts to marginalize not only their languages but also their culture.

In this chapter, we address the issue of language prejudice from the perspective of sign language linguistics. We choose complex sentences, and more specifically conjunctions, as our domain of inquiry, on the one hand because there have been claims in the literature that certain types of clause combinations either do not exist in sign languages or are not marked as such and on the other hand because there is a growing body of research showing that conjunctions may emerge over time in sign languages – just as they do in spoken languages. We start in section "Structural Complexity and Language Status" by addressing claims regarding the relation between the presence or absence of certain grammatical categories and the status of a language. Section "On Clause Combinations and (the Absence of) Conjunctions in Sign Languages" offers an overview of work on clause combinations and (the absence of) conjunctions in various sign languages. In this section, we also address ways in which conjunctions may enter the lexicon of a sign language. In section "Conjunctions in Brazilian Sign Languages", we then turn to Brazilian Sign Language (Libras) and show that conjunctions have indeed emerged in this sign language following the diachronic strategies discussed in section "On Clause Combinations and (the Absence of) Conjunctions in Sign Languages." Section "Conclusion" concludes the chapter.

Structural Complexity and Language Status

Thanks to a plethora of studies on typologically diverse languages, we know that languages may differ from each other considerably with respect to structural complexity in the domains of phonology, morphology, and syntax. It has also been demonstrated that, notwithstanding such structural differences, no one natural language would be superior when it comes to satisfying the communicative needs of its community of users. Yet, in studies from the nineteenth and early twentieth century, linguists and anthropologists were not hesitant to apply certain, often rather arbitrary, measures of complexity in order to prove that a given language was a "primitive language." When describing a language as "primitive," scholars have commonly emphasized the lack of certain lexical categories or grammatical phenomena: Language X does not distinguish between nouns and verbs? Language Y does not mark tense on the verb? These must be primitive languages then – where "primitive" is clearly a comparative notion; that is, languages X and Y are compared to a standard that is either non-defined or is simply the language of the scholar making the claim.

In this section, we offer a brief discussion of some claims that have been made regarding the relationship between language structure and language status. Obviously, we cannot do justice to the complex argumentation surrounding this topic. In section "On "Primitive Languages" and "Languages of Civilization"," we illustrate the line of reasoning alluded to in the previous paragraph by means of two representative examples, one for a spoken and one for a sign language. In section "Not So Primitive After All: Complexity Across Grammatical Domains," we discuss more recent findings that cast doubt on a categorical classification of languages based on certain grammatical features.[2]

On "Primitive Languages" and "Languages of Civilization"

The view that Aboriginal Australian languages are primitive languages endured well into the twentieth century and is reflected in Sommerfelt's (1938) account of the Aranda language of Central Australia. Sommerfelt, a Norwegian structuralist who had never visited Australia, considered Aranda as an extremely "archaic" language, claiming, for instance, that within the domain of phonology "quantity and accent do not play any role in the language" and that "vocalic quantity is without phonological significance."[3] As for word classes, Sommerfelt argues that "Aranda does not know real grammatical categories comparable to those of more developed languages, and it ignores the grammatical elements that correspond with them,"

---

[2] For reasons of space, we do not include a discussion of creole languages. It has been argued that creole languages as a group display less grammatical complexity (e.g., McWhorter, 2001), but this claim is highly controversial (e.g., DeGraff, 2003; Aboh, 2016). In this context, it is interesting to note that sign languages have sometimes been argued to share certain linguistic and sociolinguistic characteristics with creole languages (see, e.g., Lupton & Salmons, 1996, and Adone, 2012, for discussion).

[3] "Quantité et accent ne jouent aucun rôle dans la langue [...] la quantité vocalique est sans importance phonologique" (Sommerfelt, 1938:48). All translations from the French original to English are ours.

more specifically, that "Aranda knows no difference between the noun, the adjective, and the verb,"[4]

Twenty years later, Laycock (1960) reviewed Sommerfelt's book, his motivation being that Sommerfelt's claims were still perpetuated in the linguistic literature, and he clearly demonstrated that many of Sommerfelt's assertions – including the ones above – are wrong. Laycock notes that there are "two main factors conducive to error in Sommerfelt's work: the generally unsatisfactory nature of his sources, and his own views on language and society" (p. 17), and he concludes "that Aranda structure is far more complex, both phonetically and morphologically, than Sommerfelt believed" (p. 28).

Importantly, the aim of Sommerfelt (and other scholars of the period) goes beyond demonstrating that a given language is primitive or archaic. Rather, the commonly associated assumption is that primitive languages are spoken by members of primitive cultures – a view adopted from nineteenth-century moralists "for whom "high culture" stood in sharp contrast to the uncouth customs of the savage" (Kalmár, 1985:148). Indeed, Sommerfelt's starting point is that if "we want to try to determine the relations that exist between language and society, it goes without saying that we must start with the languages of societies that belong to the most archaic types known."[5] In the case of Aranda, he writes, "we are in the fortunate position of possessing linguistic materials which make an in-depth study possible."[6] However, as shown by Laycock (1960), Sommerfelt's interpretation of the available linguistic materials is, for the most part, unsatisfactory, and therefore, his conclusion that "among the Aranta, there is thus, in certain important respects, a correlation between language and society" is unjustified.[7]

Not surprisingly, similar claims have been made for sign languages. For instance, in his comprehensive description of Plains Indian Sign Language (PISL), a sign language used by various North American tribes as a sort of lingua franca, Mallery (2001[1881]: 359) notes, "There is in the gesture speech no organized sentence such as is integrated in the languages of civilization" and one "must not look for articles or particles or passive voice or case […] or even what appears in those languages as a substantive or a verb. The sign radicals, without being specifically any of our parts of speech, may be all of them in turn." Later on (p. 361), Mallery also mentions the absence of a copula verb and the lack of tense inflection.

---

[4] "L'aranta ne connaît donc pas de vraies categories grammaticales, comparables à celles de langues plus développées, et il ignore les éléments grammaticaux qui y correspondent" (Sommerfelt, 1938:189). "[L]'aranta ne connaît pas de difference entre le nom, l'adjectif et le verbe" (Sommerfelt, 1938:109).

[5] "Si l'on veut essayer de déterminer les relations qui existent entre la langue et la société, il va de soi que l'on doit commencer avec les langues des sociétés qui appartiennent aux types les plus archaïques connus" (Sommerfelt, 1938:14).

[6] "[N]ous sommes […] dans l'heureuse situation de posséder des matériaux linguistiques qui rendent possible une étude approfondie" (Sommerfelt, 1938:17).

[7] "[I]l y a donc, à certains égards importants, corrélation entre la langue et la société" (Sommerfelt, 1938: 201).

What the two accounts have in common is that they attribute inferior status to the languages they study, by comparing them to "more developed languages" (Sommerfelt) or "languages of civilization" (Mallery). However, there are two crucial differences between the studies. First, while Sommerfelt's account of Aranda can safely be called an "armchair study," Mallery had investigated the language he describes himself. Second, while many of Sommerfelt's structural analyses have been shown to be flawed, at least some of Mallery's claims regarding PISL are most probably accurate – as we may infer from studies of other natural sign languages, as well as from Davis' (2010) more recent study of PISL.

Not So Primitive After All: Complexity Across Grammatical Domains

We know from the study of numerous sign languages that they indeed display some of the characteristics identified by Mallery for PISL. For instance, sign languages usually do not feature case marking, copula verbs, dedicated strategies for passive voice, or tense inflection on the verb.[8] Crucially, however, these are grammatical characteristics that also hold true for many spoken languages that Mallery would likely classify as "languages of civilization" (e.g., lack of copula in Russian, lack of tense marking in Mandarin Chinese). In other words, a broader typological coverage will often reveal that (the lack of) a specific grammatical characteristic is not confined to a specific type of language and thus that it says nothing about the status of a language. Moreover, in many comparisons, it will probably turn out that less complex structure in one domain of grammar does not necessarily imply that the language under investigation would be relatively less complex across domains (as Sommerfelt erroneously argued for Aranda).[9] Language X might, for instance, allow for more complex syllable structure than Language Y, and Language Y might in turn mark more person/number distinctions on verbs than Language X.

Focusing on the domain of inflectional morphology, and based on data from more than 2000 languages, Lupyan and Dale (2010) were able to demonstrate that languages differ greatly in morphological complexity (as measured by 28 features) and, what is more, that there is a strong relationship between complexity and

---

[8] While sign languages appear to be rather homogenous with respect to certain grammatical characteristics (e.g., Meier, 2002), they also display considerable typological variation, and thus, the generalizations made here are not without exception. For instance, Italian Sign Language has been argued to have a strategy for marking tense on the verb (Zucchi, 2009), and for ASL, the emergence of a copula has recently been described (Sampson & Mayberry, 2022).

[9] Occasionally, the lack of complexity in one area might even be compensated for by increased complexity in another area. For instance, Nettle (1995) compared languages based on two variables, size of their segment inventory and mean word length, and found a significant correlation between the two: the smaller the segment inventory, the greater the mean word length (see Sandler, 2008, for a sign language example).

demographic factors such as the number of language users and geographic spread: languages with larger speaker populations and greater geographical coverage had overall less complex morphological systems. The authors conclude that "just as biological organisms are shaped by ecological niches, language structures appear to adapt to the environment (niche) in which they are being learned and used" (Lupyan & Dale, 2010, p. 1). What is of interest in the present context is the fact that, based on the measures applied, languages such as English and French ("exoteric languages" in Lupyan and Dale's terminology) would be located toward the more "primitive" side of the continuum, while smaller and more isolated ("esoteric") languages, that is, languages that would likely fall into Sommerfelt's "archaic" category, show more complexity in this domain.[10]

In conclusion of this section, we emphasize that at times, it may not even be clear what complexity entails, that is, whether a particular strategy should be classified as more or less complex. Since our focus in the following will be on complex clauses, we illustrate this point by means of an example involving complementation. In his discussion of "primitive" versus "evolved" languages, Kalmár (1985, p. 157) emphasizes that the label "primitive" should not be taken to imply that the language is of inferior worth; it does not even necessarily imply that the language is less complex than one of the "evolved" type. It simply means that the language is "in an early stage."[11] Focusing on subordination, he states that "[p]rimitive languages do not have subordinate clauses; instead they use a bound morpheme, a word, or a phrase." He offers Inuktitut as an example, arguing that the language does not have complement clauses of the *They say/think that...*type. Rather, the equivalent of a complement clause would be expressed by one of multiple suffixes which attaches to the verb. The suffix *-guuq*, for instance, encodes the meaning that a third-person actor said something, as illustrated in (1). "As traditional Inuit did not often feel a need, in their small societies, to identify a speaker, the morpheme *guuq* generally did the job" (Kalmár, 1985, p. 161):

(1) *qangatasuug*   *tikkinniartu-ruuq*

     airplane   will.arrive-(form of *guuq*)

     "He said that the airplane would arrive."

                                   (Inuktitut – Harper, 1979, in Kalmár, 1985:159)

Yet, as far as complexity is concerned, one could argue that a strategy involving a bound morpheme is more complex than a strategy involving a matrix verb and free

---

[10] For a discussion of the impact of community characteristics on sign language structure, see Meir et al. (2012) and De Vos and Pfau (2015).

[11] Kalmár relates the evolution of certain complex features to the genesis of text permanence, that is, the appearance of non-spontaneous narrative texts. He assumes that "there is a gradient of text permanence between languages in which there is little of no composed literature [...] and those with a large body of permanent written texts. To simplify the argument let us call languages of the first extreme 'primitive' and the others 'evolved'." (Kalmár, 1985).

complementizer, especially if one assumes that the suffix derives from an underlying main verb. In fact, in Lupyan and Dale's (2010) approach to complexity, inflectional (bound) morphology is considered more complex than lexical strategies.

On Clause Combinations and (the Absence of) Conjunctions in Sign Languages

In the sign linguistic literature, the existence and absence of conjunctions is usually addressed in the context of studies investigating different types of subordination and coordination. In studies on specific sign languages, it is sometimes highlighted that conjunctions that one might expect in such complex constructions are absent. For subordination in particular, this has led to claims that sign languages may lack certain types of subordination.

While some of the relevant studies date back to the "early days" of sign language linguistics (e.g., Thompson, 1977; Baker & Padden, 1978; Liddell, 1978, 1980; Padden, 1983 – all on American Sign Language), recent years have seen numerous publications that address different types of complex clauses – from both a descriptive and formal perspective – in a wider variety of sign languages (e.g., Pfau et al., 2016; see also Tang & Lau, 2012, for an overview). In this section, we offer a brief historical outline of work on complex clauses and conjunctions in sign languages. We proceed in two steps. First, we address the fact that the absence of certain conjunctions should not be taken to imply the lack of coordination or subordination structures. Second, we demonstrate that certain conjunctions exist in sign language and that they may enter the lexicon via borrowing and grammaticalization.

Marking of Clause Combinations in Sign Language

In an early study on subordination in American Sign Language (ASL), Thompson (1977) challenges the existence of subordination in that language. His main focus of interest is relative clauses, but he also addresses various other types of clausal embedding. His claim that ASL lacks various types of subordination structures is mainly based on (i) the fact that there is "no evidence for syntactic marking of subordination" (Thompson, 1977: 184) in the form of conjunctions – e.g., no wh-words introducing relative clauses and no complementizers introducing complement clauses, and (ii) the observation that in some of the constructions that are analyzed, pauses may intervene between what one might consider the main and the subordinate clause. Many of his claims have later been criticized by Liddell (1980). We illustrate the controversy with just one representative example.

Thompson (1977: 190) argues that "there is no distinction between direct and indirect speeches in ASL," that is, no distinction comparable to English *Peter said that he met John* vs. *Peter said "I met John."* He offers (2a) as an example (slightly adapted; note that superscript "+" and "−" indicate beginning and end of eye contact), highlighting that there is no grammatical marking of subordination and that "the narration of reported speech or thought is often accompanied by a slight change in body orientation, indicating adoption of the role of the reported speaker." In other words, despite the fact that Thompson translates the utterance as indirect speech, according to his line of reasoning, what is really signed here is "I told my friend (something): 'I doubt I will go'"[12]:

(2)   a.   INDEX₁ TELL ⁺FRIEND⁻ INDEX₁ DOUBT GO

"I told my friend that I doubted I would go."

(ASL – Thompson, 1977:190)

b.   JOHN TELL FRIEND INDEX₃ DOUBT GO

"Johnᵢ told his friend that heᵢ doubted he would go."

Liddell (1980) admits that Thompson's analysis of (2a) may well be on the right track. Yet, he further argues that one of the observations that Thompson makes in the above quote, namely, that adoption of the role of the speaker occurs *often* (rather than always), in fact "support[s] the idea that ASL does distinguish between direct and indirect speech" (Liddell, 1980: 120). In order to make the distinction clear, one needs to consider examples with a third-person subject accompanying the speech act verb (which Thompson does not provide) like the one in (2b), where the third-person pronoun INDEX₃ is co-referent with the matrix subject JOHN. This is clearly indirect speech, as the direct speech counterpart would require a first-person pronoun in the second clause and what is now commonly referred to as "role shift" or "constructed action." According to Liddell (1980: 121), and a substantial body of later research, such alternative realizations do exist, and he thus concludes that "the choice between direct speech and indirect speech is a matter of style rather than

---

[12] Notation conventions: Sign language examples are glossed in SMALL CAPS in English (irrespective of the sign language), with one word representing one sign. Whenever two words are necessary to represent the meaning of a single sign, they are separated by a period (e.g., GROW.UP). The gloss INDEX/IX stands for a pointing sign (usually articulated with extended index finger); in all examples in this chapter, INDEX functions as a pronoun. Subscripts accompanying INDEX/IX or certain verb signs indicate loci in the signing space (1 = locus close to the signer; 2 = locus close to the addressee; 3/3a = locus elsewhere in the signing space). POSS is a possessive pronoun. Signs involving fingerspelling, i.e., the use of letters from the manual alphabet, are represented by lowercase letters separated by hyphens (e.g., "i-f" for a sequence of the handshapes representing the letters "i" and "f"); fingerspelled sequences used in Brazilian Sign Language examples are presented in the original Portuguese form. Lines above the gloss line indicate the presence of a non-manual marker (such as an eyebrow, mouth, or body movement) that is articulated simultaneously with one or multiple signs; the length of the line indicates the scope of the marker. The relevant abbreviations for such non-manual markers, which fulfil various grammatical functions in sign languages, will be introduced in the context of examples.

possibility" (see Lillo-Martin (2012) and Steinbach (2021) for extensive discussion of the phenomenon).

Liddell also criticizes Thompson's conclusions regarding other types of subordination (like indirect questions and complement clauses) and offers a detailed discussion of ASL relative clauses in which he shows that the crucial marker is not produced by the hands but rather by non-manual articulators, i.e., a dedicated eyebrow and head position. Moreover, he presents syntactic tests, like topicalization and pronoun copy, that allow for the distinction between coordination and subordination and that were later elaborated on by Padden (1983).

The discussion thus reveals two crucial characteristics of clause combining in sign languages: (i) subordination – and by extension coordination – is not always marked by manual grammatical markers, i.e., conjunctions, and (ii) non-manual markers play a crucial role in the domain of complex clauses and often allow for the identification of subordinate structures (Pfau & Quer, 2010; Wilbur, 2021). Obviously, the first point also holds for many spoken languages, including English, where structures like *He knew his friend would help him* (complement clause) or *She said the exam went well* (indirect speech) are common. Yet, in English, the conjunction *that* may optionally be used in such contexts, while the available research suggests that the use of a sign corresponding to English *that* is indeed very uncommon across sign languages (but see section "Grammaticalization").[13]

Recent studies have identified other sign language-specific patterns that allow for the identification of subordination in the absence of conjunctions. Göksel and Kelepir (2016), for instance, report that Turkish Sign Language (TİD) does not employ conjunctions in complement clauses either, but distinguishes between embedded clauses under "want"-type versus "know"-type predicates. The former show a strong preference for SOV order, i.e., center-embedding of the complement clause, as shown in (3a). Clearly, in this example, we cannot be dealing with a combination of two main clauses, as the subordinate clause intervenes between the matrix subject and the matrix verb. In contrast, for "know"-type predicates, at least a group of informants found only the SVO order acceptable (3b):

(3) a. MELEK [CHILD GOOD SCHOOL GO] WANT

     "Melek wants her child to go to a good school."

  b. ALI3 SELF3 THINK [AYŞE REST]

     "Ali himself thinks that Ayşe is resting."

                                        (TİD – Göksel and Kelepir, 2016:70,71)

---

[13] The same seems to hold for signs corresponding to the conjunction *whether*, which introduces embedded polar interrogatives under matrix predicates like *ask* or *wonder*. Davidson and Caponigro (2016) demonstrate that, notwithstanding the absence of a sign that would translate as "whether," embedded polar interrogatives exist in ASL.

While the focus so far has been on the identification of subordination in the absence of conjunctions, it has to be noted that for certain meanings, the use of manual conjunctions has been reported in the literature. Two examples from Sign Language of the Netherlands (NGT) are given in (4). In (4a), we observe the use of the conjunction BECAUSE introducing an adverbial clause specifying a reason, while in (4b), we are dealing with a conditional clause that is introduced by the conjunction SUPPOSE-1 ("br" = brow raise, a marker frequently accompanying conditional clauses; "hn" = head nod):[14]

(4)   a.   INDEX₁ ANGRY [**BECAUSE** INDEX3a ALWAYS COME LATE]

      "I am angry because s/he always comes late."   (NGT – Pfau, 2016:156)

_____ hn
_____ br

  b.   **SUPPOSE-1** CHILD   UNDERSTAND   / PALM.UP OTHER.WAY

      "If the child understands it, it can go the other way."

(NGT – adapted from Klomp, 2019:372)

Yet, while for the first type of adverbial clause, the use of a manual conjunction (or another dedicated construction type) appears to be obligatory in NGT, conditional clauses can also be realized without a conjunction introducing the subordinate clause. Looking only at the manual signs in example (5), one might be tempted to analyze this example as a sequence of two main clauses. The non-manual marker "brow raise," which is also present in (4b), however, indicates that we are dealing with a conditional clause. Similar patterns have been described for other sign languages: i.e., a manual conjunction may exist, but a non-manual marker alone is sufficient to mark the conditional clause:[15]

_____ br

(5)   MUCH SAME USE INDEX3   / MUST 3INCORPORATE1

      "[If] it is used much, it must be incorporated."   (NGT – Klomp, 2019: 323)

Finally, we briefly turn to coordination, for which similar observations have been made for some sign languages. In ASL, the two conjuncts in a coordination

---

[14] Note that the sign glossed as SUPPOSE-1 (in Dutch *stel*) is a conjunction, not a verb. It cannot be used for the verbal meaning "suppose" as in "I suppose he's right." Further note that Klomp (2019) reports, based on naturalistic corpus data, that NGT actually has seven conjunctions for introducing conditional clauses, SUPPOSE-1 being the most frequent one.

[15] Klomp (2019) bases her description on naturalistic corpus data, and she finds that brow raise is not the only non-manual accompanying conditional clauses. Rather, these clauses may also be accompanied by furrowed eyebrows, head movements, or head tilts, and none of these markers needs to accompany the entire conditional clause. Moreover, some conditional clauses in her data set were not accompanied by (visible) non-manual signals at all.

structure may be marked by a manual sign glossed as COORD-L, which precedes both conjuncts, as can be seen in (6a). COORD-L is a two-handed sign, which involves a handshape with two extended fingers (e.g., index and middle finger) on the non-dominant hand and the index finger of the dominant hand pointing first to one of the extended fingers (COORD-L$_1$) and then to the other one (COORD-L$_2$). Alternatively, signers may use a non-manual strategy, which Davidson (2013) labels "COORD-shift" and which involves slight body leans toward contrasting sides of the signing space, as shown in (6b) (where we refer to the contrasting sides as "a" and "b" in the non-manual line). Note that both examples receive the same translation:[16]

(6)   a.   **COORD-L1** [POSS3 PARENTS WILL BUY POSS3 CAR] **COORD-L2** [INDEX3 WILL

       TRAVEL]

                                        body lean-a   body lean-b
      b.   [POSS3 PARENTS WILL BUY POSS3 CAR]   [INDEX3 WILL TRAVEL]

      "Her parents will buy her a car, and (then) she will travel."

                                                    (ASL – adapted from Davidson, 2013:7, 9)

Both strategies can be considered as instances of bisyndetic coordination (Haspelmath, 2007), as both conjuncts are marked, be it by a manual conjunction or a non-manual marker.

Taken together, the examples discussed in this section reveal that conjunctions exist in sign languages but that their use is not always obligatory. In addition, for certain types of clause combinations, it may well be the case that no manual conjunction is available in a given sign language. However, this should not be taken to imply that this sign language lacks the respective type of clause combination (e.g., complementation). Rather, the researcher would be well-advised to check for the presence of non-manual markers, which may be indicative of subordination or coordination. Moreover, syntactic tests might reveal whether a combination of clauses should be analyzed as a subordination or coordination structure. In the next section, we discuss in more detail how manual conjunctions may enter the lexicon of a sign language.

Emergence of Conjunctions

Sign languages, just like spoken languages, are subject to diachronic change, which must be understood as an effect of the dynamics of communicative interaction. In a sense, the lexicon and the grammar of a language are like a malleable fabric that

---

[16] We are neglecting the fact that Davidson (2013) shows that we are actually dealing with "general use coordination" in both examples, as, depending on the context, they could also be translated as disjunction, that is, "Her parents will buy her a car, or she will travel" (see Asada, 2019, for Japanese Sign Language).

adapts to the expressive needs of the speakers. One of these expressive needs may be the avoidance of ambiguities, and conjunctions may be a convenient tool for achieving this purpose.

Diachronic changes may be triggered by external factors, such as language contact or standardization, or by internal factors, for instance, a pressure toward ease of production and/or perception of the linguistic signal (see, e.g., Frishberg, 1975, for phonological changes in ASL that are motivated by such pressures). In the following subsections, we address how conjunctions may emerge in sign languages by means of borrowing, an external process (Section "Borrowing"), or grammaticalization, a language-internal process which affects elements stored in the lexicon (Section "Grammaticalization").

Borrowing

Sign languages are usually in contact with the spoken language used in the surrounding hearing community, and, to an increasing extent, with other sign languages. They may thus borrow elements from both spoken and sign languages. It is the former type of borrowing that we are focusing on in the present context, more specifically, borrowing from a spoken language mediated by the written form of that language. Most sign languages employ manual alphabets, whereby handshapes or combinations of handshapes represent letters from the alphabet (or characters in the case of some East Asian sign languages; cf. Ann, 1998). Fingerspelling is used, for instance, to represent proper names or concepts for which no sign exists (yet), but it may also undergo a process of nativization, whereby short fingerspelled sequences or single letters are integrated into the lexicon of a sign language, often undergoing certain phonological changes in order to be more consistent with the rules of the recipient language (see, e.g., Battison, 1978; Cormier et al., 2008; and chapters in Brentari, 2001, for this type of borrowing; for discussion of the sign language lexicon, see, e.g., Padden, 1998, and Brentari & Padden, 2001).

In some sign languages, conjunctions have been borrowed in this way from the surrounding spoken languages. Two examples are provided in (7). In the ASL example in (7a), the disjunctive conjunction "or" is composed of two letters from the manual alphabet,[17] and in the example from Australian Sign Language (Auslan) in (7b), the conjunction "if" is borrowed from English in the same way ("htb" = head tilt back; "bf" = furrowed brows). Obviously, these two conjunctions make for good candidates for this type of borrowing, as their corresponding English forms are very short.

---

[17] Davidson (2011) notes that the two ASL coordination strategies presented in (6) can be combined with the use of the fingerspelled conjunction "o-r" in order to disambiguate the coordination type.

(7)   a.   MARY HAVE COFFEE **o-r** TEA

"Did Mary have coffee or tea?"   (ASL – Davidson, 2011:81)

<u>   br+htb   </u>   <u>   bf   </u>

b.   **i-f** WIN L-O-T-T-O /   WHAT D-O INDEX$_2$

"If you won lotto, what would you do?"

(Auslan – adapted from Johnston and Schembri, 2007:214)

c.   [WOULD.LIKE SUITCASE] **PLUS** [BIRD^CAGE WOULD.LIKE TAKE.WITH] LEAVE

"I would like to take my suitcase and birdcage with me as I leave."

(NGT – Klomp, 2021: 339)

A different type of borrowing from the written script is observed in the NGT example in (7c). What is used here to coordinate the two clauses is not based on letters but rather on the additive symbol "+," which is formed by two hands with extended index fingers. Work based on corpus data has demonstrated that this form is commonly used by native signers – although coordination can also be realized without the use of a manual conjunction (see also Hartmann et al., 2021).

Besides borrowing from the written form of a language, sign languages can also borrow elements from the gestural repertoire of the surrounding community. Such co-speech gestures may be used as lexical items (e.g., "thumbs up" gesture for sign GOOD), but they may also serve grammatical functions (e.g., pointing used for pronominal functions; cf. Pfau, 2011; Fenlon et al., 2019). Of interest in the present context is the gesture "palm-up," which consists of a rotation of the forearms such that the palms are oriented upward and which has been shown to fulfil various functions in both spoken and sign languages (Cooperrider et al., 2018; Volk & Herrmann, 2021). It has been observed that in some sign language, this manual form can be used to connect clauses and thus functions like a conjunction. Two examples, from New Zealand Sign Language (NZSL) and NGT, respectively, are provided in (8); in both, "palm-up" marks disjunctive coordination. Note that in (8a), the authors do not gloss this form as a sign (i.e., in small caps), but rather as "palm up," while in (8b), a similar form is glossed as the sign OR – we will return to this glossing difference in the next section.

(8)   a.   […] THERE REDUCE FIVE WEEK **palm-up** THIRTY DOLLAR WEEK […]

"You could reduce it to five dollars a week, or thirty dollars a week […]."

(NZSL – McKee and Wallingford, 2011: 230)

b.   SUPPOSE [HEAR INDEX$_1$ IN.LOVE] **OR** [DEAF INDEX$_1$ IN.LOVE]

"Suppose that a hearing person and I are in love, or a deaf person

and I are in love."   (NGT – Hartmann et al., 2021: 14)

Of course, the emergence of conjunctions via borrowing is not a phenomenon that would be restricted to sign languages. In her discussion of the emergence of conjunctions in spoken languages, Mithun (1988:351), for instance, points out that, although coordinating conjunctions may have various sources, a common characteristic is that they are generally very recent in languages. Evidence from several languages shows that bilingualism is a significant factor in the development of conjunctions. Mithun offers Mexican languages as an example, where the vast majority of coordinating conjunctions are actually borrowings from Spanish.

Grammaticalization

Grammaticalization is a language-internal diachronic change, whereby lexical elements turn into free grammatical markers (and sometimes, in a second step, into grammatical affixes); a noun, for instance, may turn into a pronoun, or a verb may turn into a tense marker (Kuteva et al., 2019). It has been shown that grammaticalization processes are also responsible for diachronic change in sign languages and, interestingly, that the attested pathways are for the most part the same in the two modalities, that is, they are modality-independent (for overviews, see Pfau & Steinbach, 2011, and Janzen, 2012).

In his pioneering work, Meillet (1915), to whom coinage of the term "grammaticalization" is usually ascribed, emphasizes that the disappearance and renewal of conjunctions are motivated by repetition, which commonly leads to the weakening of the expressive value of a conjunction and the loss of "phonetic volume" (Meillet, 1915: 15–17). Cross-linguistically common sources for conjunctions are nouns, verbs, and question words – and all of these have been identified as sources in different sign languages.

For instance, in German Sign Language (DGS), the noun REASON has turned into a conjunction introducing reason/purpose clauses, as can be seen in (9a). Crucially, when used as a noun, REASON, which is a two-handed sign, is characterized by repetition of movement. In contrast, in its grammatical use, this repetition is usually lost, that is, we are dealing with phonetic reduction. ASL presents us with another example. In this sign language, the verb UNDERSTAND is the source for a complementizer introducing adverbial clauses, which can roughly be translated as "provided that."[18] Crucially, in (9b) UNDERSTAND' does not function as a verb; in particular, it cannot appear with an overt subject. In other words, we observe decategorialization, another hallmark of grammaticalization:

---

[18] Fischer and Lillo-Martin (1990) gloss the conjunction as UNDERSTAND', in order to distinguish it from its verbal source; also, they observe that it is accompanied by the non-manual marker "brow raise."

(9) a.   INDEX₁ SAD **REASON** POSS₁ DOG DIE

      "I am sad because my dog died." (DGS – Pfau and Steinbach, 2011:686)

$$\overline{\qquad\qquad\quad\text{br}}$$

    b.   ME GO.TO STORE NOW NIGHT,   **UNDERSTAND**' YOU WATCH

      MY CHILDREN, OK

      "I'll go to the store tonight provided that you babysit, ok?"

                          (ASL – Fischer and Lillo-Martin, 1990:72)

Recently, Khristoforova (in press) has reported that in Russian Sign Language (RSL), the wh- pronoun WHAT can be used for introducing complement clauses (see (10)). Clearly, this phenomenon mirrors the grammaticalization of complementizers in Romance languages (including Portuguese):

(10) INDEX₁ THINK [**WHAT** WOMAN ₃ₐCOME₁]

     "I thought that the woman would come to me."

                            (RSL – Khristoforova, in press)

However, besides such modality-independent pathways, sign languages present us with a type of grammaticalization specific to the visual-spatial modality: the grammaticalization of gestures. As mentioned in the previous section, gestures may lexicalize. Building on work by Janzen and Shaffer (2002) on ASL modal verbs, Wilcox (2004) argues that gestures, after having been incorporated into the lexicon as lexical items, may acquire a grammatical function over time (e.g., gesture expressing upper body strength > adjective STRONG > modal verb CAN). As for the second step, the transition from lexical to grammatical element, Xavier and Wilcox (2014) make a similar point for Libras, showing that modal verbs may grammaticalize along a trajectory that is also commonly attested in spoken languages, that is, from lexical sources with more concrete meaning related to possibility, obligation, and necessity.

Yet, there may also be instances whereby a (manual or non-manual) gesture enters the lexicon of a sign language as a grammatical marker, thus skipping the lexicalization stage. This particular pathway might, for instance, apply to the "palm-up" gesture discussed in the previous section. Obviously, deciding whether a particular form, which exists as co-speech gesture, is a gesture or a sign when used in signed discourse may not always be straightforward and may have to be investigated on a case-by-case basis, applying criteria like systematicity, obligatoriness, and/or language-specific behavior (see, e.g., Pfau, 2015, for the negative headshake). Looking again at the examples in (8), we may infer, based on the gloss, that McKee and Wallingford (2011) assume that "palm-up," when used as a clause linker, is still closer to the gestural source, while Hartmann et al. (2021) analyze it as a grammaticalized functional element (see also Van Loon et al., 2014; Volk & Herrmann, 2021).

Conjunctions in Brazilian Sign Language

In Libras – just as in many other sign languages – various types of coordination and subordination are commonly expressed through the juxtaposition of two (or more) clauses, without the use of a manual conjunction. In fact, as pointed out by Tang and Lau (2012:344), across sign languages, juxtaposition "appears to be more common than coordination involving manual conjunctions." The authors further highlight the important role of non-manual markers for the identification of complex sentences in sign languages.

Although, until recently, the structure of complex sentences had not been studied in detail for Libras, it is clear from examples provided in various sources that non-manuals indeed play a crucial role when it comes to marking different types of clause combinations – in line with what we discussed in section "Marking of Clause Combinations in Sign Language". Our focus, however, will be on the use of manual conjunctions, a phenomenon that, to date, has only received little attention. In particular, we will demonstrate, based on naturalistic data, that coordinating and subordinating conjunctions have entered the lexicon of Libras, exploiting the diachronic pathways described in the previous section, that is, by means of borrowing (Section "Borrowing") and grammaticalization (Section "Grammaticalization"). As for types of complex clauses, we will include in our discussion disjunctive and adversative coordination, as well as causal and conditional subordination.

Borrowing

We start by demonstrating that some manual conjunctions in Libras can be considered non-native signs, as discussed in Brentari and Padden (2001), as they are either borrowed from the surrounding spoken language, Portuguese, via fingerspelling (Section "Fingerspelling: Disjunctive Coordination") or from a co-speech gesture used in the hearing community (Section "Borrowing from Gesture: Adversative Coordination"). That is, these conjunctions are the result of externally motivated changes.

Fingerspelling: Disjunctive Coordination

Chiodi and Rodrigues (in preparation) observe that for the marking of disjunctive coordination, Libras signers consistently use the fingerspelled sequence "o-u" to manually represent the Portuguese conjunction *ou* ("or"). Two versions of this manual conjunction are shown in Fig. 10.1. In Fig. 10.1a, the signer spells the two letters O (left image) and U (right image) sequentially, changing also the orientation of the hand; the example is thus comparable to the ASL example in (7a). In contrast, in Fig. 10.1b, the signer fuses the two letters, such that the thumb, pinky, and ring

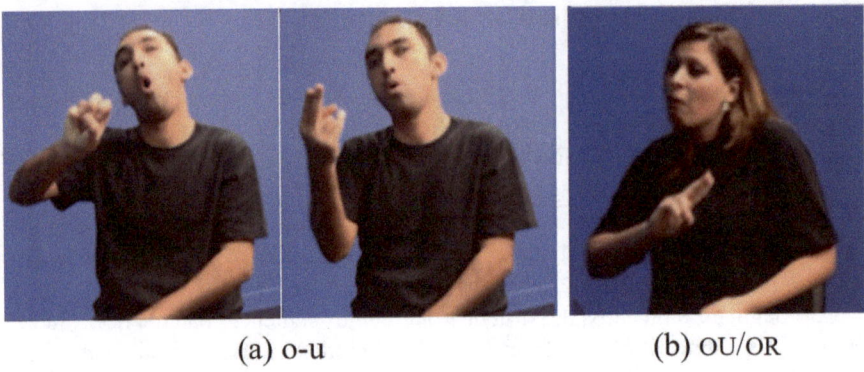

(a) o-u   (b) OU/OR

Fig. 10.1 Two versions of the Libras conjunction meaning "or": (a) fingerspelled version and (b) nativized (fused) version

fingers form the letter O, while the index and middle fingers are extended to represent the U. This latter form represents a more advanced case of lexicalization (or nativization) of fingerspelling, and this is why the form is glossed as OU/OR. Looking at the mouth configuration of the signers, we can see that in both cases, the manual forms are accompanied by mouthings, i.e., by the silent articulation of the corresponding Portuguese word – in this case, the conjunction *ou*.[19]

In (11), we present the two examples that the screenshots in Fig. 10.1 have been taken from. Mouthings, just like other non-manual markers, are indicated above the gloss line ("bl" = body lean; "el" = eyebrows lowered). In (11a), two noun phrases are coordinated, while for (11b), we may assume that two clauses are coordinated, with identical material being elided in the second clause (in (11a), we abbreviate longer fingerspelled sequences by means of "[…]"):

$$\frac{\qquad\qquad\qquad\qquad\qquad\qquad\qquad\qquad}{\text{/ou/}}\quad\overline{\text{br+bl}}$$

(11) a. ENGINEERING COURSE c-o-m[...] COMPUTER   **o-r** t-e-c-[...] TECHNOLOGY

         "In the computer engineering or technology course…"

$$\frac{\overline{\text{bl+el}}}{\text{/ou/}}$$

      b. GOVERNMENT ACCEPT   **OR** NOT

         "Does the government accept that or not?"

                                          (Libras – Chiodi and Rodrigues, in preparation)

---

[19] All the examples we present in section "Conjunctions in Brazilian Sign Languages" have been extracted from Corpus Libras, an open-access online resource (https://corpuslibras.ufsc.br/). Unless indicated otherwise, the images are screenshots from corpus videos and are reproduced from Rodrigues (2022) and Chiodi and Rodrigues (in preparation).

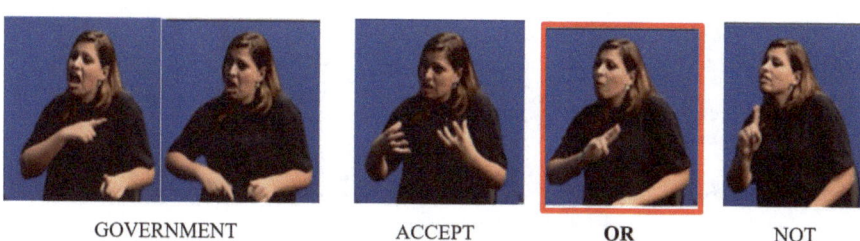

| GOVERNMENT | ACCEPT | **OR** | NOT |

Fig. 10.2 An example of disjunctive coordination in Libras

Fig. 10.3 Gesture "stop/wait" and adversative conjunction BUT. (*In*: Rodrigues (2022))

Example (11b) is further illustrated in Fig. 10.2. As the images show, disjunctive coordination in Libras can be marked both manually and non-manually, as the manual conjunction OR and the negator are accompanied by a body lean and lowered/furrowed eyebrows (as also indicated in the gloss in (11)).

Borrowing from Gesture: Adversative Coordination

Rodrigues (2019, 2022) proposes that the *open hand prone* gesture has been the source for the emergence of the adversative conjunction BUT (MAS) in Libras. According to Kendon (2004: 248–249), in spoken language discourse, this gesture commonly signals the interruption or reformulation of an action or proposition. Consequently, the manual form depicted in Fig. 10.3 can either be interpreted as expressing the meaning "stop/wait," when used as a co-speech gesture, or as an adversative conjunction, when used in a Libras sentence like the one in (12), where it links two clauses:

Fig. 10.4 An example of adversative coordination in Libras

$$\underline{\quad\quad\quad\quad\quad\text{br}\quad\quad\quad\quad}$$

```
                                          br
                      br          /m/
(12)   IF INTERPRETER HELP GOOD   BUT AUDITORIUM IMPORTANT
```

"If there is an interpreter working, that's good, but only in the auditorium

(not at schools)."   (Libras – Rodrigues, 2022:76)

The sentence in (12) is illustrated in Fig. 10.4. Note that in this particular example, BUT is articulated with only the dominant (right) hand, as the non-dominant (left) hand is maintained from a previous sign; also, the conjunction is accompanied by the mouthing /m/ (from Portuguese *mas* "but"). Clearly, in the context of this utterance, this manual form can only be interpreted with an adversative meaning, not with the gestural meaning "stop/wait" (note further that the lexical sign STOP/WAIT has a different form in Libras).

Grammaticalization

Grammaticalization from Lexical Item

Having addressed cases of borrowing, we now turn to instances of grammaticalization, and we start with the grammaticalization of a conditional conjunction from the noun EXAMPLE. Aleixo (2021) and Rodrigues (2022) propose that this case presents us with a diachronic development familiar from the study of spoken languages, that is, a pathway from lexical item (noun) to conjunction.

Conditional clauses in Libras can be juxtaposed without manual marking (similar to what we described in section "Marking of Clause Combinations in Sign

Fig. 10.5 The noun / conditional conjunction EXAMPLE in Libras. (*In*: Rodrigues (2022))

EXAMPLE   WANT   CI   WANT-NOT   CI   DEPEND

Fig. 10.6. A conditional clause introduced by EXAMPLE in Libras

Language," example (5), for NGT) or be introduced by two different manual conjunctions: IF (SE) and EXAMPLE (EXEMPLO). However, in Libras dictionaries, only the conjunction IF is mentioned for this function; the use of the sign EXAMPLE for introducing conditional clauses has only recently been identified by Rodrigues (2022). In dictionaries, such as Capovilla et al. (2017:1233), EXAMPLE (EXEMPLO) is only listed as a noun, as used in sentences like "I will show you an example" (see Fig. 10.5 for illustration of this sign).

Yet, we observe in (13) that EXAMPLE is used to introduce a conditional clause (which is also non-manually marked by brow raise); the example is illustrated by screenshots in Fig. 10.6 (CI = cochlear implant). Clearly, in this case, an analysis of this sign as a noun is not possible:

$$\overline{\qquad\qquad\qquad\text{br}\qquad\qquad}$$

(13)   **EXAMPLE** WANT CI WANT-NOT CI   DEPEND

"If the person wants or doesn't want a cochlear implant, it's up to her/his wishes."

(Libras – Rodrigues, 2022:139)

To account for this multifunctionality, Rodrigues (2022) proposes that EXAMPLE underwent a grammaticalization process, by which a lexical sign takes on a grammatical function (see section "Emergence of Conjunctions"). This hypothesis is supported by the observation that mechanisms which commonly characterize grammaticalization processes in spoken languages, namely, desemanticization, decategorialization, and extension (Heine, 2003), also operate in the change of EXAMPLE from a noun to a conditional conjunction in Libras.

In her discussion of the emergence of conditional conjunctions in spoken languages, Traugott (1985:291–292) argues that among the most common sources for such conjunctions are elements that indicate that something is known or given or that are usually used as topic markers or demonstratives. Clearly, the semantics of the underlying noun EXAMPLE involves the presentation of evidence that is known or given. Moreover, in Libras, EXAMPLE can be used as a topic marker in sentences like (14). Taken together, these properties explain why EXAMPLE makes for a convenient source for the development of a conditional marker, confirming also the overlapping of conditional and topical meanings, as proposed for spoken languages by Haiman (1978) (for sign language, see Janzen, 1999):

(14)   SOMETIMES DEAF LIKE EXAMPLE LIKE IX$_1$ **EXAMPLE** DEPEND MOTHER HELP

"There are different types of deaf people, such as, for example, deaf who

depend on their mother's help."   (Libras – Rodrigues, 2022:147)

In its lexical meaning, EXAMPLE has a concrete, demonstrative value, which becomes more abstract when it starts to function as a topic marker and even more so when it is used as a conditional conjunction. We thus observe desemanticization. Additionally, when used as a conditional conjunction, EXAMPLE gains morphosyntactic features while at the same time losing other properties related to the source meaning. As a conditional conjunction, it can only appear in the initial position of the conditional clause. Hence, the process is also characterized by decategorialization.

The second example of grammaticalization attested in the Libras data is the development of a causal conjunction from the noun REASON (MOTIVO). This sign, which is illustrated in Fig. 10.7, is described in the dictionary by Capovilla et al. (2017: 1896) as a noun which can be used in sentences like "The reason the teacher did not come today is that he is sick."

However, in (15), the same manual form is used to connect two clauses that convey a causal relation between two states of affairs (Rodrigues & Souza, 2019): the influence of sexism is the reason why a certain behavior is taboo. In this way, Libras displays the same pattern described for DGS in section "Emergence of Conjunctions" – a pattern that is also familiar from the study of spoken languages:

(15)   INDEX$_3$ t-a-b-u INDEX$_3$ **REASON** INDEX$_1$ MAN SEXISM INFLUENCE

"This is a taboo because of the influence of sexism."

(Libras – Rodrigues, 2022:108)

Fig. 10.7 The noun/causal conjunction REASON in Libras. (*In*: Rodrigues (2022))

Grammaticalization from Gesture

The grammaticalization of EXAMPLE and REASON discussed in the previous section should be understood as a modality-independent process, reflecting pathways that are also commonly observed in spoken languages. However, as previously argued by Wilcox (2004) and Pfau and Steinbach (2011) for other sign languages, Libras also presents us with a modality-specific phenomenon, that is, a grammaticalization process that starts from a gestural source.

In section "Borrowing from Gesture: Adversative Coordination," we proposed that the adversative conjunction BUT has entered the lexicon of Libras through a borrowing process, namely, borrowing of a co-speech gesture with the meaning "wait/stop." Following Rodrigues (2019, 2022), we argue that the process in fact also involves grammaticalization. As pointed out by Rodrigues, in its use as adversative conjunction, BUT exhibits properties different from the source gesture that are compatible with a grammaticalization scenario. First, as an adversative conjunction, BUT is always accompanied by non-manual markers such as mouthing, brow raise, and head movement (see example (12)). Second, the idea of interruption, associated with the source meaning "stop/wait," is only partially preserved in the target meaning, indicating that the adversative clause can also transmit the meaning of a cutoff, as it involves canceling (part of) the presupposition or even an interruption in the flow of thought expressed in the first clause. The function of BUT is therefore to signal to the interlocutor that the conclusion initially considered must be discarded. In this way, the meaning of the source form is updated in a metaphorical sense of interruption (Hopper, 1991).

Taken together, we argue that the integration of BUT into the grammar of Libras combines an externally motivated change (borrowing) with an internally motivated change (grammaticalization). As proposed by Rodrigues (2019, 2022), BUT has developed from the gesture "wait/stop," but in taking on grammatical meaning, it skipped the intermediate stage at which it would be used as a lexical element (e.g., a verb). That is, the borrowed gesture directly grammaticalized into a conjunction, different from the processes that Wilcox (2004) initially described (for ASL and Catalan Sign Language).

Conclusion

Within linguistic circles, it is – thanks to 60 years of research on many different sign languages – probably no longer necessary to argue that sign languages are full-fledged natural languages with complex grammatical structure at all levels of linguistic description. However, in the general public, prejudices persist, and some of these prejudices are not unlike those that indigenous languages have traditionally been confronted with. There is, for instance, the common assumption that there would be a universal sign language, that sign languages are basically an elaborate form of pantomime, and that they thus lack many of the grammatical characteristics of "normal," i.e., spoken languages. The latter argument in particular has also been applied to indigenous languages, in an effort to demonstrate that they are "primitive," given that they are allegedly structurally less complex than "more evolved" languages. This linguistic division, in turn, was taken to be a reflection of the division between primitive and more developed cultures.

Our aim in this chapter has been to rebut such arguments, thereby making an – albeit modest – contribution to the status of sign languages and of Libras in particular. We started by showing that arguments regarding structural complexity that have been put forward in the past (e.g., lack of word class distinctions or certain inflectional categories) are either wrong, overly simplistic, or just uninformative, as they only reflect part of a much more varied picture – a picture in which an indigenous language may well turn out to be more complex in a given grammatical domain than the language of comparison. As for sign languages, we then zoomed in on one specific grammatical domain, viz., complex sentences. Based on previous studies, we showed (i) that the absence of a manual conjunction should not be taken to imply that the clause combination is not marked – rather, non-manual markers also have to be taken into account, and (ii) that for some construction types, manual markers actually do exist and that they may enter the lexicon of a sign language by means of modality-independent diachronic processes, namely, borrowing and grammaticalization. What is modality-specific about these changes is the fact that for both these processes, sign languages can draw from the repertoire of co-speech gestures. As already shown by Meillet (1915) in his seminal study, conjunctions represent a grammatical class that commonly emerges and is renewed in the course of time. The fact that sign languages are young languages may thus explain why many of them lack certain types of conjunctions (see Aronoff et al., 2005, for a similar argument).

We were able to identify all of the aforementioned diachronic changes in Libras, i.e., instances of borrowing and grammaticalization of conjunctions, thus providing clear evidence for (the emergence of) complexity in this domain. It remains to be said that, beyond the diachronic and grammatical aspects that were at the center of our attention, sign languages actually add a non-trivial component to the discussion, as they are the target of prejudice not only because of misguided linguistic arguments but also because they are commonly approached from an ableist perspective involving a deficit rhetoric. Taking contributions of Disability Studies and Crip Theory as point of departure, we argue that, in the same sense that deaf people should not be described in terms of what they lack (when compared to what our society considers able bodies), sign languages – or any language for that matter – should also not be described or classified based on the lack of complexity in certain domains of grammar.

Acknowledgments We are thankful to our colleagues Enoch Aboh and Claude Mauk for inspiration and bibliographic references. We also thank our colleague Rimar Segala for providing his image to illustrate Libras examples used throughout the chapter. The research on conjunctions in Libras was initially carried out at the University of Amsterdam with the support of FAPESP (Process 2015/23541-2), for which we are grateful.

References

Aboh, E. O. (2016). Creole distinctiveness: A dead end. *Journal of Pidgin and Creole Languages, 31*(2), 400–418.

Adone, D. (2012). Language emergence and creolisation. In R. Pfau, M. Steinbach, & B. Woll (Eds.), *Sign language. An international handbook* (pp. 862–889). De Gruyter Mouton.

Aleixo, F. (2021). *Orações condicionais na Língua Brasileira de Sinais (Libras): uma análise funcionalista*. PhD dissertation, UNESP.

Ann, J. (1998). Contact between a sign language and a written language: Character signs in Taiwan Sign Language. In C. Lucas (Ed.), *Pinky extension and eye gaze: Language use in deaf communities* (pp. 59–99). Gallaudet University Press.

Aronoff, M., Meir, I., & Sandler, W. (2005). The paradox of sign language morphology. *Language, 81*(2), 301–344.

Asada, Y. (2019). General use coordination in Japanese and Japanese Sign Language. *Sign Language & Linguistics, 22*(1), 44–82.

Baker, C., & Padden, C. A. (1978). Focusing on the nonmanual components of American Sign Language. In P. Siple (Ed.), *Understanding language through sign language research* (pp. 27–57). Academic Press.

Battison, R. (1978). *Lexical borrowing in American Sign Language*. Linstok Press.

Brentari, D. (Ed.). (2001). *Foreign vocabulary in sign languages. A cross-linguistic investigation of word formation*. Erlbaum.

Brentari, D., & Padden, C. (2001). Native and foreign vocabulary in American Sign Language: A lexicon with multiple origins. In D. Brentari (Ed.), *Foreign vocabulary in sign languages* (pp. 87–119). Lawrence Erlbaum.

Capovilla, F. C., Raphael, W. D., Temoteo, J. G., & Martins, A. C. (2017). *Dicionário da Língua de Sinais do Brasil: A Libras em suas mãos*. Editora da Universidade de São Paulo.

Chiodi, S., & Rodrigues, A. (In preparation). O papel dos marcadores não-manuais na expressão da relação de disjunção na língua brasileira de sinais.

Cooperrider, K., Abner, N., & Goldin-Meadow, S. (2018). The palm-up puzzle: Meanings and origins of a widespread form in gesture and sign. *Frontiers in Communication, 3*, 23. https://doi.org/10.3389/fcomm.2018.00023

Cormier, K., Schembri, A., & Tyrone, M. (2008). One hand or two? Nativisation of fingerspelling in ASL and BANZSL. *Sign Language & Linguistics, 11*(1), 3–44.

Davidson, K. (2011). *The nature of the semantic scale: Evidence from sign language research.* PhD dissertation, University of California.

Davidson, K. (2013). 'And' or 'or': General use coordination in ASL. *Semantics & Pragmatics, 6*, 1–44.

Davidson, K., & Caponigro, I. (2016). Embedding polar interrogative clauses in American Sign Language. In R. Pfau, M. Steinbach, & A. Herrmann (Eds.), *A matter of complexity: Subordination in sign languages* (pp. 151–181). De Gruyter Mouton.

Davis, J. (2010). *Hand talk: Sign language among American Indian nations.* Cambridge University Press.

De Vos, C., & Pfau, R. (2015). Sign language typology: The contribution of rural sign languages. *Annual Review of Linguistics, 1*, 265–288. https://doi.org/10.1146/annurev-linguist-030514-124958

DeGraff, M. (2003). Against Creole exceptionalism. *Language, 79*(2), 391–410.

Fenlon, J., Cooperrider, K., Keane, J., Brentari, D., & Goldin-Meadow, S. (2019). Comparing sign language and gesture: Insights from pointing. *Glossa: A Journal of General Linguistics, 4*(1), 2: 1–26.

Fischer, S., & Lillo-Martin, D. (1990). Understanding conjunctions. *International Journal of Sign Linguistics, 1*(2), 71–80.

Friedner, M., & Kusters, A. (2020). Deaf anthropology. *Annual Review of Anthropology, 49*, 31–47.

Frishberg, N. (1975). Arbitrariness and iconicity: Historical change in American Sign Language. *Language, 51*, 696–719.

Geraci, C., Pfau, R., Braione, P., Cecchetto, C., & Quer, J. (2019). Hidden languages in a digital world: The case of sign language archives. *Journal of the Italian Association of Speech Sciences (Studi AISV), 6*, 31–47. https://doi.org/10.17469/O2106AISV000002

Göksel, A., & Kelepir, M. (2016). Observations on clausal complementation in Turkish Sign Language. In R. Pfau, M. Steinbach, & A. Herrmann (Eds.), *A matter of complexity: Subordination in sign languages* (pp. 65–94). De Gruyter Mouton.

Haiman, J. (1978). Conditionals are topics. *Language, 54*, 564–589.

Hartmann, K., Pfau, R., & Legeland, I. (2021). Asymmetry and contrast: Coordination in Sign Language of the Netherlands. *Glossa: A Journal of General Linguistics, 6*(1), 101: 1–33. https://doi.org/10.16995/glossa.5872

Haspelmath, M. (2007). Coordination. In T. Shopen (Ed.), *Language typology and syntactic description. Vol. II: Complex constructions* (2nd ed., pp. 1–51). Cambridge University Press.

Haugen, E. (1966). Dialect, language, nation. *American Anthropologist, 68*(4), 922–935.

Heine, B. (2003). Grammaticalization. In B. Joseph & R. D. Janda (Eds.), *The handbook of historical linguistics* (pp. 573–601). Blackwell.

Hopper, P. J. (1991). On some principles of grammaticalization. In E. Traugott & B. Heine (Eds.), *Approaches to grammaticalization. Vol. I: Theoretical and methodological issues* (pp. 17–35). John Benjamins.

Janzen, T. (1999). The grammaticization of topics in American Sign Language. *Studies in Language, 23*(2), 271–306.

Janzen, T. (2012). Lexicalization and grammaticalization. In R. Pfau, M. Steinbach, & B. Woll (Eds.), *Sign language. An international handbook* (pp. 816–841). De Gruyter Mouton.

Janzen, T., & Shaffer, B. (2002). Gesture as the substrate in the process of ASL grammaticization. In R. P. Meier, K. A. Cormier, & D. G. Quinto-Pozos (Eds.), *Modality and structure in signed and spoken languages* (pp. 199–223). Cambridge University Press.

Johnston, T., & Schembri, A. (2007). *Australian sign language. An introduction to sign language linguistics.* Cambridge University Press.

Kafer, A. (2013). *Feminist, queer, crip.* Indiana University Press.

Kalmár, I. (1985). Are there really no primitive languages? In D. R. Olson, N. Torrance, & A. Hildyard (Eds.), *Literacy, language and learning* (pp. 148–166). Cambridge University Press.

Kendon, A. (2004). *Gesture: Visible action as utterance*. Cambridge University Press.

Khristoforova, E. (in press). Subject agreement in control and modal constructions in Russian Sign Language: Implications for the hierarchy of person features. *To appear in Sign Language & Linguistics, 26*(1).

Klima, E., & Bellugi, U. (1979). *The signs of language*. Harvard University Press.

Klomp, U. (2019). Conditional clauses in Sign Language of The Netherlands: A corpus-based study. *Sign Language Studies, 19*(3), 309–347.

Klomp, U. (2021). *A descriptive grammar of Sign Language of The Netherlands*. PhD dissertation, University of Amsterdam. LOT.

Kuteva, T., Heine, B., Hong, B., Long, H., Narrog, H., & Rhee, S. (2019). *World lexicon of grammaticalization* (2nd ed.). Cambridge University Press.

Labov, W. (1972). *Sociolinguistic patterns*. University of Pennsylvania Press.

Ladd, P. (2003). *Understanding deaf culture: In search of Deafhood*. Multilingual Matters.

Lane, H. (2002). Do deaf people have a disability? *Sign Language Studies, 2*(4), 356–379.

Laycock, D. (1960). Language and society. Twenty years after. *Lingua, 9*, 16–29.

Legg, J. (2016). Exploring the promise of digital deaf histories. *Sign Language Studies, 17*(1), 42–58.

Liddell, S. K. (1978). Nonmanual signals and relative clauses in American Sign Language. In P. Siple (Ed.), *Understanding language through sign language research* (pp. 59–90). Academic.

Liddell, S. K. (1980). *American Sign Language syntax*. Mouton.

Lillo-Martin, D. (2012). Utterance reports and constructed action. In R. Pfau, M. Steinbach, & B. Woll (Eds.), *Sign language. An international handbook* (pp. 365–387). De Gruyter Mouton.

Loon, V., Esther, R. P., & Steinbach, M. (2014). The grammaticalization of gestures in sign languages. In C. Müller, A. Cienki, E. Fricke, S. H. Ladewig, D. McNeill, & S. Tessendorf (Eds.), *Body – Language – Communication: An international handbook on multimodality in human interaction* (pp. 2133–2149). De Gruyter Mouton.

Lupton, L., & Salmons, J. (1996). A re-analysis of the creole status of American Sign Language. *Sign Language Studies, 90*, 80–94.

Lupyan, G., & Dale, R. (2010). Language structure is partly determined by social structure. *PLoS One, 5*, e8559.

Lyons, J. (1981). *Language and linguistics: An introduction*. Cambridge University Press.

Mallery, G. (2001[1881]). *Sign language among north American Indians*. Dover Publications.

McKee, R. L., & Wallingford, S. (2011). 'So, well, whatever': Discourse functions of *palm-up* in New Zealand Sign Language. *Sign Language & Linguistics, 14*(2), 213–247.

McWhorter, J. H. (2001). The world's simplest grammars are creole grammars. *Linguistic Typology, 5*, 125–166.

Meier, R. P. (2002). Why different, why the same? Explaining effects and non-effects of modality upon linguistic structure in sign and speech. In R. P. Meier, K. A. Cormier, & D. G. Quinto-Pozos (Eds.), *Modality and structure in signed and spoken languages* (pp. 1–25). Cambridge University Press.

Meillet, A. (1915). Le renouvellement des conjonctions. In *École pratique des hautes études, Section des sciences historiques et philologiques*. Annuaire 1915–1916: 9–28.

Meir, I., Israel, A., Sandler, W., Padden, C., & Aronoff, M. (2012). The influence of community size on language structure: Evidence from two young sign languages. *Linguistic Variation, 12*(2), 247–291.

Mithun, M. (1988). The grammaticization of coordination. In J. Haiman & S. A. Thompson (Eds.), *Clause combining in grammar and discourse* (pp. 331–359). John Benjamins.

Nettle, D. (1995). Segmental inventory size, word length, and communicative efficiency. *Linguistics, 33*, 359–367.

Padden, C. (1983). *Interaction of morphology and syntax in American Sign Language*. PhD dissertation, University of California at San Diego [Published 1988 by Garland Outstanding Dissertations in Linguistics, New York].

Padden, C. (1998). The ASL lexicon. *Sign Language & Linguistics, 1*(1), 39–60.

Padden, C., & Humphries, T. (1988). *Deaf in America: Voices from a culture*. Harvard University Press.

Pfau, R. (2011). A point well taken: On the typology and diachrony of pointing. In G. Mathur & D. J. Napoli (Eds.), *Deaf around the world. The impact of language* (pp. 144–163). Oxford University Press.

Pfau, R. (2015). The grammaticalization of headshakes: From head movement to negative head. In A. D. M. Smith, G. Trousdale, & R. Waltereit (Eds.), *New directions in grammaticalization research* (pp. 9–50). John Benjamins.

Pfau, R. (2016). Syntax: Complex sentences. In A. Baker, B. van den Bogaerde, R. Pfau, & T. Schermer (Eds.), *The linguistics of sign languages: An introduction* (pp. 149–172). John Benjamins.

Pfau, R., & Quer, J. (2010). Nonmanuals: Their grammatical and prosodic roles. In D. Brentari (Ed.), *Sign languages (Cambridge language surveys)* (pp. 381–402). Cambridge University Press.

Pfau, R., & Steinbach, M. (2011). Grammaticalization in sign languages. In H. Narrog & B. Heine (Eds.), *The Oxford handbook of grammaticalization* (pp. 683–695). Oxford University Press.

Pfau, R., & Zeshan, U. (2016). Positive signs: How sign language typology benefits deaf communities and linguistic theory. *Linguistic Typology, 20*(3), 547–559. https://doi.org/10.1515/lingty-2016-0026

Pfau, R., Steinbach, M., & Herrmann, A. (Eds.). (2016). *A matter of complexity: Subordination in sign languages*. De Gruyter Mouton.

Quer, J., Pfau, R., & Herrmann, A. (Eds.). (2021). *The Routledge handbook of theoretical and experimental sign language research*. Routledge.

Rodrigues, A. (2019). As orações adversativas na Língua Brasileira de Sinais: uma abordagem semântico-funcional. *Sensos-e: Revista multimédia de investigação em educação, VI*, 90–103.

Rodrigues, A. (2022). *Gramaticalização de conjunções na Língua Brasileira de Sinais: um estudo sobre a mudança linguística nas línguas de sinais*. Tese de Livre Docência, Department of Linguistics, Literature, and Classical Languages, UNESP.

Rodrigues, A., & Souza, J. C. (2019). Gramaticalização do sinal MOTIVO na Língua Brasileira de Sinais: uma análise baseada no uso. *Revista do GEL, 16*, 53–82.

Sampson, T., & Mayberry, R. I. (2022). An emerging SELF: The copula cycle in American Sign Language. *Language, 98*(2), 327–358.

Sandler, W. (2008). The syllable in sign language: Considering the other natural language modality. In B. L. Davis & K. Zajdó (Eds.), *The syllable in speech production* (pp. 379–407). Lawrence Erlbaum.

Scherre, M. M. P., & Naro, A. J. (1998). Sobre a concordância de número no português falado do Brasil. In G. Ruffino (Ed.), *Dialettologia, geolinguistica, sociolinguistica (Atti del XXI Congresso Internazionale di Linguistica e Filologia Romanza)* (pp. 509–523). Niemeyer.

Senghas, R. J., & Monaghan, L. (2002). Signs of their times: Deaf communities and the culture of language. *Annual Review of Anthropology, 31*, 69–97.

Sommerfelt, A. (1938). *La langue et la société: caractères sociaux d'une langue de type archaïque* (Vol. 18). H. Aschehoug & Company (W. Nygaard).

Steinbach, M. (2021). Role shift: Theoretical perspectives. In J. Quer, R. Pfau, & A. Herrmann (Eds.), *The Routledge handbook of theoretical and experimental sign language research* (pp. 351–377). Routledge.

Stokoe, W. C. (1960). Sign language structure: An outline of the visual communication systems of the American deaf. *Studies in Linguistics Occasional Papers* 8. Buffalo: University of Buffalo Press [Re-issued 2005, *Journal of Deaf Studies and Deaf Education* 10(1): 3–37].

Supalla, T. (2001). Making historical sign language materials accessible: A prototype database of early ASL. *Sign Language & Linguistics, 4*, 285–297.

Tang, G., & Lau, P. (2012). Coordination and subordination. In R. Pfau, M. Steinbach, & B. Woll (Eds.), *Sign language. An international handbook* (pp. 340–365). De Gruyter Mouton.

Thompson, H. (1977). The lack of subordination in American Sign Language. In L. A. Friedman (Ed.), *On the other hand: New perspectives on American Sign Language* (pp. 181–195). Academic Press.

Traugott, E. C. (1985). Conditional markers. In J. Haiman (Ed.), *Iconicity in syntax* (pp. 289–307). John Benjamins.

Volk, E., & Herrmann, A. (2021). Discourse particles: Theoretical perspectives. In J. Quer, R. Pfau, & A. Herrmann (Eds.), *The Routledge handbook of theoretical and experimental sign language research* (pp. 480–499). Routledge.

Wilbur, R. (2021). Non-manual markers: Theoretical and experimental perspectives. In J. Quer, R. Pfau, & A. Herrmann (Eds.), *The Routledge handbook of theoretical and experimental sign language research* (pp. 530–565). Routledge.

Wilcox, S. (2004). Gesture and language: Cross-linguistic and historical data from signed languages. *Gesture, 4*, 43–73.

Xavier, A. N., & Wilcox, S. (2014). Necessity and possibility modals in Brazilian Sign Language (Libras). *Linguistic Typology, 18*, 449–488.

Zeshan, U., & Palfreyman, N. (2017). Sign language typology. In A. Y. Aikhenvald & R. M. W. Dixon (Eds.), *The Cambridge handbook of linguistic typology* (pp. 178–216). Cambridge University Press.

Zeshan, U., & Palfreyman, N. (2020). Comparability of signed and spoken languages: Absolute and relative modality effects in cross-modal typology. *Linguistic Typology, 24*(3), 527–562.

Zucchi, S. (2009). Along the time line: Tense and time adverbs in Italian Sign Language. *Natural Language Semantics, 17*, 99–139.

Chapter 11
Indigenous Languages in Brazil: Unveiling Linguistic Prejudice

Cristina Martins Fargetti ⓘ and Mateus Cruz Maciel de Carvalho ⓘ

Introduction

From a past with greater linguistic diversity, Brazil now has approximately 200 languages, including emigration languages and indigenous languages. Today's number may seem large to most people, who are unaware that our country already had, according to estimates, more than 1000 languages in the first moments of the arrival of the European colonizer. Why is greater diversity unknown and even surprising? What are the effects of this ignorance? We intend to address the problem of lack of knowledge about Brazilian languages and its relationship with prejudice, observed even in the media and in teaching materials.

Estimates

After all, how many languages would there be in our country? This is a big question, which, despite all efforts, does not have a clear answer, for several reasons. First of all, it must be said that we hardly know the Portuguese language in Brazil, as there is a lack of linguistic studies on the varieties that occur in a large country. There are even proposals to assume Brazilian Portuguese as a type of creole or Portuguese that has undergone a *nativization* (Naro & Scherre, 2007) or even a language structurally different from European Portuguese (Bagno, 2001). There is no consensus among specialists on this point, which highlights the always open discussion about

C. M. Fargetti (✉)
Unesp Sao Paulo State University, Araraquara, Sao Paulo, Brazil
e-mail: cristina.fargetti@unesp.br

M. C. M. de Carvalho
Instituto Federal de Educação, Ciência e Tecnologia de São Paulo, Salto, Sao Paulo, Brazil

© The Author(s), under exclusive license to Springer Nature Switzerland AG 2023
G. Massini-Cagliari et al. (eds.), *Understanding Linguistic Prejudice*,
https://doi.org/10.1007/978-3-031-25806-0_11

variation and about the distinction between language and dialect, which, as some authors point out, may actually be due to a political position, as can be seen from the quote attributed to Max Weinreich "A language is a dialect with an army and navy" (Weinreich, 1945). So, if we don't know for sure what the varieties of Portuguese are like, whether they would be independent languages or not, what can we know about little-known languages? What are their varieties? What are the limits to say where one language ends and another begins?

This problem appears in the observation of data from the 2010 Census, whose estimate of indigenous languages in Brazil differs from what linguists had determined until then. This Census deals with the amount of 305 ethnicities and 274 indigenous languages. We do not know its criteria, its data collection methodology, and its analysis. It would be very good if such data were verified, as they would raise the estimate of linguists, anthropologists, and even Funai, who have always dealt with the amount of just over 200 peoples and 150/180 indigenous languages.

How to know for sure? For this, we would need research, with adequate methodology, for which sufficient financial support could exist. An initiative of the federal government was given, in this sense, with Decree No. 7387 that established the National Inventory of Linguistic Diversity (INDL) on December 9, 2010. It provided for efforts to study languages and language dialects in our country. It started with a public notice for pilot projects, by IPHAN, which, after the completion of the projects, prepared two guides for language research and documentation (IPHAN, 2016a, 2016b). However, the INDL did not progress further, without financial support precisely for what it set out to do: research and documentation of our linguistic diversity. And what would our past have been like? If today there are an estimated 800,000 indigenous people in the country, at the time of the first contacts, the estimate was from two to five million indigenous people, who suffered from brutal extermination due to the violent process of conquest of their territory by the Portuguese crown and/or the forced assimilation in marriages of indigenous women with men of European origin. What must have happened throughout the country, as stated in historical documents and reports, as well as current genetic studies?

As for indigenous languages, Rodrigues (1993) estimates 1175 in the entire national territory, shortly after the first contact, around the year 1580. To this end, he had access to data from a survey of indigenous languages, carried out by a priest, Fernão Cardim, in a region that today covers the states of Sergipe, Bahia, Espírito Santo, and Rio de Janeiro, and with such data, made the projection for the rest of the national territory. Thus, it is assumed that we lost a large part of our linguistic diversity, around 85%, with the death and/or forced assimilation of people who lived here.

What We (Don't) Know About Indigenous Languages

Today, we have several postgraduate programs and research institutes dedicated to the study of Brazilian indigenous languages, with significant academic production on the subject.[1] Thanks to such studies, we understand the genetic affiliation of known languages, with consistent proposals arising from historical-comparative research; complementing, for example, the pioneering work of Rodrigues (1986); and seeking to face the tasks he pointed out decades ago (Rodrigues, 1966) and confirmed by Seki (2000). It is known that the situation of indigenous languages is varied; each case presents a situation of use. There are peoples who no longer speak their languages, and there are languages on the verge of extinction (with only one or two elderly speakers), languages whose younger generation does not speak them, languages spoken by the entire population (which may or may not be multilingual), and cases of monolingualism in indigenous language. We can count on works that seek to present the state of the art, such as the reference guide for studies of indigenous languages, which has more than 500 pages, prepared by a team from the National Museum (Soares, 2013), as well as works aimed at a wider audience (Fargetti, 2022). With different theoretical-methodological approaches, including other linguistic levels, the studies already carried out reveal a great deal of determination of their researchers, indigenous and non-indigenous, in the face of adversities such as lack of financial support, lack of interdisciplinary teams of researchers, lack of more adequate equipment, and transportation difficulties to overcome long distances to the communities, among others.

Scientific studies of Brazilian indigenous languages began in the mid-1960s. What we know of what previously existed is mostly due to studies carried out by missionaries, whose objectives have always been to know the languages to catechize those who speak them, not caring, generally, to record in depth the knowledge of each ethnic group. Therefore, we do not have records of the past in greater detail about indigenous cultures, since they wanted to impose a faith and a new culture, in order to save them from themselves.

Could this be the root of prejudice? Certainly, each era has its ways of understanding the world, its ideologies, and thoughts. What missionaries and colonizers did in the past is today vehemently criticized in academic circles, with their prejudice, ethnocentrism, and intolerance seen as something to be fought. And we could ask: but are we so far from them? When society doesn't know and doesn't recognize the indigenous people, when it thinks that only Portuguese is spoken (badly) in our

---

[1] We highlight, as an example, the initiatives of universities with training courses for indigenous people in intercultural graduation teachers' formation courses, which have relied on the production of academic works by indigenous professors. Among them, we can mention UFG, UFRJ, UNEMAT, and UNB. There are other proposals that are being studied, such as the one currently developed by UNIFESP, with the participation of UNESP.

country, in short, when it doesn't know about diversity, wouldn't that be showing the basis of their prejudiced attitudes? Where do such attitudes appear? We will reflect on this in the continuation of this text.

Lack of Knowledge and Media

Adequate information in the media about indigenous peoples, their languages, and cultures is not available in great quantity and reliability. With the exception of websites with information provided by anthropologists and linguists, such as the ISA website[2] (Instituto Socioambiental), there is actually a lot of misinformation. During the COVID-19 pandemic, for example, data on infected indigenous people were difficult to obtain, but we know that in peoples with threatened languages, many deaths due to infection brought even more danger to the fragile linguistic situation of the people, which, obviously, it was not publicized by the mainstream media:

> As of April 26 (2021), 1,048 indigenous people have died from Covid in Brazil – more than the total number of deaths from the disease in countries such as Australia and Mozambique – according to an autonomous survey by the Articulation of Indigenous Peoples of Brazil (Apib). Of this total, at least ten were from peoples whose languages are listed as "critically endangered" in UNESCO's World Atlas of Languages in Danger. If we consider all the peoples of the Legal Amazon who have had some contact with the disease, there are sixteen languages at risk of disappearing. In cultures that depend on oral knowledge for the survival of their identity, each death is felt by an entire village. (Queiroz, 2021, no pagination)[3]

We observe in the media a dubious attitude. On the one hand, there are some publications that show an interest in linguistic matters, such as indigenous languages and their speakers, seeking to transmit adequate and up-to-date information, although they are often limited to curiosities about etymologies.[4] On the other hand, there are publications that denigrate the image of linguists and even of languages and indigenous peoples, pointing out researchers in the humanities as leftists and indigenous peoples as savages (as could be seen in spiteful posts on social networks in the

---

[2] ISA. Povos indígenas no Brasil. Available at: https://pib.socioambiental.org/pt/P%C3%A1gina_principal. Accessed on: May 7, 2022.

[3] "Até o dia 26 de abril (2021), 1.048 indígenas morreram de Covid no Brasil – mais do que o total de mortos pela doença em países como Austrália e Moçambique – segundo levantamento autônomo da Articulação dos Povos Indígenas do Brasil (Apib). Deste total, ao menos dez eram de povos cujos idiomas estão listados como 'criticamente ameaçados' no Atlas Mundial das Línguas em Perigo, da Unesco. Se considerados todos os povos da Amazônia Legal que tiveram algum contato com a doença, há dezesseis idiomas em risco de desaparecimento. Em culturas que dependem do conhecimento oral para a sobrevivência de sua identidade, cada morte é sentida por uma aldeia inteira" (Queiroz, 2021, sem paginação).

[4] The decade of indigenous languages, 2022–2032, proclaimed by UNESCO, for example, is only published on news sites focused on indigenous languages only or on linguistic diversity, such as IPOL. The mainstream media practically does not expose the subject, which has worldwide relevance.

current political period). Of course, here is our position of disagreement with this second type of publications, which unequivocally reveal a prejudiced, biased posture, and an attempt to hide all research efforts and even knowledge about the existence and relevance of linguistic and ethnic diversity in our country.

As mentioned, Brazil is still a plurilingual country – although not as much as during the colonial period, when we had, according to Rodrigues (1993), more than 1000 languages being spoken in our territory. However, in the media we only see Portuguese, which causes this (obviously false) impression of monolingualism, that in Brazil only Portuguese is spoken. This silencing is a form of power, a way of purposefully trying to hide linguistic and cultural diversity in an act that, since the formation of the country, has been reflected in the erroneous idea of "one nation, one language."

Although Portuguese is the official language of Brazil, according to Article 13 of the Federal Constitution of 1988, paragraph 2 of Article 210 states that indigenous communities are guaranteed the right to have primary education in their mother language, in addition to their own learning processes. This, however, does not happen, given the difficulty that many indigenous communities (and not only these, but many riverside communities, as mentioned above) face in relation to basic education. And even when there are proposals that favor these communities, they can be vetoed, as was the case with the veto of the bill by Cristovam Buarque, PL 5954/2013. Vetoed in 2015 by the PT government, the bill was considered contrary to the public interest, when it proposed the use of indigenous languages throughout the educational path – from basic to higher education – with specific assessment methods in indigenous schools. The veto was an unfortunate decision and virtually unreported in the media:

> What draws our attention, on the other hand, is the apparent absence of media coverage about the veto of the Bill, although the matter involves linguistic issues and the large and traditional media often embark on these fields not always actually considering the scientific findings about language – as we could witness in the exaggerated polemic about the book *Por uma vida Melhor* (For a better life). The absence of coverage implies the non-visibility of the indigenous cause, which is harmful to it, because thus, even the common citizen who is in favor of it can remain uninformed about the setback suffered, perhaps not supporting any mobilization or protest, for example. And we reflect that, given the clear history of media support for the "cause" of linguistic prejudice, it is obvious how things will happen: either it is published distorting the facts and concepts or it is simply not published. (Fargetti & Vaneti, 2016:15)[5]

---

[5] "O que nos chama a atenção, por outro lado, é a aparente ausência de cobertura midiática, sobre o veto ao Projeto de Lei, embora o assunto envolva questões linguísticas e a grande e tradicional mídia embarque frequentemente nessas searas nem sempre considerando de fato as constatações científicas acerca da linguagem – como pudemos testemunhar na polêmica exagerada sobre o livro Por uma vida melhor. A ausência de cobertura implica na não visibilidade da causa indígena, o que lhe é prejudicial, pois assim, mesmo o cidadão comum que lhe é favorável pode permanecer desinformado quanto ao revés sofrido, porventura não dando suporte em alguma mobilização ou protesto, por exemplo. E refletimos que, dado o claro histórico de apoio da mídia à 'causa' do preconceito linguístico, fica óbvio o desenrolar do pavio: ou se publica distorcendo os fatos e os conceitos ou simplesmente não se publica" (Fargetti & Vaneti, 2016:15).

See also the absurd and recent widely publicized story about an underground city in the Amazon called Ratanabá; in great alarm, they reported that this city is bigger than São Paulo and that its wealth justifies the international interest in the region, not the respect for indigenous and riverside peoples and cultures and not their knowledge and documentation of their languages and cultures. The curious thing is that such false news emerged precisely on the occasion of the disappearance of a former Funai employee and a journalist in the Amazon, defenders of the peoples of the Javari Valley, whose tragic end revolted many, but did little to move others about his belief in a mythical and rich Ratanabá, which can be considered denialism, pseudoscience, pseudohistory, populism, nationalism, and authoritarianism.[6]

Thus, we can conclude about the mainstream media that a lot of public effort to approach the topic of linguistic diversity and its derivatives, in the main media, is rewarded with doubts, misunderstandings, and even the continuation of prejudice, error, and misinformation.

Lack of Knowledge and Teaching Materials

In a study carried out with a corpus of 50 textbooks (Portuguese, History, and Geography) and 24 exercise books, used in state schools in São Paulo, it was noted that only 10 of them had any mention of the theme of Brazilian linguistic diversity (Fargetti & Miranda, 2016). However, the approach adopted in these ten works is full of prejudices, misinformation, and wrong analysis. This finding is discouraging and makes it possible to prove the lack of adequate information for use in the classroom, which reinforces ignorance and prejudice.

In these ten materials analyzed by Fargetti and Miranda (2016), there are statements such as:

- General languages were spoken throughout the country (in fact, in the Southeast and North).
- The general languages were equivalent to the Tupi and were created by the Jesuits (in fact, the general Amazonian language, Nheengatu, and the general language of Sao Paulo had a Tupi base and were developed in contact with the Portuguese language, having been spoken in the Southeast by the Bandeirantes, who spread them).
- Brazil is monolingual, consisting of a single people, whose language has no dialects (which denies the linguistic and cultural diversity existing in the country).
- In the country there are Macro-Tupi, Macro-Jê, Aruak, and Karib linguistic trunks (the trunk is called only Tupi; Aruak and Karib are linguistic families and not trunks, along with others not mentioned).

---

[6] https://www.revistaquestaodeciencia.com.br/index.php/apocalipse-now/2022/06/18/ratanaba-capital-do-brasil. Accessed on: July 27, 2022

– Prejudiced statements regarding the variety of Portuguese spoken by indigenous people, which shows prejudice against indigenous people in general, showing them as ignorant.

This finding of inaccuracy and prejudice in teaching materials in relation to linguistic variety (whether different languages or varieties of Portuguese) and indigenous peoples shows the problem of developing inadequate teaching materials in our country, which is serious if we consider that such books are believed to be correct and reliable. That is, their incorrectness and prejudice are assimilated, giving rise to inappropriate and sometimes spiteful discourses in relation to what is different, to what is found outside the common discourse.

How to Resolve Prejudice

The knowledge of indigenous peoples is a complex construct resulting from observation and relationship with the environment in which they live. Thus, centuries of living with the environment have provided many indigenous peoples with an infinity of knowledge about fauna, flora, hunting and fishing techniques, and cosmology, among many others. Indigenous peoples' knowledge is often devalued, seen as unscientific, simply because it is different from Western knowledge. Science, by the way, is heavily rooted in the West, and all knowledge that differs from this set of knowledge is stigmatized, seen as exotic, mystical, and outside the field of science.

As they are societies that for a long time were non-technological, the experience (here in the sense of experimenting) with the local raw material is what allowed and allows the construction and development of the knowledge of many indigenous peoples. This knowledge is transmitted from generation to generation through their languages, through cultural practices, such as hunting and fishing techniques, building houses, planting and harvesting, and using plants for medicinal purposes, among many others. It is worth mentioning that much of this knowledge was used or incorporated by non-indigenous societies, which benefit greatly from the traditional knowledge of indigenous peoples. Let's look at an example in the field of pharmacology.

The greatest biodiversity in the world is in Brazil, accounting for about 20% of the total number of all species on the planet:

Brazil has different biomes that reflect the richness of Brazilian flora and fauna (Amazon Forest, Pantanal, Cerrado, Pampas and the Atlantic Forest). This wealth positions our country as the one with the greatest biodiversity on the planet. The Xingu Indigenous Park is located in a transition area between the Cerrado and the Amazon Forest. These biomes are the ones with the greatest extension in area, with the Amazon with 49.29% and the Cerrado with 22% of the national territory. In the Amazon there are about 2,500 forest species (in world terms, equivalent to 1/3 of these) and 30,000 plant species (in South America there are 100,000 plant species cataloged). The Cerrado has 11,627 plant species already cataloged and about 20% of the native and endemic species are threatened with extinction. The recognition of the Cerrado's biological importance still does not influence the percentage of protected area. Currently 8.21% are protected by conservation units, of which 2.85% are fully protected conservation units and 5.36% are sustainable use conservation units (BRASIL, 2014). An immeasurable amount of plants is threatened with extinction, both because there are many plant species not yet taxonomically identified (not recognized as being identical to a previously classified one) and because there are many species with deficient data on their geographic distribution, threats/ impacts and uses – which does not allow them to be classified as threatened. (Fargetti & Martins, 2016: 39-40)[7]

This, consequently, attracts the attention of a large number of countries, since this biodiversity represents an immeasurable economic value, especially in the field of drug development, a field that has been growing significantly. However, it is worth mentioning the investments and risks associated with the production of medicines:

> [...] statistics show that of every 30 thousand compounds synthesized by industries, 20 thousand (6.7%) enter pre-clinical studies; of these, 200 (0.67%) reach clinical phase I; 40 (013%) move to clinical phase II; and 12 (0.004%) reach clinical phase III. Only eight of them (0.027%) are approved and in general 0.003% manage to obtain a satisfactory market. (Calixto, 2003: 37)[8]

In this sense, the knowledge that indigenous peoples have about the flora is of inestimable value to the pharmaceutical industry, as it can help speed up processes and represent enormous savings in the development of new medicines. Rodrigues et al. (2007: 6) point out that "of the 120 pharmaceutical products derived from plants in 1985, 75% were developed from traditional knowledge."[9] This shows that the knowledge of indigenous peoples can make invaluable contributions to other societies. And such knowledge is conveyed by their languages, which, with their loss, take with them all the knowledge organized by the people over many centuries.

---

[7] "O Brasil possui diferentes biomas que refletem a riqueza da flora e da fauna brasileiras (Floresta Amazônica, Pantanal, Cerrado, Pampas e a Mata Atlântica). Essa riqueza posiciona nosso país como o que possui a maior biodiversidade do planeta. O Parque Indígena do Xingu localiza-se em uma área de transição entre Cerrado e Floresta Amazônica. Esses biomas são os que possuem maior extensão em área, sendo a Amazônia com 49.29% e o Cerrado com 22% do território nacional. Na Amazônia há cerca de 2.500 espécies florestais (em termos mundiais, equivale a 1/3 dessas) e 30 mil espécies vegetais (na América do Sul há 100 mil espécies vegetais catalogadas). O Cerrado possui 11.627 espécies de plantas já catalogadas e cerca de 20% das espécies nativas e endêmicas estão ameaçadas de extinção. O reconhecimento da importância biológica do Cerrado ainda não influi no porcentual de área protegida. Atualmente 8.21% está protegido por unidades de conservação, sendo que, desses, 2.85% são unidades de conservação de proteção integral e 5.36% de unidades de conservação de uso sustentável (BRASIL, 2014). Uma quantidade não mensurável de plantas está ameaçada de extinção, tanto pelo fato de existir muitas espécies vegetais ainda não identificadas taxonomicamente (não reconhecidas como sendo idênticas a uma anteriormente classificada) quanto por existir muitas espécies com deficiência de dados sobre sua distribuição geográfica, ameaças/impactos e usos – o que não permite enquadrá-las nas condições de ameaçadas" (Fargetti & Martins, 2016: 39–40).

[8] "[...] as estatísticas mostram que de cada 30 mil compostos sintetizados pelas indústrias, 20 mil (6.7%) entram nos estudos pré-clínicos; desses, 200 (0.67%) atingem a fase clínica I; 40 (013%) passam para a fase clínica II; e 12 (0.004%) chegam à fase clínica III. Apenas oito deles (0.027%) são aprovados e em geral 0.003% consegue obter mercado satisfatório" (Calixto, 2003: 37).

[9] "dos 120 produtos farmacêuticos derivados de plantas em 1985, 75% foram desenvolvidos a partir do conhecimento tradicional."

Fargetti and Martins (2016) approach the work of Loh and Harmon (2014) and agree with the authors that lower biodiversity has been related to places with lower linguistic and cultural diversity. This shows the need also pointed out by Franchetto (2021) to take care of indigenous languages, remnants of strong loss over the centuries, and threats due to several factors:

Statistically comparing data on the world's languages, in relation to animals such as birds, mammals, amphibians and reptiles, note (Loh & Harmon, 2014) that the world's languages are much worse off than animals, given the speed of its extinction. They become extinct, in most cases, not because the people who speak them disappear, but because they are replaced by languages of the majority societies, such as Portuguese, in Brazil. Of the 7,000 languages in the world, half of the world's population speaks only 24 of them, leaving the other half of the world with the vast majority of languages, in varying degrees of threat to their existence. Regarding Latin America, according to the authors, from 1970 onwards, the loss of biodiversity was smaller than the linguistic loss, considering that 60% of the languages are, in this period, in serious threat or already in extinction, although in global terms the two losses are comparable, according to the available data. (Fargetti & Martins, 2016: 41)[10]

Therefore, indigenous knowledge must be valued, as well as each language that conveys it. This finding should be made public, replacing "Indian Day" initiatives that point to them as exotic, as former inhabitants of a country today without their presence. These attitudes are common, unfortunately, and we wonder how we could have innovative and more honest initiatives in this regard.

There is certainly an intention to get to know the indigenous people better, which can be seen in the fascination that exhibitions, videos, and photos cause for non-indigenous adolescents and children. But the Indian is not just a static museum piece.[11] In an unexpected way, many times (as a presence in publishers' stands, in concerts, and in lectures), this young audience comes into contact with the real indigenous, which still exists. A non-indigenous child personally knows an indigenous child, and this meeting can be the beginning of a dialogue between different cultures, depending on the attitude of those responsible for the children so that this dialogue is respectful and non-violent.

We believe that much of the work in this regard can be done at school, where knowledge about indigenous peoples, their languages, and cultures is gradually arriving. If not out of intellectual curiosity, at least as a result of legislation this has

---

[10] "Comparando estatisticamente os dados sobre línguas do mundo, em relação com animais como aves, mamíferos, anfíbios e répteis, notam (Loh & Harmon, 2014) que as línguas do mundo estão em muito pior situação do que os animais, tendo-se em vista a velocidade de sua extinção. Elas se extinguem, na maior parte dos casos, não porque os povos que as falam desapareçam, mas sim que as substituam por línguas das sociedades majoritárias, como o português, no Brasil. Das 7.000 línguas do mundo, metade da população mundial fala apenas 24 delas, ficando a outra metade do mundo com a grande maioria das línguas, em variados graus de ameaça a sua existência. Com relação à América Latina, segundo os autores, a partir de 1970, a perda da biodiversidade foi menor do que a perda linguística, tendo-se em vista que 60% das línguas estão, nesse período, em séria ameaça ou já em extinção, embora em termos globais as duas perdas sejam equiparáveis, segundo os dados disponíveis" (Fargetti & Martins, 2016: 41).

[11] See, for example, the video "Menos preconceito e mais índio," available at https://campanhas. socioambiental.org/maisindio/. Accessed on: July 27, 2022.

occurred: Law 11,645/2008 determined the inclusion of Afro-Brazilian and indigenous histories and cultures in school curricula. But we ask ourselves how this has been done, what knowledge about the indigenous reaches the schools, and how it is used by the teachers. Would the teachers have the preparation to deal with this issue, or has the determination of the law been fulfilled with celebrations for the day of the Indian only? From what we have observed, unfortunately there is little training, and as we said earlier, the available teaching materials have serious problems and should be rethought.

A proposal that we made in the past[12] was the assembly of exhibitions in a pedagogical museum for the visitation, mainly, of the schools in the municipality of Piracicaba. There were, in addition to the exhibition of material culture pieces, games and hobbies in magazines that brought words from the language of the people thematized in the exhibition. After all, we do not have "the" Indian, but indigenous, peoples, in the plural, with a plurality of cultures and languages.

As a result of this legislation, there are currently, mainly, publications aimed at training teachers for indigenous themes in the classroom. Among them, we can mention Andrade and Silva (2017), Russo and Paladino (2016), Wapichana and Munduruku (2019),[13] and Silva and Silva (2020). An earlier material, a reference still today, is Silva and Grupioni (1995). However, teachers resent the lack of training in this regard.

As pointed out, exhibits in museums, with better preparation, including monitors to receive students and teachers from the basic education network and the community in general, can and should bring better knowledge, creating a dialogue between academia and society. It should also be noted that there are successful proposals in which representatives of indigenous communities work directly in the curatorship of such exhibitions, which allows for more direct dialogues with ethnic groups.

Art can bring differentiated knowledge and experiences of wonder, of satisfaction. It can be enjoyed in music and videos, whether they are alert or not.[14] About music, a study of the lullabies of the Juruna people can be appreciated in Fargetti (2017), with a relationship between linguistic, anthropological, and musicological studies. There are CDs of music from different peoples, made in the community itself, or in artistic interpretations such as the one made of Juruna music by Marlui Miranda (2016), in addition to studies on Brazilian indigenous music aimed mainly at elementary school (Pucci & Almeida, 2014, 2017). There are indigenous writers already recognized for their work, such as Daniel Munduruku, Cristino Wapichana, and Olívio Jekupé, among others; reading his books is a new and exciting experience. We also have indigenous filmmakers with amazing projects like the one

---

[12] See about this in Fargetti (2021), a work in which the material culture of the Juruna is thematized, richly illustrated with photos, including an exhibition held.

[13] This is a recent material produced by two indigenous writers, to be approached with teachers from the São Paulo state school system.

[14] For example, ISA. **Para onde foram as andorinhas?** Video. 2016. Available at: https://vimeo.com/179228552. Accessed on: July 4, 2022.

promoted by Vincent Carelli.[15] There is, therefore, a considerable indigenous artistic production that is available and that must be sought, enjoyed, and admired.

Finally, resolving prejudice is a very complex task, due to the difficulty of accessing knowledge, the existence of *fake news* that denigrate the image of indigenous people and researchers, as well as research institutions. It is necessary to seek ways of (re)knowing indigenous languages and cultures, which are not in the past, they still exist, is in constant movement, variation, and sometimes revitalization.

Conclusions

Each society, each ethnic group, carries with it a particular way of seeing the world and dealing with it, and this is especially manifested through language. Given that language and culture are intertwined, linguistic diversity is a facet of cultural diversity, a way for cultural diversity to show itself and to make itself more evident. Recognizing diversity, therefore, is a step on the way to reducing prejudice, accepting, and valuing different types of knowledge. The knowledge of indigenous peoples is a complex construct resulting from the observation and relationship with the environment in which they have lived for centuries, and the language that conveys them has in itself marks appropriate to such knowledge.

In this text, we undertake a path of questioning the lack of knowledge, showing prejudices in the place where they should not exist: the school. We also question the way in which the media treats linguistic diversity and the maneuvers used to hide and even reduce the importance of facts that should be known to thse population. But in addition to denouncing and lamenting this type of situation, we set ourselves the task of showing some ways to overcome it. These paths can go through raising awareness of the contribution of knowledge from traditional populations (among them the management of natural resources that can revert to pharmaceuticals), the improvement of teaching materials (incorporating excellent contributions from cited works of dissemination), and the (re)knowledge of the beauty of the art of indigenous peoples.

References

Andrade, J. A. d., & Silva, T. A. A. d. (2017). *O ensino da temática indígena – subsídios didáticos para o estudo das sociodiversidades indígenas*. Edições Rascunhos. http://www.ufrpe.br/br/content/especializa%C3%A7%C3%A3o-em-culturas-e-hist%C3%B3ria-dos-povos-ind%C3%ADgenas-disponibiliza-livro-para-download

Bagno, M. (2001). *Português ou brasileiro? – um convite à pesquisa*. Parábola.

---

[15] http://www.videonasaldeias.org.br/2009/. Accessed on: July 27, 2022.

Calixto, J. B. (2003). Biodiversidade como fonte de medicamentos. *Ciência e Cultura*. Jul/Set. 2003, *55*(3). http://cienciaecultura.bvs.br/pdf/cic/v55n3/a22v55n3.pdf

Fargetti, C. M. (2017). *Fala de bicho, fala de gente* – Cantigas de ninar do povo juruna. In *Com a participação de Marlui Miranda*. Edições SESC.

Fargetti, C. M. (2021). *Terminologia da Cultura Material Juruna*. Letraria. https://www.letraria. net/terminologia-da-cultura-material-juruna/

Fargetti, C. M. (2022). Tronco Tupí, suas famílias e línguas. In A. C. Mori & P. H. Felipe (Eds.), *Introdução às Línguas Indígenas do Brasil* (Vol. I). Mercado de Letras (on Press).

Fargetti, C. M., & Martins, M. (2016). Léxico de plantas em dicionários indígenas. In C. A. A. Murakawa, O. L. Nadin, & A. A. G. D. Ferreira (Eds.), *Léxico em cena: contribuições para os estudos lexicais* (pp. 35–56). São Paulo. https://www.fclar.unesp.br/Home/Instituicao/Administracao/DivisaoTecnicaAcademica/ApoioaoEnsino/LaboratorioEditorial/serie-trilhas-linguisticas-n28---e-book.pdf

Fargetti, C. M., & Miranda, T. (2016). Plurilinguismo: a diversidade que não é abordada nos livros didáticos. *Letras Raras, 5*, 79–88. http://revistas.ufcg.edu.br/ch/index.php/RLR/article/view/699

Fargetti, C. M., & Vaneti, L. (2016). Políticas linguísticas e a mídia. *Letras Raras, 5*, 9–24. http://revistas.ufcg.edu.br/ch/index.php/RLR/article/view/695

Franchetto, B. (2021). Diversidade linguística e biodiversidade. In M. C. da Cunha, S. B. Magalhães, & C. Adams (Eds.), *Povos tradicionais e biodiversidade no Brasil: contribuições dos povos indígenas, quilombolas e comunidades tradicionais para a biodiversidade, políticas e ameaças*. SBPC. http://portal.sbpcnet.org.br/livro/povostradicionais8.pdf

IPHAN. (2016a). *Guia de pesquisa e documentação para o INDL: patrimônio cultural e diversidade linguística*. IPHAN. http://portal.iphan.gov.br/uploads/ckfinder/arquivos/Guia%20de%20Pesquisa%20e%20Documenta%C3%A7%C3%A3o%20para%20o%20INDL%20-%20Volume%201.pdf

IPHAN. (2016b). *Guia de pesquisa e documentação para o INDL: formulário e roteiro de pesquisa*. IPHAN. http://portal.iphan.gov.br/uploads/ckfinder/arquivos/INDL_Guia_vol2.pdf

ISA. *Menos preconceito, mais índio*. https://campanhas.socioambiental.org/maisindio/

ISA. *Como valorizar as línguas indígenas*. https://mirim.org/pt-br/linguas-indigenas/como-valorizar

ISA. *Povos indígenas no Brasil*. https://pib.socioambiental.org/pt/P%C3%A1gina_principal

ISA. (2016). *Para onde foram as andorinhas?* https://vimeo.com/179228552

Loh, J., & Harmon, D. (2014). *Biocultural diversity: Threatened species, endangered languages*. WWF. https://wwfint.awsassets.panda.org/downloads/biocultural_report__june_2014.pdf

Miranda, M. (2016). *Fala de bicho, fala de gente*. CD. Selo SESC.

Naro, A. J., & Scherre, M. M. P. (2007). *Origens do Português Brasileiro*. Parábola.

Pucci, M., & Almeida, B. d. (2014). *A floresta canta – uma expedição sonora por terras indígenas do Brasil*. Peirópolis.

Pucci, M., & Almeida, B. d. (2017). *Cantos da floresta – iniciação ao universo musical indígena*. Peirópolis.

Queiroz, G. (2021). Silêncio na aldeia. Folha Piauí. 27 de abril de 2021. https://piaui.folha.uol.com.br/silencio-na-aldeia/

Rodrigues, A. D.'. I. (1966). Tarefas da lingüística no Brasil. *Estudos Lingüísticos (Revista Brasileira de Lingüística Teórica e Aplicada), 1*(1), 4–15. http://www.etnolinguistica.org/text:rodrigues-1966-tarefas

Rodrigues, A. D.'. I. (1986). *Línguas Brasileiras. Para o conhecimento das línguas indígenas*. Loyola. http://www.etnolinguistica.org/biblio:rodrigues-1986-linguas

Rodrigues, A. D.'. I. (1993). Línguas indígenas: 500 anos de descobertas e perdas. *D.E.L.T.A., 9*(1), 83–103, São Paulo: PUC-SP. https://revistas.pucsp.br/index.php/delta/article/view/45596

Rodrigues, C. R. B., de Oliveira, I. L., & Kovaleski, J. L. (2007). Conhecimento tradicional associado, patrimônio genético, pesquisa e patente de novos fármacos. XXVII Encontro Nacional de Engenharia de Produção. Foz do Iguaçu. https://abepro.org.br/biblioteca/enegep2007_TR640474_8951.pdf.

Russo, K., & Paladino, M. (Eds.). (2016). *Ciências, tecnologias, artes e povos indígenas no Brasil: subsídios e debates a partir da Lei 11.645/2008.* Garamond. http://www.promovide.febf.uerj. br/biblioteca/nepie/ciencia_tecnologia_indigena_ebook.pdf

Seki, L. (2000). Línguas indígenas do Brasil no limiar do século XXI. *Impulso*, volume 12, n. 27, (edição sobre os 500 anos do Brasil). Piracicaba: UNIMEP, p. 233–256. http://www.etnolin-guistica.org/artigo:seki-2000

Silva, A. L. d., & Grupioni, L. D. B. (Eds.). (1995). *A temática indígena na escola: novos subsídios para professores de 1° e 2° graus.* MEC/MARI/UNESCO. http://www.pineb.ffch.ufba.br/ downloads/1244392794A_Tematica_Indigena_na_Escola_Aracy.pdf

Silva, E., & Silva, M. d. P. (2020). *A temática indígena na sala de aula: reflexões para o ensino a partir da Lei 11.645/2008* (3rd ed.). Ed. UFPE. http://www.editoraufpe.com. br/a-tematica-indigena-na-sala-de-aula/

Soares, M. F. (Ed.). (2013). *Guia de Fontes e Bibliografia sobre Línguas Indígenas e Produção Associada – Documentos do CELIN.* Museu Nacional. https://www.museunacional.ufrj.br/dir/ celin/docs/Soares_org_2013_Guia_CELIN.pdf

Wapichana, C., & Munduruku, D. (2019). *Currículo da cidade: povos indígenas: orientações pedagógicas.* SME / COPED. https://educacao.sme.prefeitura.sp.gov.br/wp-content/uploads/ Portals/1/Files/53254.pdf

Weinreich, M. (1945). Der YIVO un di problemen fun undzer tsayt (רעד ןוא ןיא ייווע די דיי ףראבלעמעוו ןופ זוו טניצ רעוודנוא) **YIVO** Bleter (vol. 25 nr. 1)» (em Yiddish). Janeiro–fevereiro de 1945.

Index